More Praise for *The Least Among Us*

"Rosa is a passionate and unrelenting champion for women, children, and working people, and now she shares the lessons we can learn from the many tough fights she has led in Congress. Rosa makes a powerful case for protecting and expanding America's safety net so that every kid in this country has a real opportunity to get ahead."

—U.S. Senator Elizabeth Warren

"Can you imagine how cool the world would be if we had Rosa DeLauro getting s*** done instead of Congress being held hostage by terrible people!"

—*Wonkette*

"Congresswoman Rosa DeLauro is a one-woman truth squad when it comes to calling out the falsehoods and cruelties of current right-wing efforts to slash Social Security, health insurance, and other safety net programs. Her vividly narrated book weaves together policy ideas and personal stories to highlight stakes in the current battles."

—Theda Skocpol, Victor S. Thomas Professor
of Government and Sociology, Harvard University

"Rosa has fought tirelessly, passionately, and courageously for the weakest and most vulnerable among us. In this compelling book, she both records the battles from the inside, and offers a comprehensive blueprint for the future."

—Norm Ornstein, resident scholar,
American Enterprise Institute

"If you care about our nation in these turbulent times, read *The Least Among Us* and engage in our political process. We need more people with Rosa DeLauro's passion for justice."

—Sister Simone Campbell, SSS, executive director,
Network Lobby for Catholic Social Justice

"*The Least Among Us* brings center-stage Rosa DeLauro's strong, intellectual understanding of the issues with a visceral commitment to protect those who most need our help. This book provides an important look back on the fights we have won and lost and a roadmap forward to achieve this most noble and necessary pursuit."

—Former U.S. Senator Christopher J. Dodd

"Congresswoman DeLauro has been at the pinnacle of national power for a quarter century, and yet she's never forgotten where she came from. Read this memoir-manifesto and come away inspired."

—Jacob Hacker, Stanley B. Resor
Professor of Political Science, Yale University

"Rosa's book rings to me like the political analog of what Peter, Paul, and Mary aspired to achieve for us in activist/musical terms. We sought to inspire a thirst for justice and fairness in our songs, but Rosa's tenacious advocacy translates these values into action. Read this book and restore your faith in the woolly world of politics. For those like Rosa, principle, love of justice, and humility remain uncorrupted, even if the "F" word is unceremoniously dropped from time to time."

—Peter Yarrow of Peter, Paul, and Mary

The Least Among Us

WAGING THE BATTLE FOR
THE VULNERABLE

CONGRESSWOMAN
Rosa L. DeLauro

THE NEW PRESS

25 YEARS

NEW YORK
LONDON

Requests for permission to reproduce selections from this book
should be mailed to: Permissions Department, The New Press,
120 Wall Street, 31st floor, New York, NY 10005.

Published in the United States by The New Press, New York, 2017
Distributed by Perseus Distribution

ISBN 978-1-62097-220-5 (hc)
ISBN 978-1-62097-221-2 (e-book)
CIP data is available

The New Press publishes books that promote and enrich public discussion and
understanding of the issues vital to our democracy and to a more equitable world.
These books are made possible by the enthusiasm of our readers; the support
of a committed group of donors, large and small; the collaboration of our many
partners in the independent media and the not-for-profit sector; booksellers, who
often hand-sell New Press books; librarians; and above all by our authors.

www.thenewpress.com

Composition by dix!
This book was set in Fairfield LH

Printed in the United States of America

2   4   6   8   10   9   7   5   3   1

To
the past, my parents, Ted and Luisa,
the present, my husband, Stan Greenberg,
and
the future, my grandchildren, Rigby, Teo, Sadie, and Jasper

Contents

Introduction: Our Safety Net

IT BEARS REPEATING THAT THE reason companies do not feel free to poison us, sell us spoiled meat, lock our daughters up in ninth-floor sweatshops with no fire escapes, employ our underage sons in coal mines, force us to work thirteen-hour shifts without overtime or a break, or call in private armies to fire rifles at those of us who dare strike for higher wages is not because companies experienced a moment of Zen and decided to evolve. No. They were forced into greater accountability and social concern by the legitimate actions of a democratic government. In other words, if we depend on good-will, we are all screwed.

Growing up in New Haven, Connecticut, I saw ample evidence all around me of just how vulnerable hardworking people are in the face of business indifference. In 1957, when I was a barely a teen-ager, the Franklin Street fire claimed the life of my friend's mother. Fifteen people died in that fire because they couldn't escape the smoke and flames. A fire escape was locked, and the ladder would not extend to the ground; there had been no fire drills, and doors opened the wrong way, blocking exits. It was a disaster, and it happened down the street from my house. It is impossible to be an eyewitness to events like that and not be touched by the gravity of our responsibility to one another. The enforcement of fire safety laws and other workplace safety laws is one way to ensure that employers fulfill their obligations to employees.

Technically speaking, the social safety net is an array of government programs that ensure that no American will fall so far down the socioeconomic ladder that getting back on their feet becomes impossible. The social safety net was built up throughout the twentieth century to help working people in times of need—and make sure kids do not get punished for their parents' poverty. Morally speaking, the social safety net acknowledges that we are accountable to one another. It originated from our recognition that the vulnerable and the poor are not alien populations; they are us, in certain times and sometimes unforeseen circumstances. Economically speaking, having a social safety net makes sense, as I hope I will make clear in the course of this book.

Our safety net is one of our country's greatest legacies, and it set the stage for a century of unparalleled prosperity that made the United States a beacon for the world. It was not something dreamed up by ideologues with a perverse agenda to weaken the average American's moral fiber—as some of my colleagues now allege. The safety net's growth was incremental and in response to genuine systemic crises. Republicans and Democrats alike supported it. That is why the attacks on it now keep me up at night.

When I interview somebody for a job in my congressional office, I warn them that they need to know I swear a lot. I compete with Rahm Emanuel on the use of the F-word. (He trails me because I am older than he is.) You could say that I swear because I care, or because I am passionate about good policy, or because a colorful vocabulary helps one command attention in a town that is still getting used to strong women. Honestly, I think the impulse comes from speaking with people in my district, hearing their stories, knowing they do not have the same opportunities to speak truth to power as I do. The strong words simply tumble out.

What has me swearing now are the increasingly radical

conservative arguments against the safety net. Most stem from a series of falsehoods and misapprehensions rooted in a fundamental distrust of government and people in need. Among my opponents' factually challenged assessments:

- They say the social safety net does not work.
- They say it traps people in cycles of "dependency."
- They say our money is wasted.

Ultimately, though they are often careful to couch this falsehood in softer language, they contend that the people who receive benefits are unworthy. To top it off, they will occasionally suggest that the social safety net is a betrayal of our nation's values.

In fact, the social safety net is the natural, inevitable, and morally sound embodiment of our nation's values. Our system of social insurance started with Civil War veterans and the passage of the Dependent and Disability Pension Act, under which soldiers who had spent at least ninety days in Union forces and had been honorably discharged were to receive financial assistance if they were unable to perform manual labor. The act was a long time in the making—discussions had begun in the 1860s, but the act didn't pass until 1890. Debate swirled for decades around the cost and the potential for fraud, much like today's debates over the safety net, but compassion won out. In 1904 Theodore Roosevelt took the central idea of the act—that in the United States we do not leave every man or woman to fend for him- or herself—one step further, and made all veterans, not just Union soldiers, eligible to receive a pension.

In the midst of the Great Depression, nearly every family faced the possibility of a catastrophic loss of income, wealth, and employment. America's elderly population saw their assets lose value and their life savings disappear. In 1935, Franklin D. Roosevelt signed the Social Security Act, putting forward a vision of a country in which old age would not mean automatic penury for the majority of the population. Social Security provided economic security to retired workers who would otherwise struggle to cover basic living expenses. It rewarded work and investment in the system. During their years in the labor force, workers paid a tax on earnings that was collected in the Social Security Trust Fund. Starting at the age of sixty-two, anyone who had contributed to the system could begin receiving an annuity payment throughout their retirement years.

Social Security also created intergenerational ties, linking one generation's work to the next and vice versa. It afforded people dignity. Poverty among the elderly exceeded 50 percent and began to fall with the first check issued.[1] In the 1950s, more than 30 percent of American senior citizens still lived their last years in poverty. By 2005 that figure was closer to 10 percent.

The vision did not end there. The Social Security Act also created welfare and unemployment insurance, so that people experiencing a rough patch would not lose everything at the precise moment they needed assistance the most. Federally mandated and state-run, unemployment insurance allowed people who lost their jobs and who met their state's eligibility requirements to receive financial assistance so that housing, food, and keeping the lights on did not become prohibitively expensive while they were out of work. Prior to the act's passage, only seven states had enacted similar laws.

Though it took thirty years, our social safety net grew to meet the need for healthcare as well. In 1965 Lyndon B. Johnson signed the Social Security Act amendments that created Medicaid and Medicare. Medicare provides medical coverage for people aged sixty-five and older, as well as certain disabled non-elderly individuals. Medicaid is a federally mandated, state-run program that provides hospital and medical coverage for low-income people. Johnson receives all the credit for Medicare and Medicaid, but he himself credited former president Harry Truman, as Truman had proposed a universal health insurance program at the end of World War II.[2]

Our safety net today also includes food stamps and nutrition assistance programs—both detailed at length later in the book. All of the components of our safety net were humane responses to the Industrial Revolution and the economic, geographic, and lifestyle changes that accompanied it, advancing technology, globalization, and corporate power. These laws were not written by naive people. Our social safety net programs acknowledged that progress was making us on the whole richer, more powerful—but that it also led to incredible uncertainty and volatility. The designers of our social and human safety net realized that safeguards against family financial calamity benefited both the unfortunate and those in better circumstances, by preserving broad-based stability and confidence in the future.

I dwell on Social Security in these opening pages because it is the ultimate legislative expression of the values I grew up with: working hard, giving back, and looking after one's community. At Catholic school we were lectured on how personal responsibility was never a purely private concern. Personal responsibility included thinking about one's neighbors, especially those without resources or protectors of their own. We did not call it charity, or "handouts." For us it was about values.

That philosophy—and its essential Americanness—was reflected in Franklin D. Roosevelt's words to Congress in 1934, when he said, "Security was attained in the earlier days through the interdependence of members of families upon each other and of the families within a small community upon each other. The complexities of great communities and of organized industry make less real these simple means of security. Therefore, *we are compelled to employ the active interest of the Nation as a whole through government in order to encourage a greater security for each individual who composes it. . . . This seeking for a greater measure of welfare and happiness does not indicate a change in values. It is rather a return to values lost in the course of our economic development and expansion"* (emphasis mine).

It is hard to overstate how profoundly Social Security changed American life for the better, and how wrong its doubters were. From the very beginning, high-profile critics wasted no time attacking the program. Alf Landon, Kansas governor and 1936 Republican candidate for president, called the Social Security Act "the largest tax bill in history" and as such "a fraud on the working man . . . a cruel hoax."[3] Representative John Tabor (R-New York) said it was "insidiously designed as to prevent business recovery, to enslave workers, and to prevent any possibility of the employers providing work for the people." His New York colleague Daniel Reed was even more histrionic: "The lash of the dictator will be felt."[4] Senator Daniel Hastings (R-Delaware) asserted that Social Security would "end the progress of a great country," while A. Harry Moore (D-New Jersey) said it would "take all the romance out of life." Not to be outdone, in 1961, the future president Ronald Reagan would record an LP for the American Medical Association warning about Medicare: "The consequences will be dire beyond imagining," Reagan said. "One of these days you and I are going to spend our sunset years telling our children, and our children's children, what it once was like in America when men were free."

I declared my candidacy for the U.S. Congress in 1989 because I knew that Reagan's definition of freedom was too narrow for real life. In the real world, we need each other. I had also seen firsthand what committed, passionate public servants could accomplish. I gave my announcement speech in Wooster Square, New Haven, around the corner from where I was born. I invoked my grandmother's pastry shop, and how both my father and mother, Ted and Luisa DeLauro, worked in tough jobs before serving on New Haven's Board of Aldermen, where they devoted themselves to helping people, families, neighborhoods. My folks did not develop policies or write legislation, but they made government work for people who were struggling. Their brand of politics was about helping people make their way through the system. For them, elected office was about using government to create opportunity. It meant helping out folks from the neighborhood if their sons or daughters got into trouble or were arrested, because everyone deserved a second chance, or helping their kids get a first job for the City or Public Works. Neighbors came to our house to discuss all manner of problems, while Luisa served coffee and baked cream puffs. Our kitchen table was my parents' office and nobody gave a second thought to dropping by.

To this day, people stop me and say, "I'll never forget your parents." I just ran into a man who grew up in the neighborhood who told me that my father Ted kept him "on the straight and narrow."

I shared my parents' passion for making sure that working people get a break. The memory of how effective they were helped a lot because my first campaign was the toughest I have experienced by far. My opponent was a right-wing state senator named Tom Scott who had led an anti–tax increase movement. We did not see eye to eye on anything. The debates were ugly, the ads negative. I had crafted detailed plans for universal healthcare and a middle-class tax cut during my campaign, and argued for safe, affordable, quality day care, and helping seniors living on fixed incomes. In response Scott accused me of championing the right to abortion right up until the delivery room, challenged my Catholic credentials, and made a stink of my last name. My husband, Stan Greenberg, became a focal point, especially his Jewishness. (At the time, when women ran for office, they were assumed to either be lesbians or controlled by their husbands.) Editorials against me referred to me as "Rosa L. DeLauro, as Mrs. Greenberg likes to be called." In fact Stan and I had been married since 1978, and there had never been any question of me keeping my name. The point of all these attacks, which at one point descended into a campaign event where Stan was referred to as "Stan Greenbucks," was not policy debate, or even the meaning of public service. The point was appeals to prejudice and resentment of women. I was too liberal and too pro-government. But I eked out a 52 to 48 percent victory. Scott went on to host a talk radio show.

When I entered the halls of Congress in 1991, the voices that felt it was their God-given mission to dismantle our social safety net were in a minority, though they were loudly challenging the established Republican leaders in the House. They would succeed in their revolution and attack the social safety net four years later.

In the last few years a radical Republican Party has labeled social supports like food stamps a "hammock" whose sole purpose and only effect is to allow lazy people to stay lazy. They have attacked unemployment benefits as disabling. I have been hearing the hammock argument for a while now, and the cluelessness about the human condition that sustains it never ceases to amaze me. I do not know where they get this distorted view of human nature. Most people I know want to work and be an asset to their community.

What I do know, however, is that the social safety net's attackers do not understand their American history. Many of these programs were not Democrat-only visions but developed on a bipartisan basis. Social Security passed in the House with 81 Republicans voting in favor and just 15 against. It passed in the Senate 77–6, with 16 Republicans voting for and only 5 against. Every presidential administration saw debates around safety net programs, but at stake were largely minor adjustments. Presidents Ronald Reagan, George H.W. Bush, and Bill Clinton all supported refundable tax credits that helped ensure that families facing hard times would not fall into poverty. This bipartisan support reflected a real moral seriousness.

Today politicians display increasing skill in saying things that sound promising but totally obscure their true motivations. I recall when former president George W. Bush began talking about "saving Social Security." Republicans had been whispering about this since the end of the 1990s, but now they were getting serious. I was surprised; none of the usual conservative arguments—like that it discourages work—would seem to apply to Social Security. A person's Social Security benefits are based on past earnings on which he or she paid payroll taxes. Earn more over the course of your working life (up to an annual maximum that's well into the six figures), receive more at the end of it.

The Bush administration cited projections showing that starting in 2018, benefits being paid out would exceed what Social Security took in. The truth is there was no compelling economic or budgetary urgency to address Social Security in 2005. Bush's prescriptions made it clear that his desire for change stemmed from his belief that markets produced better outcomes than government. He proposed that a third of payroll taxes would be paid into private, individual accounts that could be invested in the stock market. I did not see how diverting money from the existing system would solve the problem of an expected shortfall. Never mind that under Bush's plan, a large portion of any extra income from your private account would be offset by reductions drawn from your guaranteed Social Security check, regardless of how well your private account performed. In other words, Bush's overall point was to introduce more risk to Social Security and turn it into an individual investment tool. That is why Speaker Nancy Pelosi was determined that the Democrats in the minority oppose Bush's privatization plan and offer no alternative plan to "save" Social Security. There was tremendous pressure from elites focused on the deficit, demanding to know where our plan was. Pelosi said Social Security "has enabled our country to obey the commandment: honor thy father and mother," and held fast. Our opposition had to be to the whole idea of reform, because the changes proposed contradicted our values. That could not be compromised.

Why is this important, and why does this matter today?

Reshaping American values was the whole point of Bush's push to "save" Social Security. The idea was to end a program grounded in the idea that every man and woman is our neighbor, and to toss out any sense that we are all in this life together. Today we hear echoes of Bush's plan in House Speaker Paul Ryan's rhetoric, as well as in the views of many of those who ran for president in 2016 and sit in the U.S. Senate. They all want to privatize Social Security. They all want us to relax and let corporations govern our lives. At least they are consistent.

We don't know whether a President Donald Trump will threaten Social Security and its underlying premise of shared responsibility, though we do know his secretary of education will promote vouchers on an unprecedented scale that will undermine public education. Trump ran as an advocate for working people, but he really wasn't. He was a champion of huge tax cuts and breaks for big corporations.

It is a strange time to be an advocate for working people. To hear some of my colleagues and the popular press swooning over the brilliance of today's investors and hi-tech disrupters, you might be forgiven for thinking we rise and fall on the success of business alone. But in fact much has always depended on the people who go to work each day—and who, when circumstances force their hand, challenge those who compromise our collective health for their individual profit.

Late in 2008 I flew to Chicago to meet with president-elect Barack Obama. I arrived on a bitterly cold day but I barely noticed. The reason for my trip was an interview about a potential cabinet appointment—secretary of labor. Was I interested? I was. I prepared extensive notes. What would I do with the job? I had wrestled with that question every hour since the call came in. I read a biography of Frances Perkins, secretary of labor under Franklin D. Roosevelt and the architect of Social Security. By the time she met with Roosevelt in February 1933 to discuss what she might do as secretary of labor, Perkins had seen a lot. She had worked in settlement houses and fought for labor standards. As a young woman she watched the infamous 1911 Triangle Shirtwaist Factory fire in New York's Greenwich Village from the pavement below. The Triangle fire was far worse than the Franklin Street fire in terms of lives lost—146 total, 123 of them women and girls—but the reasons for the tragedy were roughly the same: an employer who kept exits and access to stairwells locked and bolted, and who failed to provide adequate fire escapes, leaving workers to die on the job. Perkins had seen young women hanging out of the building's upper-floor windows, many making the choice to leap to their deaths rather than be burned. "This made a terrible impression on the people of the state of New York," Perkins later recalled. "I can't begin to tell you how disturbed the people were everywhere. It was as though we had all done something wrong. It shouldn't have been. We were sorry. *Mea culpa, mea culpa.*"[5]

The scene helped steel Perkins's resolution to change lives for the better. Simply appealing to people's better angels was not enough; there needed to be laws, and public policy, and federally mandated protections. The list she presented to Roosevelt of what she wanted to accomplish was long: minimum-wage protection, work-hours legislation, workers' compensation, workplace safety regulations, federal aid for unemployment relief, and a national pension system as well as one for health insurance.

At my interview I told Obama that Perkins was my role model. I told him I wanted to be Frances Perkins and that whether or not I got the job, I would continue to advocate for what I believed in whatever forum I found myself.

I told him that the egregiousness of the Wall Street excesses that led to the Great Recession had given us an opportunity to correct the balance on behalf of the working classes. The conversation was deep, wide-ranging, and as I walked out of his office at the end I knew I did not have the job. My friends John Podesta and Rahm

Emanuel were outside the door, and I could see it in their faces. Obama's style is cerebral, cool, whereas I come in guns blazing. It would be hard to subsume my m.o. into doing and saying what was right for the administration.

But I knew what I had to do: get back to work. This is my vantage point to tell the story of the battle to defend our most vulnerable populations. We do not know how today's assault on the social safety net will play out in this very dangerous time. What we do know is that real lives are affected. What for cable news pundits is ratings fodder that appeals to the basest rather than the noblest of instincts is of life-and-death importance to a significant portion of the American populace. There is nothing I would rather be doing than sharing what I have learned in hopes that others will join the cause.

1

Preparation for Congress and Gaining a Platform

POLITICAL IMAGINATIONS ARE LINKED to one's earliest memories. In my case, my ideas about how to serve are inextricably tied up in my parents' experience as immigrants in a working-class Italian neighborhood. Applying the lessons I learned from them to the broader arena of national politics is the backdrop for everything I have been able to do. The tight-knit community I came of age in taught me humility, the importance of being willing to help, and adaptability. Being a junior congressperson taught me how the power game is played at the highest levels.

My father came to New Haven around the turn of the last century as a young boy filled with dreams. Before long he would walk out of a classroom, at the tender age of eleven, after the teacher asked him to define "janitor." He did not know much English or what it meant, but he knew the Latin word *genitori*, meaning parents or forebears or heritage. So he answered "my parents." The other kids and teachers laughed at him, and he never went back to school. He taught himself to be deeply literate in the classics in both Italian and English, an opera lover who taught himself to read music and play the clarinet.

During the Depression, he got a job as a City Court interpreter in New Haven, Connecticut, translating for new immigrants who had a shaky command of English. He became a strong advocate of the Italian language being taught in the public schools—the exact opposite of the conservatives' call for "English only." Off the job, people in the neighborhood would ask him to translate letters from family in Italy, or just to help with personal issues. He tried his hand as an insurance salesman, going door-to-door to pick up the 50-cent premium from his clients every week. Many could not pay, and in many of those cases he paid their premiums for them. One day he complained about this to a local tough who fought under the name Midgie Renault. Midgie asked my father if he could go along to see Mrs. Carrano. "Tito, I can't pay you this week," Mrs. Carrano said. "I don't have the money." Midgie was having none of this: "No, you pay now," he said. My father pushed Midgie out of Mrs. Carrano's home. He decided his true calling lay elsewhere.

My mother left school at thirteen to help out in my grandmother's pastry shop and then went to work at the Strouse, Adler Company, a nearby garment manufacturer, as soon as she was legally allowed—at age fourteen. She studied at night for her high school diploma. The old sweatshops on State Street in New Haven were full of women bent over their sewing machines, not eating their lunches, because they were paid by the piece and to stop work for even a few minutes meant less pay. They pumped out dresses and shirt collars as fast as they could. If the sewing machine needle got stuck in your finger you just wrapped it up. You didn't go to a clinic to get a tetanus shot. You did not want to stop, and you did not want to get blood on a garment. You would not get paid.

Somehow my mother, a girl of twenty in 1933, just thirteen years after American women won the right to vote, found it in herself to remind women in an article written for the Tenth Ward Democratic Club newsletter: "We are not living in the Middle Ages when a women's part in life was merely to serve her master in her home." She urged women to get involved in the "heretofore stronghold of the male sex: politics." She envisioned a future of louder, more daring female voices in the public sphere. "Come on girls, let's make ourselves heard."

Around the same time my mother was getting involved in politics, my father was hired on a Yale University research project to track down and interview people who'd been laid off by the L. Candee Rubber Company in 1929. The experience proved radicalizing, in ways that would reverberate throughout his career and even my own. Before it closed in 1929, Candee had occupied a whole block off Greene Street and employed over a thousand people, mostly from the neighborhood, manufacturing rubber shoes. Then it was consolidated with another factory on the Naugatuck River—in other words, shut down—and most of the workers lost their jobs. Those interviews had such an impact on my father's thinking. He would always say to me, "It was the working men and women that made those businesses successful. In good times, the workers helped make the companies profitable. And in bad times they're let go." Families got into financial trouble and their lives went swiftly downhill. He thought nobody was looking out for them.

In 1953 the Democratic Party boss Arthur Barbieri asked my father if he would consider running for alderman in one of the main Italian wards that was still heavily Republican. "Teddy, we don't expect you to win the seat," Barbieri told him. "Democrats usually lose the ward by twelve hundred votes. If you can knock that number down, it will help us win the mayor's election citywide."

My father went on foot to every house and apartment in the ward. I often trudged along with him, house to house, apartment to apartment, in the rain and snow. Sometimes we stood in the doorway and sometimes people invited us in for coffee. My father talked some, but mostly he listened. He wanted to know what they needed, how he could help. He kept a file box with every voter's name on a card inside: red for Republicans, blue for Democrats.

On election night, he won the race on the voting machine but lost because of nine absentee ballots. He would win the ward two years later, and eventually my mother ran for alderman, too, and won.

If my mother promised someone a job, she would call every agency every day until someone came through with one. Once she ran out of the house in the cold of winter when the electric power and heat failed at Winslow-Celentano, a neighborhood public housing project for seniors. She ended up canvassing every grocery store and restaurant every day on Wooster Street to get food delivered until the home could cook again.

Luisa served longer than anyone on the New Haven Board of Aldermen and was the aldermanic representative on the Board of Finance. She immersed herself in city budgets and interrogated the city department heads to make sure they did their jobs, that the taxpayers' money was not wasted, and that they looked out for the poor and working-class neighborhoods, not just the downtown and Yale University.

My father was a devout Catholic and daily communicant at St. Michael's Church next to Wooster Square Park—but a staunch anti-cleric. He thought the Church should be doing more for working people and the needy. He tried to get more than one priest removed for caring more about the collection plate than the poor. Back in Naples, his extended family, who had communist sympathies, had hung red sheets from the balconies in their villages near Naples to send a message to the *fascisti*.

My parents' brand of politics included fighting for the neighborhood and the Italians who were lower down on the social ladder. Together Teddy and Luisa stood in front of the bulldozers to prevent them from razing houses and putting a highway through our New Haven neighborhood, as happened in so many American cities in the 1950s. They wanted to protect the area from being destroyed by urban renewal, and they wanted to help neighbors receive the benefits due to them.

When I graduated from Columbia University's School of Public Law and Government with a degree in international politics, my father said, "You are equipped to lead a revolution. You have a great education and a lot of book learning, but you have to understand what's happening on the street." He feared that all my education was taking me away from our community and the family. "You think you are too good for us and our politics," he told me. "If you want to make a difference, you had better understand people and their lives."

It took me years to fully appreciate what he was telling me, however.

I also embraced the liberal agenda of my generation, though with some wrinkles of my own. I strongly opposed the Vietnam War, and supported George McGovern for president and peace candidate Joe Duffey for the U.S. Senate. (Duffey challenged the incumbent senator Tom Dodd in a bitter primary because of his support for Lyndon B. Johnson's war.) My disagreement with my father on Johnson and Vietnam was part of our estrangement. He was also upset over my moving into my own apartment as a single woman. He was no fan of the sexual revolution, and would have been happier had I stayed home until seconds before my wedding ceremony.

When my father died, we were not reconciled. He never saw me elected to the U.S. House of Representatives.

After my father died, Luisa decided she would go with her daughter and back the reform, antiwar, and anti-machine candidates that I supported. She stood out, and the local Democratic party boss did everything possible to defeat her, even taking her to court on shoddy allegations of absentee ballot fraud, but without success. (Stan and I faced physical intimidation from brawny men at the Democratic mayoral nominating convention, and my Uncle Caesar paid them a visit to make sure it didn't happen again.)

In 1968 I began my post–graduate school years as a community organizer in the War on Poverty and the National Urban Fellows program to help talented minorities across the country gain experience working at high levels in city government. I came to live and breathe campaigns, mostly in my parents' style. I did everything from volunteer canvassing and phone banking to driving around New Haven with a bullhorn urging people to vote. My file cards—red and blue, like my father's—I kept neat and orderly and always at hand. I helped lead Frank Logue's insurgent campaign to end Democratic machine control of City Hall in New Haven, and became chief of staff to Mayor Logue as well as campaign manager of his successful re-election effort. As a campaign manager, I made staffers go through every ward and every town, constantly telling them, "Give me the numbers."

I first met my husband, Stan Greenberg, during the first Logue campaign. Stan was a Yale professor and an academic pollster, and was reported to have magical methods for getting out the vote. More critically, we shared a love for anchovy pizza and coffee with milk and sugar. That placed us at the same corner of the campaign's conference table at key meetings. We quickly realized how much our backgrounds, values, and intensity would lead us to get involved in the same battles.

When my independence and strong views estranged me from the mayor, I organized the first management union in the city of New Haven. This grew into a love of organizing and gathering people united around a common cause.

Then I began looking for new opportunities to use my skills and everything I'd learned. I became campaign manager for Christopher Dodd (D-Connecticut) in his first U.S. Senate campaign and his re-election. It was a heady time. Our whole team was fired up and the stakes were very high. If people did not do their jobs, they were gone, and it was my job to hold people accountable. I gave the nephew of a close Dodd supporter a job as a driver, and when he helped Dodd make an unnecessary detour one night, I pulled him in the next morning. Election Day was getting close and we could not afford any unforced errors. "We don't need you in the campaign. Go back to D.C.," I told him. "We can find somebody who will do the job and not put the election at risk." That driver, Doug Sosnik, is now one my closest friends, and he has run more than a few campaigns himself. From there on out I directed state presidential campaigns for Gary Hart, Walter Mondale, and Michael Dukakis.

Senator Dodd asked me to be his chief of staff, and I did not hesitate. In that role I joined his successful fight against the United States' involvement in El Salvador and Nicaragua. Dodd also founded the U.S. Senate's Children's Caucus, which became a big source of inspiration for me and many others who were worried about the plight of working families.

Getting ovarian cancer was life changing. Chris Dodd put his 1986 re-election campaign on hold until I could run it. Afterward, I decided I needed to work for change on my own, leading an organization that advocated for issues I believed in or running for elected office myself, not working for someone else.

When after several years I moved on from my chief of staff post, I briefly went into business as a consultant, but quickly learned that sitting in meeting after meeting was just not for me.

I was eventually wooed by a group of West Coast philanthropists and activists to lead the national campaign to end aid to the Nicaraguan Contras, a campaign that succeeded. This prepared me for my next pre-representative job: serving as the first executive director of Emily's List, the most effective organization electing pro-choice Democratic women to national office.

Then it was time to try for myself what I had helped so many others do. After the bruising twelve-month campaign against Tom Scott, I arrived in Washington for the freshmen orientation as a newly elected member. I stopped to ask the lady at the desk, "Can I park the car there in the circle?" "Ma'am, you are a member of the

United States House of Representatives," she said, "and you can do whatever you want." I knew she was talking about the perks of this Capitol Hill job. But she might well have been talking about my faith that government can really do things that change the country for the better.

I sat at a big table at freshmen orientation and Congressman David Obey (D-Wisconsin), who was a powerful member of the Appropriations Committee, and whom I had not met before, sat at the head explaining the budget of the federal government and the federal agencies—and I thought, "Oh shit, what have I done, I'm in way over my head. What have I got myself into?" Obey doesn't suffer fools. He is very abrupt. I thought, "How will I ever have a conversation with David Obey?" I was very conscious of being a woman in a Congress dominated by men. The job demanded very different levels of performance. A new male member could drool and make a fool of himself and pay no price, but the same was not true for a woman. I realized then: you do not get two bites of the apple once they decide you are not up to it.

That thought shook me. If I was going to legislate and make government work better for everyday people, I needed a deep knowledge of how this process worked from the inside. The House Democratic leaders had turned to me right away to deal with communications and message because of my campaign experience and willingness to attack the Republicans. Accordingly, Dick Gephardt asked me to be part of the Message Group that met every morning. But when asked to head up the Democratic Congressional Campaign Committee, I said, "No." I said it emphatically and repeatedly. I refused the almost ritualistic request at the start of each Congress to head up the committee—a sure path to the Democratic leadership. I needed to be a policy person first.

Because I had crafted my own detailed plans for universal healthcare and a middle-class tax cut during my campaign, I innocently thought the committee chairs would be impressed. I sat down with a tall and intimidating John Dingell, chair of Energy and Commerce. He laughed. He was cordial, but said, "My dear, no freshmen serve on this committee." He also gave me one of the best pieces of advice I have ever received from a colleague. He said to me, "You know. Never blindside your colleagues. If you're with them, say yes. If you can't stand with them, say no, so they know where you're coming from and why. Don't blindside people. Be straight and upfront." It was excellent advice, because the only thing you have in this business is your word. If you start to vacillate, you lose respect. You have to be known as someone who is consistent and credible.

In my first year on the Hill, I wrote the Middle Class Tax Relief Act of 1991, tailored after my campaign proposal. It went nowhere.

In my second term David Obey told me, "You belong on the Appropriations Committee." The Appropriations Committee is the most influential in the Congress. He says he picked me because I had the right values and was "operational." He meant I would not be content to spout Democratic platitudes, and could handle the nuts and bolts of legislating and lining up votes.

The Appropriations Committee is also where you have the most impact on what government does. I selected my first subcommittee by instinct: Labor, Health and Human Services, Education and Related Agencies. Those were my issues. Nancy Pelosi, Nita Lowey, and I formed a bond of sisters that crashed the male-dominated Appropriations Committee and challenged any government agency to pay attention. We used the committee to take up women's health issues and descended on the male subcommittee chairman from Iowa, letting him know that it was not OK to continue in the old ways that saw women's interests as less pressing a national concern than men's. Our congressional staffs came up with a nickname for the three of us: DeLoSi. "What are DeLoSi plotting now?" people would say when they saw us together.

When I had to decide on my second Appropriations

subcommittee, I sat down with Senator Dodd. He had campaigned with me at Connecticut supermarkets when I was facing my first election and had even used his privilege as a former House member to come to the floor to see me sworn in. He stood next to me with his hand on my shoulder. My husband Stan and my mother Luisa were in the gallery.

Dodd's advice for picking a second subcommittee was to abandon my comfort zone and expand my horizons: Agriculture. "Get into their world. Understand who they are and what their concerns are." He maintained that was the only way to understand the concerns of those who did not share my background and political instincts—and I would need that understanding.

I selected the Agriculture subcommittee. "What are you doing?" many friends asked. The subcommittee is packed with members from rural districts who see its main charge as tending to the big agricultural programs and farm issues, including all crop subsidies. I replied with a canned answer that I hoped would be calming to urban progressive nerves: the "ag" subcommittee dealt with food stamps and the FDA, too.

The Agriculture subcommittee, in fact, encompassed many of my concerns. It handles the nutrition provisions that control policy regarding food stamps, school breakfasts and lunches, farmers' markets, seniors' nutrition programs, and emergency food aid. Commitments on international food aid also pass through Agriculture, as do bills regarding food safety and food imports.

In time these issues would come to dominate budget talks. But I was also determined to understand how farm programs worked. The congressional members from agriculture states invited me to come visit their rural districts and I did. Charlie Stenholm (D-Texas), the top Blue Dog and the most conservative Democrat in the House, invited Stan and me to his annual Texas barbeque. Afterward Charlie, Tom Latham (R-Iowa), and I visited a Texas slaughterhouse, the three of us in hairnets. I voted in favor of the

Agriculture Appropriations bill, with all its subsidies, every year in order to be as effective as I could on these issues.

Congress was like the tight-knit community in which I grew up in some respects. It retaught me humility, and the importance of being willing to pitch in. But learning to navigate how politics is done at this level also taught me a few things about what it takes to be effective on behalf of people.

First, it helped to realize that people come from incredibly different parts of the country with incredibly different ideologies and worldviews, and they have their own reasons why they vote the way they do. It was important to understand where my colleagues were coming from and what they cared about. Some just wanted to be re-elected. All of that is an opportunity to horsetrade, though some were thick and hopeless and didn't care one whit about the poor. Some had a strong and ethical core, and those were the people you wanted to remind why we have a safety net. This understanding proved essential in fights over Medicare and food stamps.

Second, I learned how to use "downtime." Belonging to the minority party in Congress comes with a fair number of petty frustrations. You do not chair any committees. You cannot call hearings. This makes it difficult to get legislation that you have written enacted. The marginalization is not just procedural but often literal—minority members are relegated to Capitol Hill's basement conference rooms. (When you're in the majority, you have prime real estate.) For some minority members and their staff, these House rules and traditions can feel like a demotion and are demotivating. I have found, however, that time in the minority can be well spent, particularly if one has a bill whose passage depends on getting the public more aware of how the law will benefit them. Holding press conferences, releasing statements, talking to constituents—all help get the word out. I have pressed for amendments to bills that I knew had no chance of passing—and my opponents, comfortably in the majority, accused me of pulling stunts, grumbling to the press that submitting amendments that have no prayer of passing is just political showmanship. I have come to expect this. But what are you supposed to do? Sit on your hands? Time spent raising awareness is never time wasted. This is especially true when it comes to issues that you know to be universal in scope, issues that you believe affect the American way of life on a grand scale, but that too many others are inclined to see as niche concerns. An obvious example here is what were previously seen as purely "women's issues," and were thus ignorable, but which are now understood to shape the lives of men—and children—to a tremendous degree as well.

Third, people are territorial. They can be deeply attached to their role as chair of a particular caucus or conference, or simply the deference paid them due to their seniority in the House. One has to know what boundaries matter to people, and how attached to them they are. It is important to respect people's territorialism— in the sense that one takes the consequences of running roughshod over it seriously. This does not mean that I never overstep those boundaries. I have often authored bills where I had no committee jurisdiction, but where I've staked out what in my view matters and what is important. And most great, life-changing legislation has resulted from people being willing to take tough votes and cause great offense. How does one gauge when to hang back and when to charge forward? Much depends on the demands of the political moment; at critical junctures, people will want to own the change. The more you can keep your ego in check, the better you fare in these delicate situations.

Play a long game. I learned that if you are seen as someone who wilts under the first signs of resistance, you will never command the attention you need to champion legislation that privileges people without the resources to fight for themselves. It is far better to have someone see you walking toward them in the hallway and think, "Oh God, there she comes again," because they suspect you will buttonhole them into taking a position on the Child Tax Credit for the umpteenth time than for them to see you as someone who is safely ignored.

Then there is the fact that no one who really knows their stuff can be safely ignored for long. The extent to which one cares about an issue should match the amount of information one can command about it. I mean info that one can recall on the spot, without pausing or checking email threads. This is about doing your homework, but it also concerns basic integrity. People who are passionate about an issue best demonstrate that passion by knowing their stuff inside and out. Legislation that moves this country forward, particularly when it comes how we stand up for the interests of ordinary working families, takes a long, long time to pass. Reintroducing a bill year in and year out gives one plenty of time to study. Every time I travel from New Haven to D.C. or vice versa, I get four and a half hours to read, better understand the issues my constituents face, and plot my next move on their behalf.

The next lesson took me a while to appreciate: people who are "on your side" will drive you as crazy as your opponents do, and sometimes more so, because you expect better from them. In those situations, take a long view. Be forgiving. You will need their help someday. But do not forget.

Lastly, being prepared to lose should have no bearing on how much muscle you put into the fight. You can't win if you are afraid to lose. Both of my parents exemplified this lesson like few people I have met since. It came in handy from day one on Capitol Hill.

2

Breaking the Contract with America

THE FIGHT OVER THE CONTRACT with America was a masterclass in political combat. For forty years, there had been no concerted threat to the bipartisan agreement on the social safety net. The 1994 "Gingrich Revolution" changed all that.

After the 1994 midterm elections the Republicans took over the Congress after forty years of Democratic control. Newt Gingrich was made speaker of the house, and the Republicans' plans were nothing if not ambitious. Their mission was reducing government in every possible way. They wanted, in anti-tax advocate Grover Norquist's words, to make government so small "it can be drowned in a bathtub." What that really meant—and what it still means—is that they wanted the government out of the business of helping poor people as much as it does rich people.

Gingrich and Dick Armey were co-authors of the contract and had been working to poison the well against Democrats for some time, and the drip-drip-drip of Armey's attacks had done the job over time.

At the outset of Gingrich's takeover, Democrats were demoralized. They had controlled the House for forty years. Now they had lost it and it was hard for many senior members to adjust. I knew from my organizing background that if you can get people on their feet, enthusiasm tends to follow. It helped that we felt ourselves to be on solid ground on the values front. Democrats had a strong message—and history—of caring for all people.

The Contract with America was just the opposite. It promised to bring to the floor ten bills within one hundred days—and along the way completely restructure the American safety net. The "Personal Responsibility Act" was, interestingly enough, about teen mothers. It would prohibit welfare payments to mothers under eighteen years of age, deny increased welfare payments should a woman happen to have another child while receiving welfare, and bump everyone off the welfare rolls after two years if they did not meet work requirements.[1] The "Common Sense Legal Reforms Act" would make the loser of a civil case pay his or her opponent's legal fees, as well as weakening product-liability laws and capping punitive damages. The Republicans also proposed folding food stamps into a block grant, with the money returned to the states, which is just a way to cut spending. Then, in addition to a balanced-budget law, they proposed $200 billion in tax cuts. The math for that did not work at all; calculations for the most regressive budget legislation came up $700 billion short.

I first spoke up against the Contract in September 1994, a couple of months before the midterm elections that year. I felt my Republican colleagues had representative democracy backward. Instead of making clear what they really wanted to do when they got to Washington, they promised to pass a Frank Luntz focus-group-tested package of great-sounding bills that would actually hurt a lot of people, including their own constituents, if they ever happened. I saw it as taking a blood oath to support ill-conceived proposals that were very different than anything we had seen before.

I had been in Congress for less than four years, but I knew I had to fight this. After all the votes were counted and it was clear that the Contract with America would dominate everything else, I decided to run to be head of the Democratic Study Group, the main policy and research arm of the Democratic Caucus. Obey urged me to run. Congressman David Skaggs (D-Colorado) was the frontrunner. He was greatly respected for his integrity and thoughtfulness on policy. I was pretty junior but determined, and emerging as a policy-making person with expertise. Skaggs and I tied in the secret caucus vote.

On the day the tie was announced, the Chief Whip David Bonior (D-Michigan) offered me the position of chief deputy whip. If I accepted, we would be working hand in hand to coordinate Democratic efforts to reverse the Gingrich Revolution. The whip's role is not unlike its portrayal in *House of Cards*; doing it well takes a tenacity and tactical intelligence that can border on the pathological if not tempered by a core of generosity and goodwill. Bonior had both of those latter qualities in spades, but even so I was initially reluctant. In many ways whipping was not unlike what I had been doing for years before I ran for Congress, running and winning campaigns—counting votes, assembling the support needed to pass the bill you want passed, making sure that everyone who has pledged to vote with you will actually stand up and do so. The whip's role combines counting and policy, because to be persuasive you have to know your stuff. I knew I could do it, but questioned whether I should embrace a role that—at least publicly—would primarily draw on my campaign skills.

But the more I thought about how the Contract with America promised to choke off everything I wanted to use government for, I knew I had to change course. I had a quick strategy conversation with David Obey on the floor of the House and decided that with the caucus vote tied, I would withdraw, urge my colleagues to elect Skaggs, and accept Bonior's offer to be deputy whip.

A group of Democrats quickly coalesced to confront Republican leadership in the arena of public opinion. When you are in the minority in the House, you have little chance of amending laws before they go to a vote, so making sure the public hears about what the majority party is up to and what the frightful consequences might be becomes more important. The members that Dick Gephardt assembled for this messaging group were especially dynamic. Bonior was thoughtful and a man of faith, not flashy, but focused, fearless, and unrelenting. Obey was smart, strategic, and emotive. Gephardt kept his cards close to the vest. He had learned a lot about messaging during his 1988 run for president and brought to the table valuable insights about responding to Republican attacks while initiating our own. He was our leader. George Miller (D-California), Chuck Schumer (D-New York), and Dick Durbin (D-Illinois) all lived in the same house when in Washington. Schumer and Durbin were both strategic, incisive, media-savvy. Miller I had long regarded as one of the titans of the House; he had served since 1975 and chaired Education and Labor. John Lewis (D-Georgia) was a hero of the Civil Rights Movement. I was in awe of him. He was gentle but a man of great courage, and his speaking style was bombastic, full of bravado. Patricia Schroeder (D-Colorado), Frank Pallone (D-New Jersey), and Lloyd Doggett (D-Texas) rounded out the coalition to challenge the "Contract *on* America," as some started calling it. We met every single day.

Bonior and I clicked personally. I had worked with him on the anti-Contra aid campaign, so we knew each other well. We bonded on trade, too, fighting against NAFTA. People looked to him for leadership, but he did not seek it out. Later, when he was running for House minority whip and asked me to second his nomination, I did so, which made me the only woman in Congress who supported Bonior outside of the Michigan delegation. Bonior was pro-life, so abortion groups called me, enraged. I understood their anger, but I also respected him enormously and appreciated his work.

I knew I had to fight the contract with everything I had. I also received an education in how being in the minority in the House comes with its own special privileges—like literally being relegated to lower quarters. We met every day in the basement of the Capitol, in room HC9, in the early morning. No coffee, no donuts. Durbin and I co-chaired the group, and among the first orders of business was getting our colleagues who were not as accustomed to making noise as I was more comfortable in the role of provocateur. We burned up the phone lines, and buttonholed colleagues in the hallway, on the floor of the House, as they were getting up to get a coffee.

We had a few tools at our disposal. There was a long-standing House tradition of what are called "one-minutes." Each party got ten speaking spots each day. One-minutes take place at the beginning of every day the House is in session; members are invited to come to the front of the House floor and speak at the podium on any topic they wish. End of the day, same deal—one minute, any topic. Typically the House floor is empty during these hours. Most members are in their offices, so anyone doing a one-minute is likely to be talking to empty seats. But the C-SPAN cameras are there for the viewing public, and that's the audience that matters. These one-minutes can be used strategically.

Our group wanted to paint a complete picture of what was going on in the House, so viewers and the American public would have no illusions about the Republican agenda—and ours. I did a one-minute on how Republicans did not cooperate with our efforts to ban gifts from lobbyists. Perks and privileges betrayed the public trust, I argued, and had a corrupting influence. A few days later the subject of one of these one-minutes was one of the Contract with America's centerpieces: the balanced-budget amendment. Why was the new majority leader not sharing with people which programs would be put on the chopping block? (The truth is he had said he feared the amendment would be defeated if the details were spelled out.) One week later my one-minute centered on the conflicting stories surrounding a meeting between Speaker Gingrich and Rupert Murdoch. First, the speaker's office had said they could not recall the meeting. Then a Gingrich spokesman said nothing serious was discussed. The next day, the speaker said he and Murdoch discussed the FEC complaint against Murdoch's ownership of Fox Television, but that it had only come up in passing. Then we learned that Fox's top lobbyist was also in the meeting.

Gingrich was vulnerable on ethics, and Bonior took the lead on challenging him on that front. He was relentless.

Meanwhile I started calling members to speak out on a big range of issues and ask them, "Can I count on you to do a one-minute?" I decided each morning what issue we would take up, and a rhythm was established, as members of the "opposing team" rose to meet the challenge. My Republican counterpart in the battle on the House floor was Jack Kingston (R-Georgia). Every morning and most evenings he and I argued. We agreed on no issue. But we became good friends nonetheless. I respected that he believed in what he was doing.

Eventually some of the more august older statesmen of the House, men who had felt themselves above this sort of thing, were doing one-minutes. Our messaging group grew in confidence as the fight with Republicans intensified. Eventually I was inviting members who got up to say something wonderful about people in their district—another House tradition—to go to the end of the line. Making sure people understood how corrosive the Contract with America was to our social fabric was more important. We also used "Special Orders," or speeches given at the end of the day after the House has completed all legislative business. Members deliver speeches on a topic of their choice—only now they have up to sixty minutes. These became another tool in our arsenal.

Then, the Republicans made a huge mistake in their policy proposal, cutting the "school lunch" program. That was so wrongheaded it let us claim the moral high ground. It had a human face and it exposed the anti-social-safety-net agenda for what it was: shortsighted and indifferent to the most vulnerable. After working with Tom O'Donnell in Gephardt's office, we decided to focus our fire almost totally on school lunch.

The Republicans had proposed block-granting school lunch, and we sensed this made them vulnerable. Everyone in Washington knows that block grants are a cover for cutting spending on particular programs without being too specific about whose funds are being axed; unlike federal programs that specify who exactly will be receiving benefits, block grants are given with only vague general direction as to how the money is to be allocated (so money marked for early childhood education could wind up spent on a state governor's pet project, be it roads or mass transit, while budget tricks obscure the transfer). When politicians say they want to introduce block grants in order to save on administrative costs, or give states more control, they are merely being shy about their real motivation, which is to get the federal government out of the business of helping vulnerable people. The Republicans were overplaying their hand, and would face intense opposition if enough Americans could see their plans. We could use their misguided plan to deprive kids of school lunch as a way to attack the entire contract.

The U.S. government had been in the business of school lunch since President Truman signed the National School Lunch Act into law in 1946. He had seen World War II draftees who showed evidence of malnutrition, so for him—not unreasonably—school lunches were a matter of national security. As for Gingrich, I simply wondered: How does a grown man decide that *not providing food for schoolchildren* is the answer to America's problems? What kind of values were those?

Gingrich wanted to transfer responsibility for providing school lunches to the states. Block grants to states would be more efficient, he and his colleagues argued, although in reality the school lunch program worked pretty well. Participating school districts got $1.76 for each child receiving a free lunch (those whose families had incomes below 130 percent of the poverty level), $1.36 for kids receiving a reduced-price meal (those from families earning between 130 percent and 185 percent of the poverty level), and 17 cents each for the rest. The cost to the nation was about $1.70 per lunch, and schools could charge whatever they wanted for the meals that were only slightly subsidized.

Meanwhile the number of kids who would be affected by any policy change was huge: in Washington, D.C., alone, nearly 60 percent of public school students received free or reduced-price lunches. In most states the number was between 20 and 40 percent. Worse was that the Republicans proposed that overall funding for the program be slashed, so that by 2000 there would be $2 billion less for school lunches, even before accounting for the fact that states would also be able to divert 20 percent of the block grant monies to other programs.

Our campaign to save school lunches grabbed everyone's attention. I got the idea to contact Save the Children and sell Save the Children–branded scarves and ties from my office. We also got children to hold hands and create a ring around the Capitol building, with the added incentive of ice cream donated by Ben & Jerry's, in defense of school lunches. We had 20,000 paper plates that read, "Don't End Our School Lunch!" delivered to the Capitol for them to hold. It was a Sunday afternoon in May, and an unbelievable event that worked exactly as we had hoped—it brought public attention to the issue. And it got Newt Gingrich's attention as well. The Associated Press reported that Gingrich had to cancel a speech at a Washington ballroom when five hundred protestors burst through the kitchen doors chanting "No More Cuts" and waving empty lunch trays.[2] Meanwhile our group continued calling fellow Democratic House members, giving them talking points. We mobilized every last person we could.

I had my office organize similar protests in my district. It was important to lead by example, and I tried to show other members they could take up these issues, too, and double the public pressure on Gingrich. Schumer was brilliant in getting across how much the Contract of America impacted each district and that specificity brought it home to people.

We ended up defeating the Contract of America in its first hundred days, which is quite the accomplishment since the Republicans had just taken control of the House after forty years. The Gingrich Republicans had the momentum, and we stopped them.

Gingrich was greatly weakened by our efforts to torpedo the Contract with America, but he was smart and knew how to work the rules of the House. He was determined to reduce the size of government and poison the public's view of pro-government Democrats. Gingrich was further weakened, though not defeated, when an ethics investigation led by Bonior exposed how he had cheated the system by mixing political activities with tax-exempt charitable ones.[3]

We would knock Gingrich and Dick Armey back when they turned to Medicare, a program of the Great Society that a lot of people, especially retired people, depended on.

In 1995 Gingrich told a Blue Cross/Blue Shield conference that he intended to let Medicare "wither on the vine." At this point, Armey had already gone on record saying, "We need to wean our old people away from Medicare."[4] This sounded like bluster, but they meant it. In May newspapers announced Gingrich's pledge to slash Medicare spending by one-seventh over the next seven years, to the tune of about $270 billion, "without significantly affecting anyone now enrolled in the program."[5] Senate Majority Leader Bob Dole, though he supported the overall plan, had enough integrity to refrain from suggesting that was actually possible—that we could make $270 billion in cuts and it wouldn't significantly affect people. Republicans also claimed that this action constituted an effort to "preserve, protect and strengthen" Medicare. To me it sounded more like an attempt to rob Medicare in order to give tax cuts to people who didn't need them.

Congressman Sam Gibbons (D-Florida), a member who represented a huge number of seniors, proposed GOP could stand for "Get Old People." I loved him. We had posters with that slogan printed up in Gephardt's office. My granddaughter Rigby many years later saw the framed poster on my office wall, "GOP = 'Get Old People.'" "Bubbie," she said, "Really? They want to do that?"

Every morning, every night, we took to the House floor to relay our message. We took advantage of the fact that as a minority party we chaired no committees and thus could not call hearings, and took to the outdoors instead. We held a hearing on the lawn in front of the Capitol, asking seniors to explain what these cuts would mean for them and their families. Amazingly, the Republican House leaders had the Capitol police arrest senior citizens who were protesting the cuts, and the staff ran to get pictures of them handcuffed in the hallway. We made huge posters with their pictures that stood behind us when we spoke on the House floor.

Constituents responded—some with support, others with vitriol. The fight became very, very public. My colleague Pallone shared the faxes that had started pouring into his office: "I'm sorry you joined that asshole DELAURO." "See you in the ovens."

None of it dented our determination to preserve the safety net, though. Our campaign was also working; the polls started changing in our direction. When we took to the floor during the government shutdown to declaim about the Republicans' plans for the 1996 federal budget, in particular the proposed $270 billion in Medicare cuts to pay for tax cuts for the rich (without offering any alternative healthcare plan), Republican leaders turned off the TV cameras and microphones. We stayed on the floor to protest, though we didn't have social media to bring in the outside world, as we would decades later when we protested the Republicans' refusal to address gun violence. Bill Thomas (R-California), never one to shy away from a confrontation, took the lead in shutting out the public. Then, on November 14, 1995, the Republicans shut down the government altogether.

Two days after the shutdown started, a *New York Daily News* columnist reported that he had heard Gingrich explain his reasoning for the shutdown. Gingrich had been invited by President Clinton to join him on Air Force One to fly to Israeli Prime Minister Yitzhak Rabin's funeral. Gingrich accepted the invitation and had hoped that Clinton would take the opportunity to walk back to where Gingrich was seated on the plane so they could discuss the budget deal, but that visit never happened. When the plane eventually returned to Andrews Air Force Base, Gingrich and Bob Dole were asked to deplane by the rear door. This show of disrespect, Gingrich said, led him to send the president two financing and spending bills that he knew that Clinton would have to veto, thereby shutting down the federal government.[6] Accompanying this report the *Daily News* ran a full-page front-page political cartoon depicting Newt as a diapered baby, crying and stomping his foot, the headline CRY BABY emblazoned across the top.

In some ways it was disillusioning to see personality and pettiness factor so heavily in this fight. I was not naive enough to expect all talk to center on whether a policy was good or not, but at the same time I had not expected policy debates to be subsumed, even driven, by outsized egos and other character failings more than concern for the American people.

The 1995 government shutdown ultimately lasted twenty-seven days, sidelining Congress through the first week of January 1996. Early on I had said I would not accept a salary while the government was shut down, which did not exactly thrill my husband. Dick Durbin made the same commitment. This stance seemed like a great idea at the time—and I still believe it was the right thing to do—but as the shutdown dragged on week after week, and my bills kept arriving, it seemed less smart.

When the government finally reopened, Tom DeLay (R-Texas), then the House majority whip, said ending the shutdown was the worst thing that could have happened. In this respect DeLay was an ideological and temperamental forerunner of many Republicans in the House today. They want to be employed by the government and yet tear out its foundation at the same time. Gingrich, for all his grandstanding, nonetheless fundamentally believed in the institution of the House, and I appreciated that.

I was so glad to be back at work, but I also came to see the shutdown as a singular opportunity to defeat those trying to kill government. The Republican Party in power was blamed, and Gingrich's approval ratings took a nosedive. The Democrats and their allies quickly rallied to defeat the Republicans' hundred-day plans. Most of the Contract with America never became law. And the fight over it allowed people to see the important things government does.

Still, the fight proved costly for many of us. Bonior lost his seat for going after Gingrich. Being such a visible antagonist to the Republicans and their plans for government was a mixed experience for me. I was better in this attacking role than I wanted to be. I'd never wanted to be a junkyard dog, but here I was, loud and out in front. In years to come, having been so visible during this contentious time would hurt me, particularly when I lost the race for caucus chair. I was not seen as someone who could bring people to consensus, but instead as better at highlighting and exploiting differences. Defeating the Gingrich Revolution took a personal toll, though I would soon have opportunities I did not foresee.

3

In Defense of Working Families

Nobody has ever before asked the nuclear family to live all by itself in a box the way we do. With no relatives, no support, we've put it in an impossible situation.

—Margaret Mead, *Culture and Commitment*

DOCTORS TOLD ME that I had ovarian cancer in March 1986 while I was working as Chris Dodd's chief of staff. I was about to take a leave of absence to manage Dodd's re-election, but on the day he announced his campaign, the doctors delivered the news. As my doctor talked, Stan felt nauseated and wanted to throw up. I stumbled throughout the rest of the day. All I knew about ovarian cancer was this: it is dangerous. There was no marker for early detection, and survival rates were not great.

Still, I was forty-three years old and lucky. The cancer was discovered during an unrelated medical check-up and it was Stage 1. The next day I told the senator the situation and he gave me the response that everyone in that situation wants to hear: "Go get yourself well. You are still chief of staff and the campaign doesn't start without you," he said. I would undergo radiation treatment for two and a half months without the added worry that my job would not be there when I returned.

Now, I am fortunate to say that by the grace of God and the hard work of biomedical researchers I have been cancer-free for thirty years. At the time, however, surgery and radiation treatment left me exhausted—but also galvanized to lead Dodd's re-election because he understood the importance of legislation that protects men and women from bosses less enlightened than mine.

1986 was the same year that Dodd wrote and first introduced the Family and Medical Leave Act (FMLA). It is one of those pieces of legislation that at first glance appears "soft"—and not something for serious politicians to waste their time on. In fact family and medical leave speaks volumes about the kind of society we hope to create. The fight to pass FMLA also taught me a lot about tenacity.

Dodd had been interested in children's issues for some time. With Republican senator Arlen Specter he founded the Children's Caucus in 1983. He also was keenly aware of how caretaking and work life could never be kept entirely separate, not in the real world. As Dodd recalls, he would see senators occasionally miss votes because family issues had temporarily pulled them away from Capitol Hill. Some of these legislators later voted against FMLA, seemingly unaware of the hypocrisy involved.

We knew that not having job security in the midst of rocky times affected everyone, at all levels of American society, but the forces aligned to defend the status quo were firmly entrenched. The Chamber of Commerce was notoriously averse to policies like the Family and Medical Leave Act. Dodd and I crisscrossed the state to meet with business groups to present the bill and ask: Any objections? If so, what are they? I put together a bipartisan women's advisory committee of about two dozen people to advocate for the bill and approach Connecticut business leaders to be spokespeople.

In 1988 Connecticut became the first state in the nation to enact legislation that provided unpaid leave from work for workers in the event of a serious illness in the family or the birth or adoption of a child. John Larson, now of Connecticut's First Congressional

District, then president of the state senate, was instrumental in getting it passed. Advocates like Judy Lichtman of the National Partnership for Women and Families and Marcia Greenberger of the National Women's Law Center were also tireless in their efforts. In fact it is hard to imagine what family policy would look like now in the United States were it not for these two women.

Yet the statistics overall, nationwide, remained dispiriting. Getting traction for family and medical leave on the federal level was a tough sell. Doggedness was critical to its ultimate success, and Dodd provided an excellent model for how to fight when victory lies far beyond the horizon. He introduced the bill every year for eight years, over and over and over again. It was a tremendous lesson in taking the long view and abiding by your convictions in the face of defeat after defeat. Dodd's bill for FMLA passed both the House and Senate twice, but passage was not easy, and both times it passed, President George H.W. Bush vetoed it. Dodd, undeterred, kept bringing it up—and so did advocates. The National Partnership led the lobbying and grassroots efforts, with the support of the American Academy of Pediatrics and Ed Zigler of the Yale Child Study Center and other organizations.

During the 1992 presidential campaign—by then I had been serving in the House for a little over a year—Dodd was raising family and medical leave as a campaign issue. He recalls a meeting with James Baker, who was then White House chief of staff and trying to help President Bush revive his stalling campaign for a second term. In the course of their conversation Dodd brought up his struggles passing the bill. As Dodd remembers it, Baker was taken aback for a second. Dodd explained the policy in full, after which Baker asked, "Why are we against that?"

Most objections to the Family and Medical Leave Act reveal painfully privileged mind-sets and zero compassion. Some people imagine the law is for people who demand more time off to drive their kid to tennis lessons. They imagine that it licenses indulgent behavior, and that if we continue down this road of acknowledging that work and family are sometimes in tension, American productivity and our global competitiveness will suffer, and we will end up like France or Spain, with a moribund economy and only memories of past glories. Nothing could be further from the truth.

Another objection to family and medical leave is a pure head-in-the-sand approach to lives of families today. Some opponents imagine that we still inhabit a culture wherein every wage earner has a partner at home who is both willing and able to take care of messy, dirty, time-consuming family stuff while they devote themselves solely to bringing home the bacon. As the writer Irin Carmon put it: "Get a wife. The United States' approach to work-life balance more or less boils down to that."[1] But the days of one-income families are long gone, and they are not coming back.

For some families, honestly, it is not a matter of those days being long gone. For many of us, cruising along on a one-earner household was never an option. My family, for instance. When my father came down with tuberculosis in 1942, not only was he out of work but he spent a year at Gaylord Sanatorium in Wallingford, Connecticut. My mother traveled by bus every day after quitting time to visit him—an hour's trek each way, and then a walk uphill.

Finally, February 5, 1993, the Family and Medical Leave Act became law. President Bill Clinton made it the law of the land when he made it the first bill he signed. Since then it has been used more than 200 million times by workers needing time off to care for themselves or their families.

Many of the collaborations and relationships that resulted from the fight for family and medical leave would sustain me for years to come, and the central question of how to ensure that women can achieve greater economic security continues to guide my work.

The results of having Family and Medical Leave Act as the law of the land have been gratifying. Those who argued that it would dampen productivity have been proven wrong. According to the Labor Department's surveys, nine out of ten covered employers report that the law has either a positive or neutral effect on their productivity and growth. Giving employees a modicum of leave to care for family has proven good for businesses as well. Any productivity losses that could conceivably be traced back to the Family and Medical Leave Act are dwarfed by the costs that would be incurred if good, reliable employees did not have the freedom to tend to their families when tragedy struck—or when they had the joys of ushering in new life.

The Family and Medical Leave Act was always meant as a first step toward securing broader provisions to benefit workers and families, however. As is, it provides unpaid, job-protected leave for roughly 60 percent of the private workforce—those in salaried positions at employers above a certain size. Forty percent of the private-sector workforce still has no access to family leave protections; the law does not apply to people in their job situation. Further, the law's unpaid status continues to be an obstacle to more families benefiting from the law. With just 13 percent having paid family leave from their private-sector employer, many simply cannot afford to take advantage of it.

During the administration of President George W. Bush, a coalition of progressive legislators and activists decided to tackle short-term paid leave and sick days, leaving the question of paid long-term leave to the side for a while. The coalition that had pushed for FMLA was in agreement: President Bush would never sign anything that came close to providing paid family leave, so better to go for a policy we can realize.

Our doubts about Bush's discomfort with paid leave proved correct. Prompted by the Chamber of Commerce, Bush fought to curtail the Family and Medical Leave Act as it existed, and put forth a proposal to diminish the short-term leave that it already allowed.

Bush and his allies wanted a more precise definition of "serious ill-ness" in the law, and they wanted to prohibit using the law to take short chunks of time off.

While family leave opponents recognized that some people used the law to receive radiation treatments for cancer, and others to sit bedside with dying children, they genuinely seemed to believe that first and foremost people used it to avoid work. Testimony from those who advocated for ending FMLA was rife with stories of employees faking migraines just so that they could cover their coming into the office half an hour late each day.[2] As we find with many Republican objections to our social safety net, the concern is that somewhere out there, someone unworthy is getting away with something. In fact the vast majority of people are just trying to honor their family commitments and keep their jobs.

If passing paid leave was a political impossibility, pushing for paid sick days was not exactly throwing in the towel. Paid sick days are a big issue. It is a stark and disheartening fact about work in America today. Nearly half of all private-sector employees do not get paid sick days—not even a single day a year.[3] So what do people do? They work while sick, or take a day or two off to recuperate but pay a stiff financial penalty. They deal with the heartbreak of send-ing sick children to school simply because they cannot afford to take an unpaid day to care for them. Often a consequence of being sick is not having enough money to pay the bills. The situation for low-wage workers is abysmal: more than 80 percent of low-wage workers do not get paid sick days.

Senator Ted Kennedy (D-Massachusetts) and his staff on the Health, Education, Labor and Pensions committee were develop-ing legislation to tackle the issue of paid sick leave. I found in him the ideal partner for action on the problem. He had firsthand ex-perience with the agony of having to choose between professional obligations and family—and understood how family rightly won most of the time. Senator Kennedy focused on what providing paid sick days would mean to public health. I focused on paid sick days as a basic workplace protection, a new and critical labor standard. Together I thought we had a powerful argument—but it would take a while, and in fact the fight continues.

We called our bill the Healthy Families Act (HFA) and began making the case for it in 2004. The legislation was simple. HFA would allow workers to earn paid sick leave that they could use when sick, or to care for a sick family member, to obtain preventive care, or address the impacts of domestic violence, stalking, or sexual assault. It would require employers with fifteen or more employees (for twenty or more workweeks a year, thereby excluding most seasonal employers) to allow each employee to earn one hour of paid sick time for every thirty hours worked.

A broad coalition supported the bill: women's groups, teachers, healthcare workers, children's advocates, unions, and civil rights and religious organizations. The bill anticipated the concerns of business owners by declaring that an employer would not be required to permit an employee to earn more than fifty-six hours of paid sick time per calendar year, though the employer could opt to set a higher limit if they wanted to. Employers could also require workers to provide documentation, for example a doctor's note, to support any request for leave longer than three consecutive days. The bill was designed to balance the needs of workers and employers.

Even people working for very small businesses, those with fewer than fifteen employees, could benefit from the Healthy Families Act—they could earn up to seven job-protected days of unpaid sick leave annually. Our point was simple: having to choose between a paycheck and physical recovery should not be the American way. This principle is especially important for women. Despite several legislative attempts to address the problem, women still overwhelmingly bear the burden of caretaking.

The Healthy Families Act did not pass. Kennedy's statement

upon reintroducing the bill in April 2005 on Administrative Professionals' Day, formerly known as Secretary's Day, called the status quo "unacceptable" and a public health risk. I added that paid sick leave was a necessity; it was nuts that the United States did not have it.[4]

The bill was brought up again in 2007, and again in 2009. Repeatedly we encountered opponents who did not take it or family and medical leave seriously. They seemed to think it was OK—even a smart strategy, business-wise—to place workers in untenable positions. Even the Supreme Court seemed infected with a bias against people who dared get sick. In early 2006 I had the opportunity to speak against the confirmation of Supreme Court Justice Samuel Alito. As an appellate court judge Alito had handed down rulings that weakened the Family and Medical Leave Act; he wanted to overturn it because he felt it created an unwarranted "substantive entitlement to sick leave."

In 2009, it seemed like we might have an opening for the Healthy Families Act. After eight long years of Bush, President Barack Obama was in office. By this time Senator Kennedy, the lion of the Senate, had died, and Dodd had taken over as the primary sponsor of the bill in the Senate. With the backing of the National Partnership for Women and Families, the American Association of University Women (AAUW), and the National Women's Law Center, plus grassroots advocates, we were able to keep up the drumbeat on HFA.

Dodd scheduled a hearing on it. Stakes were high; Democrats were now in the majority in the House, we had a sympathetic White House, and we had been working on this bill for five years. In the end, however, competing bills served as a distraction from the substance of HFA. The window on being able to pass HFA as a national standard quickly closed.

Without federal legislation, the fight turned fast and furiously to the states. In 2011 Connecticut became the first state to pass a paid sick days law—mandating one paid sick day earned for every thirty days worked. The bill was first introduced in the Connecticut State Senate in 2007, and had repeatedly failed to pass because business associations persuaded legislators that it would hinder them from being able to run their businesses properly and profitably. I spoke out at rallies and lobbied across the state. When it finally passed, it barely squeaked by; eighteen to seventeen votes in the State Senate, seventy-six to seventy-five in the State House. But a majority is a majority and this was a major victory for Connecticut's working people.

Now reports on the state of business in Connecticut indicate that paid sick days have not done the damage their early detractors said they would. Most business owners say they do not notice a difference.

Since 2011 paid sick days have spread to California, Massachusetts, Oregon, and most recently Vermont. Nearly twenty cities in New Jersey and Pennsylvania, and now Cook County, Illinois, have passed paid sick day legislation. Grassroots groups like AAUW and Moms Rising were critical to these state victories. Recent polls show that an overwhelming majority of Americans support it.[5] I lobbied for it in New York City and was thrilled to see it signed into law by Mayor Bill de Blasio in 2014.

After two decades of the Family and Medical Leave Act, some facts remain startling: not many American workers take parental leave. Very few men do. Disparities in parental leave rates have not changed much over time. The less-educated take less time off. The more-educated and wealthier take more time off.

These facts explain the weakness of FMLA. As long as family leave remains unpaid, most American families simply cannot afford to take leave. And as long as family leave remains unpaid, men will be less likely to take it.

In the spring of 2010, economist Heather Boushey was working at the Center for American Progress (CAP) and brought to my staff a proposal she termed "Social Security Cares." My former legislative director Becky Salay was also at CAP at the time, and they were talking to a range of groups. Heather's idea was that family and medical leave could be paid if individual employers were not asked to cover the costs. Boushey proposed instead a system that worked more like Social Security. Individuals pay in, individuals get back benefits.

Having paid leave covered by a universal pool means that employers will not be smacked with added expenses that they might not be able to cover in a given year. It means that no worker employed by a business that's too small or financially shaky to provide them with paid leave would be denied the opportunity to take paid leave to help his or her family.

Translating Boushey's proposal into legislative language took time to get right. Letty Mederos on my staff and I worked with the National Partnership for Women and Families and the Center for American Progress, who were doing the groundwork on the policy outside of Congress. We convened meetings with groups including the National Women's Law Center and Family Values at Work to build support for the proposal. Advocates who had been weathering ongoing attacks on Social Security were slow to warm up to the idea, perhaps wearied from the work to protect Social Security itself. I understood their concerns but was also convinced that a social insurance program with a universal benefit was the way to go.

In late 2013 Senator Kirsten Gillibrand (D-New York) and I introduced the Family and Medical Insurance Leave Act—or FAMILY Act. This would make family and medical leave paid through the creation of a national family and medical leave insurance program. Workers who took leave would receive 66 percent of their wages, up to a capped monthly amount, for up to twelve weeks in a one-year period. They could use it to address their own serious health conditions, including pregnancy or childbirth; to deal with the serious health condition of a parent, spouse, domestic partner, or child; to care for a new child; and/or for specific military caregiving and leave purposes. The definition of "serious health condition" would be the same as that used in the FMLA. The leave would be paid for out of a .02% increase in the Social Security tax withheld from paychecks. Contributions would cover both benefits and administrative costs. It is an extraordinary piece of legislation to benefit American workers.

How much would it cost, for most workers? Less than two dollars a week. An employee whose annual salary is $32,196 would pay about $1.24 per week into the insurance program. A full-time worker who earned $43,579 would pay $1.68 per week.

The cost is small, but the economic benefits are large. Leave programs and other flexible options help people remain in the workforce rather than dropping out. Employees who use family and medical leave tend to stick with their employer once they return from leave, so employee retention rises. Leave insurance programs also boost lifetime earnings, because people are not forced to choose between their job and the needs of their family. This is particularly important for women. Last but not least, when fathers take advantage of the leave option, it starts to erode the assumption that women are always the primary caregivers for their families—an assumption that depresses women's wages across industries and labor sectors.

Even some conservatives like the idea of a government response to the pressures facing modern families. 2016 Republican candidate for president Marco Rubio presented a family leave policy that offered businesses that gave employees four to twelve weeks of paid leave a tax break of up to $4,000 per employee. Among the commentary from those to his right, however, we heard comments like this: "Wanna get paid for watching Bobbie's soccer game? Marco Rubio is here to help."[6]

To me the lines are clear. As a nation, we cannot force individuals to absorb more risk—as the Republican plans for Social Security do. Nor can we toss out the role government plays in the lives of vulnerable populations as the Contract with America did. Objections to family and medical leave, or fighting against paid sick days, are a refusal to recognize modern times—and by extension, a reluctance to trust people, especially women, to know what's best for their families and livelihoods. More than coercive force against American workers, we need policies that aid them in good times and bad. Family leave, ultimately, is about basic trust in humanity.

But in no arena does basic trust in humanity factor in more than when talk turns to food stamps. To that epic food fight we turn next.

4

In Defense of the Hungry

When I give food to the poor they call me a saint. When I ask
why the poor have no food, they call me a communist.

—Dom Hélder Pessoa Câmara,
Archbishop of Olinda and Recife, Brazil

THE FIRST FOOD STAMP PROGRAM was piloted in 1939 in response to
a systemic crisis that caused massive crop surpluses in the United
States. Globalization, combined with the effects of the Great Depression, caused farmers to produce vastly more than our urban
factory workers could afford to purchase. Everyone experienced
hardship as farm incomes crashed while city dwellers grew hun-
grier. Soup kitchens struggled to keep up with demand, resulting
in some of the iconic images from the Depression of breadlines
snaking around city blocks. This crisis produced a cruel societal
juxtaposition in which food riots were not uncommon, even though
food was going to waste.

Food stamps were not the first solution to this problem. At one
point, FDR's Agricultural Adjustment Administration paid farmers to plow under surplus crops and ordered the slaughter of hogs,
effectively destroying usable food. Not surprisingly, millions of
unemployed, malnourished Americans opposed these attempts to

increase crop and commodity prices at the expense of feeding the hungry.

Any permanent solution had to take into account not just the farmers who grew the food, but also those who consumed it—or would, if it was affordable. Milo Perkins, the first administrator of the food stamp program, emphasized the critical linking of fates for urban and rural populations, declaring, "We got a picture of a gorge, with farm surpluses on one cliff and under-nourished city folks on the other. We set out to find a practical way to build a bridge across that chasm."

There was another misstep, however, before food stamps came to fruition. The Federal Surplus Relief Corporation first tried to distribute food from farmers directly to consumers, bypassing regular market channels. Naturally, this course of action upset food retailers because it diminished their role in the marketplace.

Eventually the government inaugurated a food stamp program in a handful of "stamp towns." The first food stamps were literally orange stamps that people could purchase just like any other commodity. For every dollar of orange stamps purchased, they would also receive 50 cents' worth of blue stamps. The orange stamps could be traded for any type of food, while the blue stamps could only be spent on food deemed surplus by the Department of Agriculture. The immediate results of this pilot food stamp program were striking: people living and shopping in stamp towns experienced a significant increase in their food purchasing power, farmers saw their incomes rise, and grocery store receipts in participating areas increased 15 percent.

The program worked, but it ground to a halt in 1943, when a wartime economy put many Americans back to work again in defense manufacturing. With the higher incomes that accompanied the strong economy, Americans did not need food support.

However, in 1962 President John F. Kennedy revived the program to again address poverty and hunger. Two years later, President

Lyndon B. Johnson signed the Food Stamp Act, heralding it as a triumph of marrying humanitarian instincts with free enterprise. The system of purchasing coupons of greater monetary value remained, while the provision that the food bought be labeled surplus was eliminated.

Hunger has been a persistent problem throughout American history, but attention to it and attempts to address it have varied. In 1967 Robert F. Kennedy helped bring national attention to hunger when he toured Mississippi and saw children so much thinner than he thought was possible in the United States. At the same time diseases thought only to affect undernourished populations in underdeveloped countries were being found in the United States as well. A growing sense of crisis helped make the problem of hunger seem like an American problem, not just the hungry person's problem, and the effect of the emerging crisis was to make hunger-fighting efforts bipartisan.

When the United States Senate formed its Select Committee on Nutrition and Human Needs, the liberal senator George McGovern (D-South Dakota) took the helm, but his team of eight Democrats and five Republicans was equally committed to the task. They visited migrant farm workers in Florida and people living in gutted-out neighborhoods in the Bronx, New York. In 1974 they expanded their focus to include nutrition policy, because it was increasingly evident that chronic illnesses resulting from eating too much were also becoming a problem.

Addressing hunger through food stamps has always received bipartisan presidential support. In 1971, President Richard Nixon signed legislation that required that allotments be equal to the cost of a nutritionally adequate diet, and established uniform national eligibility standards. Then, the 1977 Food Stamp Act signed by President Jimmy Carter eliminated the requirement that participants purchase their stamps. Senators McGovern, Dole, Jacob Javits (R-New York), and Ernest Hollings (D-South Carolina) shepherded this legislation through the Senate. Looking back on this push, Dole would years later remark on how food stamps, the school lunch program, and WIC (Women, Infants, and Children) brought leaders together to help low-income Americans. "As I look at it," he said, "no first-class democracy can treat its people like second-class citizens."

Today, one in four Americans under the age of nineteen lives in a household served by food stamps. However, despite this prevalence, food stamps are the orphan in the policy process, with few willing to champion the cause. People who depend on them are frequently dismissed and vilified.

Battling to expand and preserve food stamps has been one of the fights of my life.

The people who think they can dismantle nutrition programs try to do so often—every four years or so at least—and they never tire of their pursuit. The food stamps program faces ongoing, determined, intensely ideological opposition from those in Congress who argue that it enables sloth, poor household management, and even drug use. They make these claims despite clear evidence that demonstrates that it is an effective, efficient program.

Opponents argue further that the issue is not whether hungry Americans are fed, but that the government play no part in the feeding. The only way to maintain sanity while explaining to colleagues that accepting food stamps is not a "lifestyle" is to remind yourself that millions of people would go to bed with aching stomachs if you did not fight on behalf of this program.

Because Congress must periodically reauthorize it, funding for food stamps is not automatic. Since 1973, that reauthorization has been included in the Farm Bill, which typically comes up for renegotiation every five years. A wide variety of groups see the Farm Bill as an opportunity to achieve policy goals—from ending subsidies of biofuels, to ending crop subsidies, to bolstering commodity subsidies, to addressing obesity and the overuse of antibiotics. Every renegotiation is fraught, drawn-out, and contentious.

One morning early in the new session in 2005, Marcy Kaptur, then the ranking Democrat on the Agriculture Appropriations Subcommittee, called me to say she was selecting another subcommittee, which meant I would become the ranking Democrat on Agriculture. I tried to persuade her to stay, because if she did, and Democrats won the House in the next election, she would become the chair—thus one of the so-called "cardinals" in Congress who have a significant role in funding key domestic policy initiatives. However, she opted to move over to the Defense Appropriations Subcommittee, which meant that when Democrats did win control of the Congress in 2006, I became the chair of the Agriculture Appropriations Subcommittee. This proved a blessing. The subcommittee had jurisdiction for the traditional "ag issues," but I also brought a different perspective to them. Even more important, it was the committee responsible for nutrition. I also now listened to people in my district with a new ear, including a woman with five kids who told me, "I just don't have enough food. Some weeks I feed my sons more and my daughters less."

Because the Farm Bill renegotiation is intense, protracted, and often ugly, prep work starts early. In May of 2007, I, along with Representative Wayne Gilchrest (R-Maryland), introduced with a bipartisan group of twenty-two members of Congress an alternative Farm Bill—the Farm, Nutrition, and Community Investment Act—that sought to ensure that issues impacting other regions of the country, specifically the Mid-Atlantic states, the Northeast, and California, should be taken into consideration when drafting the bill.

These were not traditional "ag" states, but places where specialty crops and environmental conservation were major concerns. In the past, their interests as contributors to our national "breadbasket" had not been well-represented. The Farm, Nutrition, and Community Investment Act was an attempt to shift this prevailing attitude, as well as to strengthen support for food stamps and other nutrition programs. We wanted to signal that if these issues of regional equity were not addressed, we would champion this alternative bill.

By the end of 2007, the statistics on food stamp usage were alarming. An array of states were experiencing massive increases in food stamp caseloads that year, and contrary to popular perception, this was not just an urban problem. Among the states where we were seeing large increases in the numbers of food stamp recipients were Nevada, North Dakota, Vermont, Maryland, Mississippi, and North and South Carolina.

Knowing of my deep interest in anti-hunger and nutrition issues, House Speaker Nancy Pelosi appointed me to the Farm Bill Conference Committee in 2008 to help defend food stamp funding in the House version of the bill. Typically, the farm bill conference committee is comprised only of members of the House Agriculture Committee and other authorizing committees, none of which I sat on. I also represented an urban and suburban district in a state that has no high-profile agricultural interests. According to how business is normally conducted in the House, I was considered, to borrow an agricultural term, an invasive species.

But while I was not a member of that committee, I had extensive knowledge of farm bill programs by virtue of being the chair of the House Agriculture Appropriations Subcommittee, which provides the actual funding for these programs. So, I was not a complete stranger to the farm bill, especially the anti-hunger and nutrition programs. When some senators objected strongly to my being there, the House Agriculture Committee chairman, Collin Peterson (D-Minnesota), rose to my defense and said, "Rosa speaks for us on nutrition." He promised to me personally that I could take the lead on the nutrition title, and he never went back on that

promise, although he probably cringed whenever he heard that I was trying to reach him.

By April 2008, unemployment was rising, and the number of Americans receiving food stamps was projected to reach 28 million in the coming year, the highest participation rate since the late 1960s. Given what was at stake, I determined that it was in everyone's best interest that I stay out of the way of the other sections in the farm bill, and focus on being the sole spokesperson for food stamps during conference deliberations. A significant undertaking such as this required assistance, and I was fortunate to have the support of my colleague Jim McGovern (D-Massachusetts), as well as the support of key advocacy groups, such as the Food Research and Action Center (FRAC) and the Center for Budget and Policy Priorities (CBPP). Their support throughout the process was invaluable.

At the outset of the farm bill debate, I was optimistic that we could address a number of problems surrounding food stamps, including the biggest one: the current food stamp benefit was about $1 per person per meal. That is a paltry amount of money for food necessities to support health, energy, and good nutrition. Through the bill, supporters of the food stamp program wanted to:

1) Stop the slide in value of food stamps and index benefit amounts to inflation. Benefit levels had been eroding in purchasing power since 1996 because they were not indexed to inflation. The 1996 Personal Responsibility and Work Opportunity Reconciliation Act—aka the "workfare" bill—signed by President Clinton not only disqualified Able-Bodied Adults Without Dependents (ABAWDs, or *a-bods*, as they are called in policy circles) from receiving benefits if they failed to work twenty-plus hours a week, but it also froze the standard income deduction

for everybody. So a food stamp recipient eligible to receive a particular dollar amount in 1996 was eligible to receive the exact same amount in early 2008, and no more. For a working parent with two kids, that meant they were receiving about $37 a month less than if the benefit had kept up with inflation.

2) Increase the benefit to make up for those twelve years of lost value.

3) Raise the household asset ceiling. The limit was $2,000 in assets, and had not been raised in twenty years. As a result, many households with very modest savings were barred from receiving benefits.

4) Eliminate the unreasonably low cap on the childcare deduction. Food stamp recipients could deduct childcare expenses from their income up to $175 a month per child (or $200 per infant), which is well below what even many low-income families pay for childcare. This stingy deduction punishes working parents by forcing them to choose between securing adequate childcare and securing food for their kids.

5) Raise the minimum benefit. In early 2008, the minimum benefit was just $10 a month, and had not been adjusted for inflation in thirty years. The minimum benefit goes primarily to the elderly and disabled.

6) Eliminate some paperwork and bureaucratic hurdles. One hurdle required recipients to report a change in their situation if their income changed by as little as $100 from the previous month.

7) Exclude combat pay from being considered as income for families of military personnel deployed to combat zones.

Late on the night before the House vote on the 2008 Farm Bill, I was one of several members of the House Democratic leadership

and staff huddled in the Red Room off of the floor of the House, where House Democrats go when we need a temporary working space. The room is not large, and the atmosphere was tense. The goal of the meeting was to find a way to extract funds from the crop insurance program and allocate it toward the nutrition title. After consulting with the group, Speaker Pelosi phoned Chairman Peterson, holed up in his office across the street in the Rayburn office building, to say we needed more funding for food stamps. Could it come from crop insurance? Peterson balked. Others in the Red Room brought up recent reports from the Government Accountability Office (GAO) that indicated that the crop insurance program was enriching insurance companies more than helping farmers.

The debate went back and forth for quite a while, and it was coming up on one or two a.m. Finally, Peterson accepted it, and that elicited a gasp from those up in the room. For Peterson, I am sure his thinking was that he could recapture these funds in the Senate, and that his concession would be excluded from the final bill. The change did not make several of my House colleagues happy, either. Afterward I was accosted out in the hall by fellow members from primarily rural districts—people who were on our side, literally in terms of side of the aisle but also broadly in support of food stamps. Although they supported the food stamp program, they were often compelled to express a preference for protecting farms. My colleague Earl Pomeroy (D-North Dakota), a good friend and ally, was incensed, and came up to me as I was putting on my coat. "What are you trying to do? Destroy the crop insurance program? I've been with you all along!" He was angry—he and I had worked closely together on food issues and he felt genuinely betrayed.

I was singularly focused on the goal of funding the improvements to the food stamp program, and was willing to go as far as necessary to accomplish that goal. But even I had limits, as I learned when I was extended an offer I could not in good conscience accept.

Another claustrophobic meeting had members of my staff and I huddled in Senator Tom Harkin's "hideaway"—a room that senators have in the Capitol building in addition to their office where they can hold private meetings in the immediate vicinity of the Senate floor without having to go back and forth to their offices. Bob Goodlatte (R-Virginia), who was then ranking member of the House Agriculture Committee, was present for the meeting, too.

During this meeting, Harkin presented an offer that would find the $1 billion in funding we were seeking in exchange for my support of his plan to make dietary supplements eligible for purchase under the food stamp program. He argued that the increased use of dietary supplements could provide a nutritional benefit for those on food stamps, and even contacted one of my closest friends in an attempt to convince me. I responded to Harkin that I would have to resign my chairmanship of the Agriculture Appropriations Subcommittee if I agreed to allow unregulated products that are unproven to benefit anyone, let alone women and children, to be purchased with food stamps. (In addition to the lack of proven nutritional benefits from taking dietary supplements, many of these products are expensive and thus would take up a significant portion of a person's food stamp allowance.)

The whole scene was discouraging. Senator Harkin thought so too, and proceeded to walk out of the meeting, which was awkward, considering we were occupying his personal office.

There were times when I thought I was experiencing an alternate reality. When members of the Senate Finance Committee and members of the House Agriculture Committee decided to meet, I found myself in a beautifully ornate room in the Senate that I had never seen before. With me were two Hill staffers, and around us were mostly older white men, with body language that suggested they would rather be doing anything than discussing the food stamp program.

Questions asked from both sides of the aisle betrayed a host of misconceptions about the program and who it benefits; answering them was akin to playing whack-a-mole with terrible ideas. Senator Max Baucus (D-Montana) asked me if my proposal to raise the household asset ceiling would result in a flood of people with 401ks applying for food stamps.

I was stunned. "Do you have any idea who these people are?" I finally managed to stammer out. I reminded him of the basics: to receive food stamp benefits, a person's gross monthly income has to be below 130 percent of the poverty line. This discussion continued until finally Representative Goodlatte said, "OK, Rosa's made her case."

Everything about that meeting bothered me. First, the setting. While I often appreciate being in a historic, ornate room inside the Capitol, here the opulence belied the topic of this meeting, in which were debating outcomes for millions of people whose ability to feed their families depended on what we decided in this room.

In addition, it appeared that some members seemed bored, even bothered, by this responsibility, while others seemed to outright resent it, barely disguising their contempt for food stamp recipients. I cried on the train back to my office. Based on the tone of the meeting, I thought we were going to lose this fight.

Another important component of the farm bill debate was discussions about the McGovern-Dole International Food for Education and Child Nutrition Program, which helps support food security and child development initiatives in low-income areas around the world. This program was a target for reductions in funding from those who were unconvinced that it accomplished anything.

I called former senators Dole and McGovern to inform them that funding for their program was in jeopardy, with some members expressing a desire to cut funding by more than 90 percent. Even among those who were inclined to support the program and who believed it beneficial, most did not think it was worth expending political capital to try to rescue it.

Dole and McGovern teamed up to write an op-ed for the *Washington Post* that argued for the program's effectiveness. "For just a few cents a day," they wrote, "the McGovern-Dole program has . . . promoted American values in the most positive terms, and helped achieve U.S. foreign policy and national security goals." They highlighted the benefits for young girls: school lunches helped these girls stay in school, and as their attendance increased, they married later and had fewer children.

Meanwhile, I continued to keep Speaker Pelosi apprised of the deliberations because she was a strong supporter of the food stamp program and provided support for me during times when the debate would become especially intense. We now were faced with a situation in which we were still $1 billion short of our goal, and Peterson said there would be no more money for food stamps forthcoming from the Ag Committee.

I went up to Charlie Rangel (D-New York), then chairman of the Ways and Means Committee, on the floor of the House. Rangel was great. I would even say he was a hero. He had been looking for ways to offset the cost of nutrition programs in the Farm Bill reauthorization since July 2007. His first proposal to Senate Finance Chairman Baucus had concerned international tax treaties: instead of eliminating the withholding tax, Rangel wanted to continue to levy them where the U.S. subsidiary of a foreign multinational from a low-tax country was paying out the interest. The Senate had rejected that idea because they did not want to mess with those tax laws—though later the Farm Bill they passed included almost $17 billion in tax reductions.

"What do you need?" Rangel asked me. I said we needed money for food stamps and The Emergency Food Assistance Program (TEFAP). He found us the money we needed. In the end, an extension of customs user fees (paid by importers) offset the $10 billion needed for nutrition programs.

When the 2008 Farm Bill passed in June we did a victory lap, holding a press conference, joining hands with the food advocacy groups, expressing gratitude for Chairman Peterson's support. In a situation wherein each step toward radical reform would have cost twenty to fifty votes, we had done all we could. We wanted to focus on the victory, not on how hard-won it had been. The results of the bruising 2008 Farm Bill debate went into effect in October of that year. How successful were we?

We eliminated the cap on the childcare deduction. Instead a household could deduct the full amount that they spent on childcare, reducing the chances that families would have to forgo food to pay for decent childcare.

We raised the minimum benefit to 8 percent of the maximum, or approximately $14, and the standard deduction to $144. We also indexed benefits to inflation.

We reformed how assets are counted. Tax-preferred retirement accounts and education accounts were no longer counted toward the asset limit in determining eligibility and benefit amounts. We indexed the asset limit to inflation.

The bill also increased the funds for commodity purchases for TEFAP from $140 million per year to $250 million in 2008, with adjustments for food price increases in later years.

The food stamp program was renamed the Supplemental Nutritional Assistance Program, or SNAP, and changes in eligibility requirements made it easier to qualify.

The numbers spoke to the size of the shift in priorities. The 2002 Farm Bill had been approximately $75 billion over "baseline," or current spending at the time, and the nutrition title's share of that increase came to approximately $5.4 billion. The 2008 Farm Bill was $10.36 billion over baseline, and the nutrition title's share was $10.36 billion. Spending on crop insurance was cut by $5.7 billion, and spending on commodity programs was cut by $1.7 billion.

Support for corn ethanol production was reduced from fifty-one cents per gallon to forty-five cents to reduce the incentive to shift corn production from feed to fuel.

My one regret was that Jim McGovern and I didn't get the level of funding that we thought was needed for McGovern-Dole, the international food aid program that relieves worldwide hunger, particularly for young girls. I looked to Jim on this issue; he was deeply troubled by the funding and fought just as hard. Congressman Jim McGovern is one of the great champions in the battle against hunger here and worldwide and co-chairs the Congressional Hunger Caucus.

We thought that would be the end of the food stamp fight for a while. Then a recession of historic proportions happened.

The 2009 American Recovery and Reinvestment Act (ARRA) was an attempt to help Americans navigate through a calamitous economic environment. Legislators faced the question: How do we get money in people's hands quickly? At a congressional hearing about the stimulus I asked the economist Mark Zandi what the quickest way to stimulate the economy was. Zandi came back with three recommendations: extend unemployment benefits, enact or expand refundable tax credits, and boost food stamps. The last was especially important because hungry people spend money; they do not hoard it. Every dollar spent at a grocery store then has a ripple effect; it pays cashiers, stock personnel, the truckers who move the product from state to state, and the farmers who grew the food. Research backed up Zandi's claim: various studies have estimated that every dollar spent on SNAP generates between $1.56 and $1.84 in increased economic activity.

During economic downturns, food stamps operate counter-cyclically. They serve as an "automatic stabilizer," stimulating the economy and absorbing some of the shock of sudden increases in unemployment and poverty.

When the recession hit, changes to eligibility requirements, combined with a surge in the ranks of the unemployed, produced a surge of new recipients. In pre-recession 2007, fifty-four million Americans lived in households with incomes below 130 percent of the poverty line, which is SNAP's federal income limit (some states have lower or higher limits). In 2009 that number rose to sixty million—and it would keep rising until 2013.

Suddenly people who had objected to SNAP during times of economic growth were more open to it. The initial package for the Economic Recovery and Reinvestment Act, however, did not include additional funding for SNAP. Although many in Congress recognized that the program represented a sound investment, no one thought we could get more than $4 billion for SNAP into the Recovery Act. Some feared how increased funding for SNAP would impact their political fortunes at home. This was especially true for Democratic members from swing districts.

The White House also did not think we could get anywhere near $4 billion, and a key advocacy group, the Center for Budget and Policy Priorities, thought that $8 billion was the maximum that could be achieved by Congress.

Using the data provided by Zandi, I went to David Obey, chairman of the House Appropriations Committee, who had introduced the first draft of the economic recovery program, and explained that increased spending on food stamps would deliver "bang for the buck." He agreed to put a package together to get food stamps into the bill.

Along the way, several options were debated on how to design the stimulus, including raising the maximum benefit amount and making more people eligible for benefits. In addition, there was the question of how to "close the faucet" once the economy recovered. Some proposed to "cliff" the benefits, which meant that after two years they would stop suddenly. Proponents of this plan argued this was stimulus money, thus it was *supposed* to end. Others argued that suddenly cutting people off after two years could prove traumatic to many families.

Because I was still the chair of the Agriculture Subcommittee on Appropriations, I was confident I would have the votes on the subcommittee to provide additional funding for SNAP. However, after a bill is moved out of the subcommittee, the process becomes more complicated. Once the subcommittee votes, you have to obtain the support of the full committee chairman—in this case, Representative Obey. The Appropriations Committee was able to structure the bill so that we would be able to obtain $20 billion for food stamps over a period of time that outlived the ARRA, while factoring in increased participation rates and rising food costs. Speaker Pelosi was fully on board, so all that remained was to get enough votes on the House floor to pass the bill.

I bombarded my colleagues with memos, urging them to go big on food stamps. Trying for $20 billion for food stamps was a significant undertaking—but still, even with this intense internal lobbying effort, it was not like trying to prevent a $40 billion cut, which we would have to do a few years later.

The American Recovery and Reinvestment Act passed the House without a single Republican vote. The Senate version passed two weeks later, with only three Republican supporting it—Senators Olympia Snowe (R-Maine), Susan Collins (R-Maine), and Arlen Specter (R-Pennsylvania).

With a few tweaks, our language on food stamps became law and provided all recipients with a temporary 13.6 percent boost in their monthly benefit. For a household of four receiving the maximum benefit, this meant an additional $80 per month. The economic recovery program also eased eligibility requirements for ABAWDs by temporarily eliminating time limits for benefit receipt. It also suspended the work requirement through 2010. According to the

Department of Agriculture, these measures reduced food insecurity among low-income households by 2.2 percentage points, and increased spending on food by 5.4 percent.

National SNAP enrollment reached an all-time high across the country during the recession.[1] The number of caseloads kept rising as lagging economic recovery led more households to apply for assistance. Some states adopted "broad-based categorical eligibility," which made most households that qualified for non-cash Temporary Assistance for Needy Families (TANF) program benefits automatically eligible for SNAP as well. This meant households just above the federal limit could receive SNAP benefits, too. Participation peaked in December 2012, and it is estimated that 10.3 million people were lifted out of poverty thanks to food stamps.

With the American Recovery and Investment Act battle behind us, one food fight I never expected to have was trying to prevent the Obama administrations from redirecting funds allocated for SNAP toward other policy priorities. When we drafted the law, we used projections for food stamp funding that assumed increased usage and rising food prices. The way the bill was written—combined with the fact that not all of these projections came to pass—meant there were excess funds in the account. This excess capacity remained a secret for a short time, but when it was revealed, it immediately became a target for raiding. After that we encountered some difficult choices.

Funds set aside for food stamps were tapped twice. The first time was for education. In August 2010, with unemployment still high, a lot of public-sector jobs were on the line, including many teachers' jobs. Medicaid needed another $26.1 billion. The White House determined they could tap food stamp funds for twelve of those billions. I essentially was faced with an excruciating choice between wanting to save teachers' jobs or keep this money for SNAP. For me it was a classic "Sophie's Choice." Because I was assured that the SNAP funding would be restored, I opted to provide funds to save teachers' jobs. But despite the assurances about restoring the SNAP funds, it never happened.

The second time the White House raided SNAP funds was to fund the Healthy, Hunger-Free Kids Act. I liked this bill and strongly supported the goals the legislation aimed to achieve. However, I was opposed to the use of $4.5 billion in SNAP program funds to help pay for it.

This position brought me and others into conflict with the White House, especially First Lady Michelle Obama. It had been well documented that the Healthy, Hunger-Free Kids Act was one of her top issue priorities. She called to urge me to lift my opposition to the funding of the bill so that the process could move forward and the bill could be passed. I explained that I was a very strong supporter of her hunger efforts for children. Having followed this issue for years, I added that I was determined to find alternative funding before taking the $4.5 billion from food stamps. Using those funds would represent a significant setback for SNAP, and the administration promises that these funds would be restored were unconvincing.

The phone call with Ms. Obama was tough, and Speaker Pelosi had virtually an identical conversation with her. We were determined to find alternative dollars.

It was late in 2010, and if we lost the midterm elections that year—and I was pretty certain we would—we could no longer pass the Healthy, Hunger-Free Kids Act. We provided the White House with a list of other places or programs where they could get the money. We proposed they get money from "Paid to Delay" programs that incentivize companies that make generic drugs to hold off on selling them for a few years. But that was refused; everything we proposed was rejected. My colleagues Jim McGovern and Barbara Lee (D-California) were also in touch with the White House to express opposition to using the SNAP funds.

After our considerable efforts were repeatedly rejected, we were finally forced to make the funds available. There are times when every option presented to you is unpleasant, but you are forced to choose anyhow. The Healthy, Hungry-Free Kids Act moved ahead and became law, and I was proud to be at the bill signing with President Barack Obama and First Lady Michelle Obama. I have a framed and signed copy of the law and signing pen in my office. I saved the telephone message from President Obama thanking me for helping pass the bill.

I tried to explain to the whole Democratic caucus, group by group, over and over again, that we were going to be all right until the American Recovery and Reinvestment Act would come to an end in 2013. At this point every food stamp beneficiary would be exposed to a severe cut in benefits.

When it was time to debate the Farm Bill in 2013, again a wide array of interests were clamoring to influence the process and ensure that their priorities were included in the bill. Some wanted to end all farm subsidies, others to legislate better treatment of animals to reduce methane emissions. Now that it had a Republican majority in the House, the Club for Growth was pushing Congress to turn over food stamps to the states.

With that backdrop, I was worried about what would happen in December when the people who had qualified for food stamps courtesy of the economic recovery program would suddenly lose them. The cliff affected approximately 1.5 million people.

For months, House Republicans outlined their plans for the Farm Bill, including a proposal that would force three hundred thousand kids out of the free school lunch program by modifying eligibility requirements. They also proposed cutting $40 billion from SNAP. Freshman Republicans, who had fueled their campaigns by promising to get tough on food stamp recipients, wanted even deeper cuts.

These draconian measures placed them at odds with some

senior committee members from their own party, who knew more about how food stamps worked, and were aware of their value, even if they did not embrace the program personally. Frank D. Lucas (R-Oklahoma), chairman of the Agriculture Committee, found himself voting with Democrats in defeating amendments advocating those deeper cuts.

In May 2013, the House Republican majority introduced a Farm Bill that would have cut almost $21 billion from SNAP over ten years and hurt the most vulnerable people. Among other measures, the bill was set to sever the "heat and eat" link between Low-Income Heating and Energy Assistance Program (LIHEAP) and SNAP benefits in the eighteen states that had it. These cuts translated into bumping 1.7 million people from the program entirely, and slashing benefits for millions more.

Groups I could normally count on to support the cause, such as the Center for Budget and Policy Priorities, a nonpartisan think tank devoted to reducing poverty and restoring fiscal responsibility, expressed support for the the proposal to separate LIHEAP from SNAP. "The optics were not good," one advocate for the separation said, because conceivably, in seventeen states, a person could get $1 in LIHEAP funding and then qualify for food stamp benefits.

I remember standing in my kitchen in New Haven talking on the phone to three other people whose stances on the issue could prove pivotal—Jim McGovern, Marcia Fudge (D-Ohio), and Senator Debbie Stabenow (D-Michigan), who was chair of the Senate Agriculture Committee. Debbie and Marcia believed the Republicans were so adamant about breaking the link that it was pointless to pursue the issue further.

Jim and I knew that we had to do whatever was necessary to prevent the cuts. I coordinated Democratic opposition to the bill, constantly asking my colleagues, "If there were these cuts . . . would you vote against it?" I convened weekly meetings in my office to whip the no vote inside the House, and the food advocacy groups whipped from the outside. On June 20, 2013, the bill failed—195 votes to 234. Sixty-two Republicans voted against it, too.

A few weeks later, the Republican majority made another attempt to implement cuts to these programs. Their new version of the Farm Bill did not include a nutrition title at all—exactly what Paul Ryan, then House Budget chairman, had been advocating. It represented a blatant disregard of bipartisanship, and of the history of the nutrition title. The way the Farm Bill is structured reflects the generally accepted truth that food stamps have always been about helping American farmers as well as Americans in poverty. Food stamps build a bridge between rural and urban workers in the United States, and many have argued that without the nutrition title, Congress would never be able to pass a farm bill. No food stamps means less rural development, trade, conservation, and support for farmers.

Leaving a nutrition title out of the Farm Bill was a dangerous procedural move that attempted to break bipartisan support for federal nutrition programs. I led 204 House Democrats in opposition to this maneuvering, and wrote to Speaker John Boehner to insist that he include a nutrition title. However, our efforts were unsuccessful, as the bill passed the House without a single Democratic vote.

The Senate, which had by then already passed a version of the Farm Bill that included a nutrition title, then amended the House bill to reinstate its own version.

On September 16, 2013, just two weeks before the 2008 Farm Bill and its SNAP authorization was to expire, the Republican House majority introduced a separate bill for federal nutrition programs. The purpose of introducing this stand-alone nutrition bill was to allow them to argue that they were not walking away from food stamps entirely. Their proposal would have reauthorized SNAP for three years, not the standard five, and authorized states to establish pilot programs under which all adults receiving food stamps, except parents with infants at home, would be required to work or take part in job training for twenty hours a week. If this requirement was not met, the entire household would be disqualified for noncompliance.

The bill also would have allowed states to drug test food stamp applicants. It would have restricted outreach activities as well, because its proponents believed that educating people about benefits was tantamount to recruitment.[2] (They do not, I should add, have similar concerns over the notifications the USDA sends out to alert farmers to enrollment periods for benefits and subsidies.) Jim McGovern called it "one of the most heartless bills I have ever seen."[3]

Meanwhile, the version of the farm bill that proposed cuts to food stamp funding was still very much alive. Because of these proposed cuts, I organized 103 votes against the bill and called every member of the caucus to ask, "If they cut food stamps, will you vote against?"

My frantic activity led to a tense exchange with Pelosi on the floor of the House. She asked me if I was really trying to defeat the farm bill, to which I replied that the bill would not fail. We both knew it was going to pass, but I was not about to let it go unnoticed that people would go hungry as a result.

The bill passed the House, but when the Senate weighed in, SNAP was reauthorized for a full five years and broad-based categorical eligibility remained intact. The drug-testing idea was not, thankfully, enacted. Those with felony convictions faced limited access, and states' data collection and reporting requirements were increased. The law restricted SNAP outreach along the lines proposed by the House majority, and established the LIHEAP threshold at $20 per year—in effect, a benefit cut of $8.6 billion over ten years.

Once the final Farm Bill passed in February 2014, total cuts to food stamps amounted to $20 billion over ten years. These cuts

were coming on top of each other for millions of beneficiaries—
$12 billion with the expiration of the American Recovery and Rein-
vestment Act in 2013 and $8.6 billion with the ending of eligibility
for people getting help with energy costs.

The effects of these cuts were felt immediately. In the month
after the economic recovery program increase expired, more than
half of New York City food pantries and soup kitchens reported a
rise in visitors, with the average increase amounting to 25 percent.
A family of four receiving the maximum food stamp benefit lost
$396 in financial support in 2014.

This ongoing battle is discouraging. Critics of food stamps continue to ignore the fact that the high number of food stamp recipients was a direct result of the recession and slow recovery.[4]
Between 2007 and 2013 the participation rate increased among
families that had earnings, but this fact suggests that the working
poor were having a tough time—not that people suddenly got lazy.
Critics say that SNAP caseloads have not fallen in step with falling
unemployment numbers, but the poverty rate is a better indication
of the need for food stamps than the unemployment rate. By 2015
the poverty rate had not fallen significantly since the end of the
recession.

Those who say food stamps discourage people from working ignore the fact that 98 percent of households that qualify for SNAP
thanks to categorical eligibility include an able-bodied adult who
has a job. The ugly rhetoric used against people who use food
stamps rarely matches reality. So what is there to say to those who
think people on food stamps are lazy and refuse to work for life's
barest necessities?

First of all, people do not stay on food stamps for long. After that
2012 peak, government spending on SNAP began falling, as did
the caseload.[5] Half of all new SNAP participants leave the program
within ten months. Seventy-four percent leave within two years.

According to the CBPP, SNAP spending fell for the second consecutive year in 2015, and is projected to keep falling.[6]

Second, many eligible people do not take advantage of the program. Around 17 percent of food stamp–eligible households do not enroll, and 8 percent of potential benefits go uncollected. Before the 2008 elimination of the childcare deduction cap, many families eligible for that deduction either did not claim it or did not claim the full amount to which they were entitled.

The reasons why people are resistant to enrolling in SNAP vary. Some potential participants simply are not fully aware of the program or their potential eligibility, while others are discouraged by the verification and reporting requirements. Some report that their sense of personal independence is offended by the idea of taking a government handout. Others have experienced bad treatment at the SNAP office or have felt embarrassed when they use their EBT card at the grocery store.

Third, it is impossible to deny that many people who harbor ugly stereotypes about food stamp recipients do so because in their mind, the recipients are minorities, live in the inner city, and are possibly criminal. In reality, a higher percentage of rural households receive SNAP benefits than do households in metropolitan areas.

Finally, for all the good that SNAP does, the average level of benefits is not enough to erase the burden of poverty. Many recipients continue to struggle to put healthy meals on the table, even when making smart shopping choices. The model used to set benefit levels makes assumptions about food preparation facilities, time, and proximity to grocery stores—and in some areas, those assumptions prove unrealistic. SNAP is not allowing people to lounge and take Caribbean vacations at the government's expense.

So if food stamps do not encourage dependency, why these persistent objections to them? And why are even people who believe food stamps work so ready to abandon the fight when it proves politically costly?

Anyone who claims that food stamps erode people's willingness to work simply has no case. Receiving food stamps is not a substitute for working for food; it gives people the food that enables them to work. The real factor keeping millions of Americans using food stamps is that there are no longer enough well-paid jobs to go around for working-class Americans. There are solutions to that problem, but cutting SNAP is not one of them.

What about waste? I emphasize this point repeatedly—SNAP is remarkably efficient. Benefits paid out represented 94.4 percent of its total federal costs in fiscal year 2014. As for fraud? Every time food stamps are discussed, my Republican colleagues claim that the program is rife with fraud and abuse. But in reality, fraud and error rates in SNAP are actually low compared to other federal programs. More than 99 percent of SNAP households are correctly deemed eligible. Only 1.3 percent of benefits are trafficked (meaning exchanged for cash), which represents an improvement from 3.8 percent in 1993. This may reflect the success of EBT cards, which replaced the physical stamp, look like regular debit cards, and have improved the program's accuracy. There is significantly more waste, fraud, and abuse involved in defense spending than in food stamps.

Another distressing aspect of this rhetoric is that it pits the middle class against the working poor. As Eric Cantor (R-Virginia) once said, "It's wrong for working, middle-class people to pay" for abuse of food stamps. Never mind that plenty of working people are *on* SNAP. Meanwhile we have congressmen like Robert Aderholt (R-Alabama) and governors like Scott Walker (R-Wisconsin) who believe we should have mandatory drug testing for all SNAP recipients. Aderholt has stated that if recipients can afford drugs, "then they have the money to buy food. The federal government should not be enabling people to fund their drug addiction at taxpayer expense." Walker chimed in to tout the drug-testing idea to the *Huffington Post*. "It's not a punitive thing, it's a progressive thing," he said. Walker's reasoning is that food stamp recipients might not be getting and keeping jobs because they abuse drugs. Once we can make sure they are drug-free, we can get them back in the workforce.

That idea would make perfect sense if drug use were rampant among public assistance recipients. As it happens, though, this is nonsense. Seven states that have drug-test requirements for TANF recipients—Arizona, Kansas, Mississippi, Missouri, Oklahoma, Tennessee, and Utah—discovered that "applicants actually test positive at a lower rate than the drug use of the general population."[7] In Florida, the results of drug testing welfare recipients showed a few things. First, just 108 of the 4,086 people who were administered a drug test failed. Second, the state lost money on the deal.[8] No matter, say testing's supporters, because the point of the law is to fight drugs.

But the larger truth exposed by results like those in Florida is the determination of the pro-drug-test crowd to punish and stigmatize people in genuine need. Given that the evidence overwhelmingly shows that drug testing for welfare recipients does not snag a lot of substance abusers, nor does it save money, I suspect Paul Waldman's blog for the *Washington Post* is on the mark: "Walker isn't trying to solve a practical problem here. He wants to test food stamp recipients as a way of expressing moral condemnation. You can get this benefit, he's saying, but we want to give you a little humiliation so you know that because you sought the government's help, we think you're a rotten person."[9]

I have asked this question several times: If you want to test food stamp recipients for drugs, why not drug test every person who benefits from USDA programs or subsidies? To those who insist that SNAP be engineered so that certain foods are off-limits: If we allow business owners to deduct money spent on business lunches from their taxes, as we do, should we demand proof that they ordered healthfully before we grant them their tax deduction?

And yet the objections to food stamps persist. During the 2013 Farm Bill debate, Representative Stephen Fincher (R-Tennessee) even quoted the Bible, saying, "the one who is unwilling to work shall not eat." Fincher's district, incidentally, received over $1.7 billion in federal agriculture subsidies between 1995 and 2014.[10] His colleague Ted Yoho (R-Florida) flatly doubted that around 50 million Americans face food insecurity. "I think there's 50 million people starving at least three times a day," he said. "We call it breakfast, lunch and dinner." If we cut food aid, "not one person would lose a calorie or crumb that deserves it." At the same time Yoho revealed that his own family had used food stamps for about two months. But the people receiving SNAP now were different, of course. For them, it had become a "lifestyle."

There are many political lessons to be derived from the ongoing food stamp fight, but here is one: many people say they care about poverty but their policy recommendations invariably entail taking food away from poor people and their kids. Their solutions to poverty will mean more people in poverty. That action is motivated by a conservative passion that has wandered far from our shared values. The only way they win the argument or achieve their goals is if those of us who know better stand idly by. That is why legislating is often a matter of educating, particularly when it comes to issues affecting the poor.

5

In Defense of Women

What was the New Deal anyhow? Was it a political plot? Was it just a name for a period in history? Was it a revolution? To all of these questions I answer "No." It was something quite different. . . . It was, I think, basically an attitude. An attitude that found voice in expressions like "the people are what matter to government," and "a government should aim to give all the people under its jurisdiction the best possible life."

—Frances Perkins, secretary of labor,
first woman to hold U.S. cabinet position

THE IMPORTANCE OF WOMEN'S economic security was drilled into me by my mother. She did not have to say much, however. I could see with my own eyes what bad work, under bad conditions, did to people.

At age fourteen, my mother went to work for the Strouse, Adler Company, a nearby garment manufacturer, as a Girl Friday. From there she went on to sew shirt collars and dresses in New Haven's old sweatshops. The pay arrangement for most of the women was "piecework," which means they were not given breaks, and worked amid clouds of dust, poor lighting, filthy bathrooms, and deafening noise. When World War II erupted my mother got a job at the

Winchester Firearms primer shop. That job paid better and had better conditions, but only lasted until her pregnancy. After I was born, she went back to work in the needle trade. Occasionally after school I would meet my mother at work. I hated it there but she made me visit and only as I got older did I understand why. She brought me there to teach me what life could be like, but did not have to be. "Rosa, get an education," she would say, "so you do not have to do this."

My mother got what she wished for: I went to college and eventually to Congress. In 1997 with that experience vivid for me, I introduced a bill to achieve pay equity for women. What struck me most of all was the indifference the issue encountered. This is roughly what you hear whenever women and equal pay come up. Ask why women earn less than men, and you get told that it is because women make different life choices. Ask why women working the same jobs as men get paid less, and it is explained to you that the difference is too small to fret about and will fix itself in time.

Years ago, you would have heard that women should not be working outside the home anyhow. While you hear that much more rarely these days, you do hear this: the government imposing more regulations on business is a recipe for killing businesses and jobs and everyone will pay the price in a stagnating economy. Tell that, I always think, to the family and friends of those who lost lives in the Franklin Street fire.

My belief is that government has a big role to play in curbing the exploitation of women, and that everyone will benefit as it does so. These convictions have led me to champion the Paycheck Fairness Act for nearly twenty years. I first introduced a bill for paycheck fairness in 1997, and then again in 1999, 2001, 2003, 2005, 2007, 2008, 2009, 2011, 2013, and 2015. Related bills have been introduced in the Senate numerous times by an array of heavy hitters, including Senators Dodd, Tom Daschle, Harry Reid, Hillary Clinton, and Barbara Mikulski. Every time we introduce the bill, we are accused of wishing to benefit trial lawyers. That accusation would be comical if it were not so willfully blind to the realities of working women's lives.

I will admit the issue of pay equity can be complex. Some jobs pay more because men dominate those job markets. Other jobs pay less because those jobs are mostly filled by women. "Comparable worth" policies aim to reset wages for female-dominated jobs so that they equal wages for male-dominated jobs of comparable worth.

A bill introduced the year before my pay equity bill, sponsored by Congresswoman Eleanor Holmes Norton (D-District of Columbia) and Senator Tom Harkin, used comparable worth as a vehicle to achieve equal pay and that was an important advance.

In the early days of the fight, the answer as to what path to take toward the goal of equal pay was by no means cut and dried. I believed that "comparable worth" was too complex and too open to legal challenge to pass the Congress. I met regularly with women from the National Women's Law Center, the American Association of University Women, and the American Civil Liberties Union, and even among all of these people ardently devoted to the cause, there was a lot of internal dissension about walking away from a comparable worth approach.

The premise of the Paycheck Fairness bill, in contrast, was simple: men and women in the same job deserve the same pay. I threw my full weight behind Paycheck Fairness when Senator Daschle picked it up in the Senate and came looking for a partner in the House.

We were not moving into uncharted territory. Federal policy regarding equal pay dated back to World War II. In 1942 the War Labor Board ruled that men and women should be paid the same job rates, but enforcement proved tough. In 1945 the first Equal Pay Bill was introduced in Congress. It was blocked from consideration but reintroduced annually for the next eighteen years as evidence piled up that unequal wages were a serious problem. A revised version of the bill eventually passed by Congress was introduced by Congresswomen Edith Green (D-Oregon) and Edith Rogers (R-Massachusetts), both members of the AAUW.

The first big breakthrough came when President Kennedy signed the Equal Pay Act in 1963. Women at the time made only 59 cents for every dollar a man made. Provisions of the Civil Rights Act of 1964 subsequently helped shore up the Equal Pay Act. Its Title VII banned employment discrimination against women—or more broadly, banned discrimination in employment on the basis of sex, race, color, national origin, and religion.

After 1964, most of the progress made was at the local level. In 1984, twenty states conducted pay equity surveys; although most states discovered inequities, only four states did anything about it. In 1991, more than a thousand women 911 operators were awarded $1 million in back pay. During this time, while examples of the harms women experienced continued to become more visible, even pay equity bills limited to federal workers repeatedly stalled in the Senate. That was disheartening. While pay equity for federal workers would not affect the lives of the vast majority of American women who don't work for the federal government, success there could have set a major precedent.

Opposition to mandating pay equity came from several corners. There was business opposition. The Chamber of Commerce hated it. Some remained stubbornly unconvinced that women's economic insecurity had real, long-lasting repercussions for women themselves, their families, or for the country. Some argued that those of us fighting for pay equity want government dictating to business what they should pay their workers. To that we answered that no, we wanted to make capitalism as we knew it work better—to get paid based on the work we did, not on our gender.

Legislation that challenges the status quo is always seen as deeply threatening. This is especially true for any legislation that places requirements on employers, let alone requirements that are actually enforceable. The National Committee on Pay Equity originated Equal Pay Day in April 1996. President Clinton later declared April 11, 1997 "National Pay Inequity Awareness Day," marking the day on a year's calendar when a woman's earnings caught up to a man's earnings from the year before. This action was designed to bring more visibility to pay equity and lessen anxiety surrounding the issue—but while effective, raising public awareness took time. Many women who suffered the effects of unequal wages were quick to assume that it was just their private, individual concern, not a systemic problem that affected millions of others.

When I introduced the Paycheck Fairness Bill in the fall of 1997, I made a statement at the press conference that was a data dump of alarming statistics: the average working man could have stopped working the previous Saturday—September 20th—and have earned as much as the average woman who continued working through the end of December. Women earned only 71 cents for every dollar that men took home, and women of color fared far worse: black women earned only 64 cents and Latino women only 53 cents for each dollar earned by a white male. As AAUW found as early as 1896, even a college education did not close the wage gap for women.

And why were women paid less, I asked? Not because they worked less hard, or weren't as good at their jobs. Women were paid less because historically society has undervalued their contribution, and not respected their work.

The political climate was not ideal for this fight. The whole battle over the Contract with America was only a few years behind us. Advocates from groups allied to fight for pay equity agreed: we did not yet have a human face for the problem that convinced people that women faced real inequalities. Finding people who were willing to be public advocates for the cause was a work in progress. At events organized nationwide we worked our tails off to get women from the audience to tell their stories, but even when we were successful in getting a good story, the mainstream press mostly ignored us and the women.

We continued holding Equal Pay Day events every April. Every year we trudged out the whole dog and pony show. Every year we elicited yawns. If we were lucky, we would get a story or two, a photo in *Roll Call*. The *New York Times*, *Wall Street Journal*, *Washington Post*? Not interested; it was not "hard news." A lot of our colleagues thought we were being ridiculous, and argued that the Paycheck Fairness Act was overkill. Conservative think tanks were publishing white papers against it. The Equal Pay Act from 1963 already outlawed paying men more than women for the same job, they all said, so there was really no problem that required our intervention.

The argument that the Equal Pay Act took care of all our concerns was easy to answer: the act had huge loopholes. The first version of the legislation had not even extended protections to white-collar professionals. Women employed in administrative jobs or executive roles were not covered. Though that oversight would be fixed in the early 1970s, other loopholes remained. Under the Equal Pay Act, federal labor law does not protect workers who share salary information with colleagues. They can be fired for doing so. That was a real problem, as I saw it. If you are prevented from discussing your earnings with your coworkers, how would you ever know you were being paid less?

The biggest problem with the Equal Pay Act is that it made it very easy to argue that slight differences between a job held by a woman and a man justified significant, life-changing pay differentials. In other words, it is only illegal to pay a woman less for the same job if her job description, her qualifications, and the geographical location of that job are *precisely identical* to a male colleague's.

Such loopholes made the Equal Pay Act toothless. It does not protect women as it should. The Paycheck Fairness Act was designed to give real teeth to existing law. It put gender discrimination on the same footing as race discrimination. It required employers to show that any pay disparity on their books was truly related to a bona fide business necessity. It also prohibited employer retaliation for sharing salary information with coworkers and increased the amount of compensation that women could seek for pay discrimination. Under Paycheck Fairness, women would be able to seek back pay plus punitive damages. That, to me, was the only legitimate response to a situation that can hobble women and their families financially for years. One paycheck is one paycheck; fine, maybe you are a big enough person to shrug it off. But paycheck after paycheck wherein you earn less than your male colleagues simply because you are female can add up to hundreds of thousands of dollars less in income over a career, along with smaller pensions and Social Security benefits and less financial security for your children. How could anyone argue that back pay is sufficient to make up for those deficits? And where's the deterrent to the employers? Many work hard to follow the law, and end up competing against bad actors who get nothing more than a slap on the wrist for paying women less.

There were also difficulties regarding reporting. Employment agencies at both the federal and state levels were not reliably collecting pay data from private-sector employers, making it harder to enforce the laws already on the books. And so we kept reintroducing Paycheck Fairness year after year, even knowing that when Republicans were in the majority we had zero chance of passing it.

Finally, in 2000, President Clinton inaugurated the Task Force on Equal Pay the last year he was in office. The purpose of the initiative was to "enhance agency enforcement and public understanding of wage discrimination in the workplace." It bolstered the Equal Employment Opportunity Commission's field staff's ability to investigate charges of pay discrimination and to take action when discrimination has occurred. At the same time that he announced the task force, Clinton renewed his call to Congress to pass Paycheck Fairness. It fell on deaf ears.

The next two years I would get renewed energy for the fight—not from any success, but from a significant setback. I ran for Democratic Caucus chair in 2002 and lost to Bob Menendez (D-New Jersey) by one vote. This loss spelled the end of my efforts to get on the Democratic leadership ladder. (I had run in 1998 and lost by six votes.) I returned to work after the Christmas break with a plan. I wanted to take a lead on women's economic issues. I was more convinced than ever that economic issues unique to women do not affect women uniquely but their entire families—partners, children, parents.

But first there were more setbacks. Senator Daschle lost his seat in 2004, and the Senate under the Bush administration was in no mood to consider paycheck legislation. Then in 2006 President Bush gave the Chamber of Commerce a gift and rolled back pay equity enforcement efforts by abolishing the survey—developed under the auspices of both Republican and Democratic administrations—which the Department of Labor had used to detect and remedy wage discrimination by federal contractors. Rather than forward motion to address pay equity, we were moving backward.

Finally, in early 2007, there was a break in the clouds. Democrats were back in the House majority for the first time in twelve years. Speaker Pelosi was a strong supporter and George Miller (D-California) became chair of the Education and the Workforce Committee, which has jurisdiction over the bill. It meant the bill really could move forward. My friend Chairman George Miller surprised me by holding the first hearing on the Paycheck Fairness Act on April 24, on Equal Pay Day, to the mischievous delight of our staffs.

At the speaker's leadership meeting just before the Memorial

Day holiday, I asked Miller: What about Paycheck Fairness? What are we doing for Paycheck Fairness? Isn't it time to bring it to the floor? Miller told me, almost as a dare, that I did not have the votes. He would move the Paycheck Fairness bill in the Committee on Education and Labor if I found at least two hundred co-sponsors.

Two hundred co-sponsors was a very high bar, but at least now I had an official target. As my friend Rahm Emanuel commented at the time, if the goal was to stall my efforts, giving me a number was a mistake. (His exact words? "Don't make the bitch mad.")

I took up the challenge. My staff and I moved aggressively to secure the number and gather co-sponsors. I called in the groups—AAUW, Business and Professional Women, the National Women's Law Center, NOW, and others. The AAUW and Lisa Maatz were pretty formidable as they crisscrossed the country for Paycheck Fairness. Their members were particularly animated by this issue. They galvanized their members and supporters across the country and showed how real the grassroots could be.

I made phone call after phone call after phone call after phone call. I buttonholed colleagues on the floor. After our first drive, right before the Memorial Day holiday, and on the heels of the U.S. Supreme Court decision in *Ledbetter v. Goodyear Tire & Rubber Co.*—and more on that in a bit—we received a big bump. Additional members signed on throughout June.[1]

Just before the July 4 recess I told Miller I had 224 votes, more than the 218 needed for passage. He scheduled a hearing—the first ever for this bill after twelve years of trying. It is an amazing feeling when something for which you have been fighting for ten years finally gets a day in the sun. I kept hearing my mother's voice: *Come on, girls, let's make ourselves heard.*

Then we endured several more months of nothing, no movement whatsoever.[2] It was disheartening.

Meanwhile champions of pay equity had an opportunity for a real breakthrough—ultimately a bittersweet one, but at its heart was something that had eluded us for some time: a real-life case, with a compelling woman to tell it. In late May the Supreme Court had handed down its decision in the Lilly Ledbetter case, a wage discrimination lawsuit that starkly exposed the realities of gender discrimination in the workplace as it is actually lived. Ledbetter was a strong, credible voice. Through her testimony all the fallacies that support discrimination against women in the workplace were exposed: she worked hard, was devoted to her job, put in hours and hours of overtime, performed well, was a team player, and still she was paid less than men doing the same job.

Ledbetter had worked as an area manager and supervisor for Goodyear for decades. For her, it was a dream job. She retired in 1998 and soon thereafter learned via an anonymous tip that Goodyear had paid her 40 percent less than her male counterparts for the exact same job. She was even paid less than men she was training. "I was actually earning 20 percent less than the lowest paid male supervisor in the same position," she testified. "Lots of men with less seniority than me were paid much more than I was." She consulted with her husband and they decided to sue, risking everything they had, because the facts were too outrageous to swallow. When she took Goodyear to court the company acknowledged they paid her less but claimed it was because she was a poor performer, and consequently got smaller raises than her male colleagues. Ledbetter did not buy that story and neither did the jury. She won her first lawsuit and was awarded $3.3 million in damages (later reduced to $360,000 because of the damages cap). The Eleventh Circuit ruled against her on appeal, however; they said any annual pay decision not contested within 180 days becomes set in stone, grandfathered, and could not be fixed by appealing to Title VII. The Supreme Court—handing down a verdict nine years after her initial complaint with the EEOC—upheld that Eleventh Circuit ruling 5–4; they said since Ledbetter had not filed a complaint within the stipulated 180 days of her pay being set, she had no case. As Ledbetter herself put it, the Supreme Court decision "essentially said my employer had been paying me unfairly for long enough to make it legal."[3]

Not every justice on the court was out of sync with the realities of life for Ledbetter and women like her. Justice Ruth Bader Ginsburg wrote a withering dissent to the majority opinion, and in a break from tradition, read her dissent aloud from the bench. Editorial cartoons at the time showed Ginsburg reading her blistering dissent with smoke coming from her ears. She noted that experiencing pay discrimination is not like getting hit by a bus. You do not always know it is happening, at least not in real time. Disparities accumulate in small increments, and the "cause to suspect that discrimination is at work develops only over time." To tell a woman that it is up to her to ferret out salary information kept secret by supervisors, or to confront coworkers and managers about pay arrangements on an ongoing basis, is somewhat like mandating a particular personality type. It rules in favor of those quick to suspect that something is amiss, and penalizes those—like Ledbetter, who oozes Southern charm—inclined to give their employers the benefit of the doubt.

Ginsburg's dissent put it well: "Small initial discrepancies may not be seen as meat for a federal case, particularly when the employee, trying to succeed in a nontraditional environment, is averse to making waves." More importantly, she noted that if the outcome of Ledbetter's case were to change, it was in the hands of Congress.

I did not need another invitation. The case had a public face in Lilly Ledbetter, and the Supreme Court's 5–4 decision added a sense of immediacy—not to mention outrage—nationwide. I met Ledbetter for the first time at a Washington function in the early days after the Supreme Court case. The equal pay coalition, led by AAUW and NWLC, would fly her out, put her up in a hotel, and bring her around to talk to members of Congress. She handled this dive into the legislative and public battle spectacularly well. We quickly became friends. She is one of the most impressive people I have ever met.

Lilly spurred the women's groups, together with my staff, staff from Miller's office, Judiciary, and Senator Kennedy's office in the Senate, to extensive discussions on how best to get redress and justice. I was pushing for the Ledbetter fix to be attached to the Paycheck Fairness Act so the legislation could move forward together, but the decision was made to focus on reversing the setback from the Ledbetter decision.

Miller, whose committee had jurisdiction, began immediately drafting the Lilly Ledbetter Fair Pay Act, which would simply reinforce the law as it stood before the Supreme Court decision of 2007. He was the author of this critical reform and said, "What better name could we use than Lilly Ledbetter?" Ted Kennedy took it up in the Senate. Neither version got far, initially. The Ledbetter Fair Pay Act was defeated in early 2008 by Senate Republicans afraid of "frivolous" lawsuits, despite the fact that Ledbetter did not force employers to do more than they already thought they had to do before the Supreme Court decision. We redoubled our efforts.

Advocates were again broadly in agreement but divided on how to reach our goal. No one disputed that the Ledbetter ruling could be used to spur momentum for a broader civil rights bill. Some wanted to focus on Title VII, the provision of the 1964 Civil Rights Act that banned employment discrimination on the basis of sex, race, color, national origin, and religion, and not overhaul or address the Equal Pay Act. I argued that Paycheck Fairness brought the EPA in line with Title VII, but the key element was lifting a cap on damages. The limits in place on compensatory or punitive damages were so paltry I believed they hardly qualified as either compensatory (of lost wages) or punitive (especially to a large employer; for example, would $300,000 really put a dent in a Fortune 500 company's coffers?)[4] I also stressed that Paycheck Fairness dealt with the cultural issues of how women are prepared for the workplace: the bill included grants and training to help women negotiate their compensation packages.

Meanwhile I continued to press Miller to move forward with Paycheck Fairness. That fall we started hearing the kinds of noises and whispers that signaled that the committee was getting ready to start moving on it. By January 2008 Miller gave us the sign that his committee staff would begin preparing the bill for markup. The Education and Labor Committee, as it had been renamed when the House came under Democratic control once again, would pore over it, go over every line—a process that can take weeks or months. AAUW's Lisa Maatz and NWLC's Jocelyn Samuels spent hours and hours with Letty Mederos of my staff, as well as Jody Calamine at the committee, getting Paycheck ready for the big day. We wanted the strongest bill possible, but also needed one that would pass muster with the Blue Dogs, or more conservative Democrats.

The tension during this time was immense. Conceivably the committee could have had the markup prep done by the end of February, but that date came and went and still no concrete sign of progress. Some members of my staff and even the advocacy community worried that we were being "slow-walked by commit-tee staff." We worked for weeks to field concerns from legislators, and translate issues they raised into tweaks to the bill's language. One amendment prevented the expansion of the Equal Pay Act from including job applicants. Another pushed the effective date back six months in deference to our small business friends, and further asked the Department of Labor to assist these businesses with compliance. Miller's committee staff asked us to clarify the legal standard for punitive damages. Under the Equal Pay Act, employees did not have to prove the employer was intentionally discriminating to receive punitive damages; but under Title VII, intent was required. We confirmed that under Paycheck Fairness, courts would have to find intent on the part of the employer before awarding punitive damages. Miller's staff also wanted to limit the scope of payscale comparisons. Would one branch of a national chain in rural Idaho, for instance, have to offer the same wages as a branch in New York City, where the cost of living is higher? We limited the scope to establishments within the same county or geopolitical subdivision. Another requested change clarified that Paycheck Fairness would not interfere with applicable immigration laws. All along we had to wrestle with the fundamental question: Would these changes water the bill down too much?

One Friday in July, Miller and Pelosi grabbed me on the House floor. I sat between the two of them at the back of the chamber as Miller explained that because Paycheck Fairness placed no cap on damages, we were sure to lose. My view, completely supported by the advocates, was that having no cap was one of the bill's strengths. Capping damages would effectively neuter the bill. With capped damages, we would never have the deterrent necessary to see a turnaround. Miller and Pelosi seemed to think that without a cap on damages, we might never pass the bill. The hearing was scheduled for July 24.

Give me the weekend, I said.

That weekend I called every single Democrat in the caucus. It turns out the big concern was not about capped damages, or class-action lawsuits, but the effect of the legislation on small businesses. We then drafted amendments on small businesses and parceled them out to be led on the floor by members who needed to show they were alert to the needs of small businesses in their district.

I stood my ground on the no-cap issue.

The House Committee on Education and Labor held the markup on July 24, 2008. Per House rules I could not be in the room because I was not a member of the committee. I channeled my nervous energy into pacing the floor and trying to gather intelligence as people came in and out. In his opening remarks, Miller pointed out how the wage gap between men and women had narrowed since the Equal Pay Act, but women still made seventy-seven cents for every dollar earned by a man, and this may cost women anywhere from $400,000 to $2 million over a lifetime, following them into a retirement of smaller Social Security checks and reduced pensions. He added that Paycheck Fairness would close the Equal Pay Act's remaining loopholes, and forbid employers from retaliating against employees who discussed their pay. Sanctions we had in place to enforce equal pay were negligible; they needed to be ramped up to have any effect. He tied it all up by nodding to how this backwardness affected American competitiveness. "By allowing wage discrimination to continue, we hold down women and their families, while harming the American economy as well. In the new global economy, those who stand in the way of equal pay are tying one hand behind America's back." The proverbial mic then passed to Howard P. "Buck" McKeon (R-California), who remarked that the bill had a "catchy name that masks its more troubling intentions," which in his view were to make wage discrimination lawsuits "more appealing to trial lawyers."

The important thing was that our amendments to the bill pass in committee. Actually, the markup took only forty-five minutes as the Republicans did not have much more than a few trial-lawyer horror stories. The markup was done, our bill survived, and our amendments passed, and I could breathe again.

The bill finally moved to the floor of the House for a vote on July 31, 2008. The timing was not accidental. It was the middle of campaign season, and there was pressure to have a good women's issue on the table. The Paycheck Fairness Act passed the House with a bipartisan vote of 247–178. Fourteen Republicans voted for the bill. No Democrats voted against it.

But the Senate did not take action on the bill. That whole fall the Senate was tied up by the debate over the bailout of the banks after the financial crisis, relegating pay equity to not-serious-enough-to-worry-about-now status. Meanwhile Ledbetter campaigned all over the country—for Obama, for Paycheck Fairness, for women candidates.

The day after the 2008 election we got back into gear, making plans for how to proceed after Obama's inauguration. Speaker Pelosi put the Lilly Ledbetter Fair Pay Act and the Paycheck Fairness Act on the floor as one bill in early 2009, and sent it to the Senate. This was a carefully thought-out procedural tactic. We wanted the Senate to consider both bills, and we felt Obama's honeymoon coattails would get us over the finish line.

It seemed natural to me that they be combined. Being voted on at the same time as Lilly Ledbetter would give Paycheck Fairness a better shot. On January 9, 2009, the day of the House vote, Lilly Ledbetter passed 247 to 171, with three Republican yes votes. Paycheck Fairness passed 256 to 163, with ten Republican votes. (Yes, Paycheck had more GOP support than the Ledbetter bill.)

Soon after that absolute thrill, I got a call from Senator Barbara Mikulski (D-Maryland). The Senate was not going to vote on Paycheck Fairness, she said. She offered no apology, just her assurance that Lilly Ledbetter would be voted on. Paycheck Fairness, she said, would be dealt with at a later time.

Nothing prepares you for that kind of call. I was devastated—and angry. I told Senator Mikulski this was a big, big, costly mistake. If we failed to do the bills together, Paycheck Fairness would never get done. We would lose momentum. Lawmakers would be able to say they voted for Ledbetter, and having checked the "women's issues" box, they could wash their hands of women's rights until next campaign season. I argued vehemently about this with Phil Schiliro and Rahm Emanuel of the new Obama White House. You know that it's true, I said: people would think the Ledbetter Act had satisfactorily addressed the issue of equal pay and nothing more needed to be done. Don't worry, they said; we'll get to Paycheck Fairness later. Look, I'm not stupid, I replied. We will never get to Paycheck Fairness if we cave now. I argued until I was blue in the face, but no one was going to cross Mikulski.

When the Lilly Ledbetter Fair Pay Act passed the Senate, it was a bittersweet victory. Party lines had hardened, but the votes of four women Republican senators—and the leadership of Senator Olympia Snowe—tipped the scales in our favor.[5] If three of them had voted no, then the bill would have been defeated. But those same Republican women never supported Paycheck Fairness; the backlash from the right after the Ledbetter bill had shocked them, and there was no mood for bucking their party leadership on further equal pay bills.

I stood in the Oval Office, along with Pelosi, Miller, and Lilly herself, when the Lilly Ledbetter Fair Pay Act was signed into law by President Obama in late January 2009. It was a great moment, and the first bill signed by our new president. After Obama signed the first copy of the bill, he handed the pen back to the legislators clustered around him. I thought it should go to Miller, but after some wrangling it ended up in the hands of Mikulski or Norton. Then when Obama continued signing his signature, he handed another pen back, Pelosi handed it to me. I still wanted to give the pen to Miller, but Pelosi said, *Hold the pen.* Miller did get the next pen. Today I keep the signing pen framed in my office.

The Ledbetter Act's success was bittersweet. The intense opposition to it showed how far we had to go to make the case to address the gender gap in pay. Opponents of the bill had argued—again— that it was just something Democrats dreamed up to suck up to trial lawyers. Paul Ryan claimed during the 2012 campaign that the Ledbetter Act "was about opening up the lawsuits and statute of limitations," proving that while unoriginal he could stay on message. Even among those who were generally inclined to be in favor of equal pay legislation, we had some explaining to do. Primarily, advocates had to explain how the Ledbetter Act did not move the ball forward on equal pay. While extremely important, it only re-affirmed rights women already had before that dismal Supreme Court ruling. It kept the courtrooms open, but it did not close the gender wage gap.

In the spring of 2009 the press reported that momentum around Paycheck Fairness was building in the Senate, but the full picture was more complicated. Hillary Clinton had introduced Paycheck in the Senate in early January; at the time she knew she was headed to the State Department, and Paycheck was the only bill she cared about enough to ensure her name was attached to it when she resigned. When she moved over to State a few weeks later, Dodd stepped in to take over the bill in the Senate. But as the economy spiraled downward, Banking Committee chairman Dodd soon became absorbed in banking reform efforts. The eventual Dodd-Frank Wall Street Reform and Consumer Protection Act was the result of that.

Senator Harry Reid had committed that this 111th Congress would not end without a vote on Paycheck Fairness. With my mentor Senator Dodd as the main sponsor, Paycheck Fairness was finally given a vote in the Senate on November 17, 2010. We had lost the majority in the House by that time. Even though the Senate bill garnered fifty-eight votes—a clear majority—we did not get the sixty votes we needed to survive the procedural cloture vote that would allow us to move forward with the bill. Two votes more and we would have had it. I had been hoping for yes votes from Olympia Snowe and Susan Collins, and when they did not support the bill—no Republican woman in the Senate did—it was a surprise and a disappointment. In fact, we only needed one of them to step up. Senator Ben Nelson (D-Nevada) also voted no, but he said he would have voted yes if a Republican had crossed party lines for equal pay.

Paycheck Fairness became a political football. In the Senate it was voted on again in 2012. Republicans again blocked it.

I kept nagging the White House to do more. Senior White House advisors Phil Schiliro, Valerie Jarrett, Tina Tchen—they all received more calls than they would have liked from me and the advocacy groups.

To win passage, I decided we needed to make the agenda for women bolder and more encompassing and enlist the support of outside groups to put pressure on everyone. I had countless conversations with Heather Boushey, including a lunch in London, to bring together the key components of a women's economic agenda. It would take almost two years for this agenda to be labeled, "when women succeed, America succeeds." My office convened meetings with the National Women's Law Center, National Partnership for Women and Families, AAUW, Center for American Progress, Moms Rising, the ACLU, and others. We developed an agenda that included Paycheck Fairness, but also paid family leave and paid sick days, quality childcare, the minimum wage, and more capital for small business women. Later, we would bring in retirement security. And with the help of Page Gardner's Women's Voices, Women Vote, we polled repeatedly in the House battleground congressional districts to create a framework for making this relevant to voters, men and women.

Remember, we had never been able to get traction before on these issues facing working families. Packaging them together as a comprehensive agenda to bolster women's economic security, we now had a much better chance of getting individual bills passed, and doing more for women.

I spoke to Leader Pelosi and she immediately saw the substantive value for women and the potential to engage the caucus, Democrats, working women, and the country. She called every female media person in her Rolodex to announce the Democratic focus on a women's economic agenda. She created the Democratic Women's Working Group, co-chaired by Congresswomen Donna Edwards of Maryland and Doris Matsui of California, to promote the agenda.

She also put this agenda at the heart of the Democrats' off-year campaigns, and she signed off on a bus tour with women and male members touring key areas of country, with a campaign bus boldly painted with the words, "When women succeed, America succeeds."

I had gotten the idea for the bus tour after sitting down with Sister Simone Campbell, whose "Nuns on the Bus" famously undermined the moral credibility of the Ryan budget. In truth, I am known to my staff as the "bus lady," having earlier prodded the Kerry presidential campaign to fund a tour, "Women on a Roll." The women in the caucus really embraced the "When Women Succeed, America Succeeds" bus tour, and they were joined by many of the men, too. It started in Seneca Falls, New York, and when Marcia Greenberger, Judy Lichtman, and Lisa Maatz joined us, we marveled, "When did our issues ever become so mainstream?" My bus tour buddies liked to say I "gave birth to the bus," and what a tour it was.

During a 2014 meeting with Jarrett and Tchen, my colleague Joyce Beatty (D-Ohio) asked President Obama if he could use the actual phrase, "when women succeed, America succeeds," in his State of the Union address. This was days before the speech. Just say the words, she said, that's all she was asking for. And he did, to great jubilation on the House floor.

In April 2014 Paycheck Fairness was again put up for a vote, this time with Mikulski as the sponsor in the Senate. Republicans blocked it again. The bill had fifty-two co-sponsors—every Senate Democrat—but needed sixty votes to overcome a Republican filibuster. It got only fifty-two.

The charge from some Republicans that it was a "show vote"—a vote we knew in advance would fail but pushed forward simply to get a message out in an election year—was more patronizing. "These are bills designed intentionally to fail so that Democrats can make campaign ads about them failing," Senate Minority Leader Mitch McConnell (R-Kentucky) remarked. What McConnell may not have realized is that the issue increasingly has clear support among the public. Poll after poll, women and men of all political stripes list pay equity as a top priority.

Changing demographics in the country demonstrated that unmarried women—single, separated, divorced, or widowed—were a growing group. In fact they comprised over a quarter of all voting-age Americans.[6] But in the 2012 election a whopping 31 percent of them were not registered to vote. We needed to engage these women in political processes.

The "When Women Succeed, America Succeeds" bus tour kicked off in Seneca Falls, New York, that June in an effort to change that. Seneca Falls was the obvious starting point because the first American women's rights convention was held there in 1848. Over four days and eight cities, a group of congressional members met with an incredible array of women eager to tell their stories. It was a spectacular experience, not least because I was reminded how powerful women are when they band together to focus on what's possible.[7]

In September Paycheck Fairness again went up for a vote in the Senate, and again went down 52–40. But earlier, in April, anticipating that Congress would not act on the wage gap, President Obama issued two executive orders, responding favorably after a year of lobbying by myself and other women's groups. One lifted the gag rule that prevented employees of federal contractors from discussing their compensation packages. Employees who shared salary info were no longer at risk of being fired, something that would help not only women but also people of color. The second executive order required federal contractors to give the Labor Department compensation data broken down by gender and race.

After a busy public comment period on the data collection, in 2016 President Obama announced that the EEOC would do the data collection, ensuring that companies with one hundred employees or more would be asked to report to the federal government summary pay data for their employees by race, gender, and ethnicity. This is huge. Not only will the newly collection data inform EEOC and DOL technical assistance and enforcement efforts, it can drive further research into the gender and racial wage gaps and help state legislatures further tailor pay equity solutions. Perhaps most importantly, it could prompt companies to do the right thing; there's nothing like a self-audit that must be turned in to the federal government to wake up the executive suite to pay issues in their company.

There are still people who claim paycheck fairness is not a substantive issue. They dramatically overplay its risks and ignore the benefits. The Heritage Foundation argues that Paycheck Fairness would place burdensome regulations on employers, and thereby "reduce the number of jobs available for women." That seems tantamount to saying that employers would rather skew the demographics of their workforce than bother to employ women. (Their math also does not add up. If paying men and women costs the same, how much would employers save by hiring only men?)

Critics also contend that Paycheck Fairness will lead to a world wherein the government determines wage rates. A memo released by the GOP argued that Paycheck Fairness would end merit pay and cut flexibility in the workplace for working mothers—though they do not say how, exactly. When these naysayers have finished explaining all the damage Paycheck Fairness will do, they say the law is already in effect thanks to the Equal Pay Act of 1963.

The conservative canard that comes up again and again is that the eighty cents a woman makes for every dollar a man makes is a misleading statistic. That number comes from comparing women's average earnings across all industries with men's average earnings.

If you compare women and men in the exact same jobs, they say, the pay gap is insignificant. In other words, the seventy-seven cents figure mainly reflects differences in the jobs men and women hold, educational attainment, years of experience, and lifestyle choices that see women, on average, working fewer hours outside the home than men do because they are working longer hours *inside* the home, taking care of children and extended family.[8]

It is true that some of the pay gap is attributable to the fact that women-dominated job sectors tend to be lower paying. Does that mean women choose lower-paying jobs? Or do the jobs become lower paying once women start outnumbering men in the industry?

Some analysts say that roughly half of the wage gap can be attributed to how women and men tend to cluster in different industries and jobs. But even here we find evidence of systemic bias against women. According to the Center for American Progress, the top ten occupations for women, including executive and administrative assistants, registered nurses, teachers, and cashiers, all pay men more on average. There are a few jobs wherein women earn more than men with the same job title—but that is more the exception than the rule. In some job sectors, like real estate, women earn closer to sixty cents for every dollar men in the same job do. The difference in take-home pay can amount to hundreds of dollars a week.

Getting a college degree does not eliminate the gender pay gap, either. AAUW research shows that just one year out of college, women working full-time are already paid less than their male colleagues, even when they work in the same field. Ten years after graduation, the pay gap widens. After controlling for factors that affect earnings—like college major, job, and hours worked per week—women are still paid an unexplained 5 percent less than men with the same major, working in the same field, one year after college graduation. This unexplained pay gap widens to 12 percent ten years after graduation, even though women are more likely to get an advanced degree. This is not chump change, especially when you remember that benefits and future raises are based on salary.

According to Cornell economists Francine D. Blau and Lawrence M. Kahn, 41.1 percent of the pay gap between men and women cannot be explained away using measurable factors like job title, educational attainment, or years on the job. Then there is the unignorable fact that unlike men, women are not likely to receive pay increases after becoming a parent. If a woman makes less than her male partner does, it makes economic sense for her to be the one to take a step back from her job should family needs require it. Unfortunately this leads to a cultural expectation that mothers are less devoted to their job because they are more distracted by family—and this assumption can depress wages for all women, even those who have no intention of having children. Further, while the gender wage gap has been narrowing at a snail's pace, the wage gap between mothers and fathers is actually widening. This "Motherhood Penalty" depresses women's pay, while men receive a fatherhood boost.

By the 2016 election season, some Republicans realized it was no longer enough to say no to equal pay and Paycheck Fairness. The issue was no longer on the fringes but front and center for Hillary Clinton, at least, who made it one of her highest priorities. Just being obstructionist proved they were behind the times. Now they had to start offering alternatives. The danger, however, is that now we will see bills designed to make it look like they are addressing the problem, but are unable to effect much change. "Faux" fair pay bills are not the answer.

The facts remain: unmarried women—single, divorced, separated, and widowed—are the fastest growing segment of women in America. The women's poverty rate is as high as it has been in seventeen years. Women are now half the workforce. Mothers are the primary breadwinner or co-breadwinner in two-thirds of American families. Women have less retirement security and pension protection. They are more reliant on Social Security, but receive lower payments. Women own 30 percent of small companies but only receive 4.4 percent of the total dollars loaned. Two out of three minimum-wage workers are women. And last but not least, the United States remains the only advanced economy in the world without paid maternity leave. Women need Paycheck Fairness.

6

"Two Women on the Ticket": Notes on Ending Sexism

WHEN I THINK BACK on my career, my gut response to much of the sexism I have encountered is "Don't dwell. Learn." Many years ago, when the mayor of New Haven was considering nominating me to be the director of the New Haven Coliseum, the local paper—the *New Haven Register*—fought hard against it. They described me as "a helluva gal around the office" and asked, how could a woman function in any leadership capacity in the male sports world?

I was the first woman to run a statewide campaign in Connecticut. Some of the old-line town party chairs wouldn't work with me. And I remember when some pols would come into the state headquarters and ask to speak to the manager. I would tell them, "You are!"

When I started my job as Senator Dodd's chief of staff, I was one of a handful of women in that role at the time. Every day I met people surprised to see a female chief of staff. I perceived early on that women had to work twice as hard to be taken seriously. That has remained true throughout my years in Congress.

Even when you are prepared, that is no guarantee you will be taken seriously. I vividly recall watching Hillary Clinton testify on healthcare when she was still first lady. It was the 1990s, not exactly the Dark Ages. All around me I heard male colleagues express surprise that Hillary actually knew what she was talking about.

When I arrived in the House in 1991, there were thirty-four women serving in Congress out of 535 total seats.[1] I was again conscious of being a woman in a field dominated by men, and again I found the job demanded very different levels of performance from men and women. As a woman you are allowed little latitude in making mistakes before people watching conclude you are not worth paying attention to anymore. People are quick to say, "She doesn't get it," "She can't answer the questions," and so on.

One small anecdote from my early days on the Hill demonstrates this reality for women legislators. A Connecticut company called Sikorsky, which makes helicopters, and another called Pratt & Whitney, which makes engines for jets, employ a lot of people in my district. When I first went to testify before a Defense Appropriations subcommittee for funding relating to an engine for the M1A1 tank, made in Stratford, Connecticut, at Textron Lycoming, I did my presentation and thought it went well. Congressman Jerry Lewis (R-California) was a member of the committee. As I finished my testimony, Lewis said to me, "Congresswoman DeLauro, can you speak about the M1A1 tank without looking at your notes?"

I said to him, "Damn straight I can." The chairman of the committee, Democrat Jack Murtha, winked at me, as if to say, "Good for you." Jack and I forged a friendship—but he did not vote for me either time I ran for chair of the Democratic Caucus.

The first time I ran for chair, I lost by six votes to Martin Frost, a senior member who chaired the Democratic Congressional Campaign Committee. The same day I was invited to join a photo op with the group that had won leadership slots, ostensibly to show the public that the Congress was not as white-male-dominated as it actually was. I declined. Gephardt subsequently called a meeting of the women members of the House so he could hear us talk about what it would have meant for there to be a woman chair of the Democratic Caucus. Gephardt was not one to emote in public but after hearing these women's stories he was nearly in tears. It led him to think about what position I could lead, and over the next few days talk among the Democratic leadership turned to the possibility of creating a new position for me. What about assistant leader? That idea was shot down—too much power. Then Steny Hoyer (D-Maryland) proposed the title "assistant to the leader" and that made everyone happy. A few years later that title would cause problems, however, when the post was being given to James E. Clyburn (D-South Carolina). A title that suggested Clyburn, who is African American, was somehow subservient to, a mere helpmate for, the Democratic leader would not go over so well. So they made him "assistant leader," and everyone was once again satisfied.

The second time I ran for chair, Murtha told me he could not support me because Pelosi was also running for minority whip at the time, and we could not have two women on the ticket. So it is important not to assume that a glimmer of feminist instincts in someone means they have no blind spots.

I am sure many women have experienced something like the following. You say something in a meeting and are ignored. A few minutes later a male at the table will say the exact same thing you said and people will say, "Gosh, that is a great idea." You might be surprised to hear this happens in Congress all the time, even today, even in leadership circles. When Pelosi made George Miller and myself co-chairs of the Democratic Steering and Policy Committee, it was often assumed I did the steering (i.e., overseeing the Democratic members' committee assignments) and Miller the policy (i.e., determining what polices the Democratic caucus would formulate and prioritize). Miller, who was sensitive on these issues, heard from Pelosi that I was not very happy with this arrangement, and he came to see me in my office. He said, "We work together like ham and eggs."

I do not know of an easy fix for this situation. So I offer these reminiscences and thoughts not as fuel for resentment, but as encouragement to get to the same "Don't dwell. Learn" place I arrived at. Today women make up roughly a fifth of the House and Senate. Progress has certainly been made. If I had to offer advice to women struggling through this stuff for the first time, I would say this: do your homework. Know what you are talking about. Do not throw in the towel until you absolutely have to.

I have found it also helps to turn oneself toward an alternative project, to build something, in the face of defeat. Not to ignore the sexism but to work around it once it is clear it will not budge—or at least not yet. Losing the race for Democratic Caucus chair led to my starting the public policy dinners at my home in Washington. For fourteen years, we've been meeting twice a month with prominent journalists, academics, and policy experts—and many members consider it one of only venues for serious policy discussion. It was an unorthodox maneuver, and risky, but at that point no one was going to get in my way.

The good news? I firmly believe that in my lifetime we will be able to put an end to women being the "cheaper" option. Then we will finally be rid of the notion once and for all that two men on a ticket is normal but two women is a tactical error.

7

Politics and Faith

A FRIEND OF MY FATHER'S died when he was still young. He left behind a widow and five boys, the youngest thirteen-year-old twins. A couple of summers later one of those boys needed a summer job, and his mother, bumping into my mother at a store one day, mentioned this in passing. Could my mother help in any way?

"Sure, bring him to my house," my mother said. "When?" the woman asked. "Whenever you want," my mother said. She did not stipulate an hour, or tell her to call first to make sure we were not in the middle of dinner. Instead she essentially said: *You know where I live. Just knock on our door.*

The religion that has influenced me throughout my life has a lot to do with my parents' faith tradition. They were Catholics for whom faith and hospitality went hand in hand. Faith was a daily practice; it meant knowing what was going on with the families around you, and knowing how to help them. Faith demanded service to one's neighbors. Our local parish, St. Michael's in New Haven's Wooster Square neighborhood, was where people gathered to share their lives and help shoulder one another's burdens. My father often squabbled with local clergy because he felt they were not acting in a way consistent with Catholic principles—and he wanted to keep them honest.

He was proud of his values, and knew there was a strong case to be made for Social Security itself having a foundation in Catholic social teaching. In Pope Leo XIII's 1891 encyclical *Rerum Novarum*, it states that "among the several purposes of a society, one should try to arrange for . . . a fund out of which the members may be effectually helped in their needs, not only in the cases of accident, but also in sickness, old age, and distress." Bear in mind that in 1891, U.S. newspapers were still carrying reports of troops firing on workers who dared demonstrate for eight-hour workdays. Catholic leaders and intellectuals were at the forefront of the fight to correct injustices across the country. The hardships that working people faced would inspire Monsignor John Ryan, who grew up in hardscrabble communities in northern Minnesota, to champion the minimum wage as early as 1906, long before it became law. Ryan's later book *A Better Economic Order* (1935) had a tremendous influence on the Roosevelt administration and the formation of the New Deal. Ryan not only served on the advisory council to the President's Committee on Economic Security during the drafting of the Social Security Act but became one of the program's most ardent defenders.

Still, we were aware that we were Catholics in a country whose political leaders on a national level were predominantly Protestant. As a student at Marymount College I tracked John F. Kennedy's path to the presidential nomination with the kind of fervor usually afforded rock stars. I tracked the delegate count state by state. I campaigned for Kennedy. I remember distinctly his now famous 1960 speech to the Greater Houston Ministerial Association, in which he assured the public that though Catholic, if elected he would not be *too* Catholic, and as president would never take marching orders from the Vatican. He affirmed his belief "in an America where the separation of church and state is absolute, where no Catholic prelate would tell the president how to act and no Protestant minister would tell his parishioners for whom to vote," a belief "in an America that is officially neither Catholic, Protestant or Jewish—where no public official either requests or accepts instructions on public policy from the Pope, the National Council of Churches or any other ecclesiastical source." Kennedy defined for me an important relationship between faith and politics.

When Kennedy was scheduled to make a campaign appearance in Waterbury, Connecticut, my father and I waited until three a.m. to see him speak. On election night, I could not sleep. I was up all night. When Kennedy won, my whole family was inspired. Here was proof positive that we Catholics had something to contribute to the national discussion. My father and several friends from the neighborhood drove down in a raging snowstorm to Washington, D.C., for the inauguration. It honestly felt like we had arrived.

For me, the appeal was also generational. People my age were eager to forge new paths but equally inspired by Kennedy's appeal for us to give ourselves to service. "Ask not what your country can do for you, but what you can do for your country"—that was an affirmation of everything we believed in as Democrats and as Catholics. Kennedy's example let us keep ties with our parents' generation while still following our own individual consciences.

Complementing this excitement were the reforms of Vatican II. Pope John XXIII's convening of the Second Vatican Council was motivated by a strong desire to see the church address social problems and economic inequality. Vatican II called Catholics to be agents of Christian living in the world as it was, in all its messiness and nitty-gritty, not the world as one might imagine it to be, sitting within the comfortable confines of a church pew.

So when I went to Congress in 1991, I never imagined my religion would be a subject of controversy. I remembered thinking how lucky I was that, unlike presidential candidate Kennedy, I did not have to battle anti-Catholic prejudice. The atmosphere on the Hill then included people from all kinds of religious backgrounds, who held their beliefs with varying degrees of intensity, from the lukewarm Episcopalian to the diehard Baptist. Religion informed our actions, but it was seen as one of many formative influences. Faith mattered, but when it came to guiding one's political stances, so did family, geography, ethnicity, and one's career before Congress.

People in Congress were understood to have a number of motivations and influences informing their votes. This is very different from the atmosphere today.

Religion had been returning to political conversation since President Jimmy Carter talked about teaching Sunday School classes, Jerry Falwell's Moral Majority formed in 1977, and Ronald Reagan put his faith front and center. But in the early 1990s it was not yet being used as a marketing tool for one's political career or policy positions—or to signal to voters whom you believed was in and who was out. Personal piety was never hauled out as a reason for policy decisions that you made. No one ran to be "pastor in chief."

But within a decade, the ecumenicalism that had characterized earlier legislative bodies had been turned on its head. The reason was abortion. The politics of abortion completely took over the conversation on faith in politics. Pro-choice Catholic Democrats increasingly came under scrutiny. For all of our advancement of programs like Social Security, Head Start, Medicare, and the Child Tax Credit, all guided by a rich history of Catholic social teaching, we were increasingly on the outs because of our views on abortion. Never mind that the right to abortion was guaranteed by the U.S. Constitution and affirmed by the U.S. Supreme Court.

I was concerned that Democrats were being viewed as godless creatures, and pilloried for not having values or morals. It made no sense to me, and so on some level I wanted to understand why, but mainly I wanted it to stop. Many of us had come to Congress fully aware of our personal histories, religious or otherwise, and we had drawn on that history and our religious upbringing when we needed fuel for the fight to bring about social justice. There was no way I was going to let people with no appreciation for the religious core of our demands that people be fed, or assisted in tough times, demean that legacy.

Unfortunately the Church itself was behind this shift. The only issue on which they judged someone's commitment to Catholic teaching was abortion. Suddenly whether one had upheld the tenets of the faith by advocating for the poor, the hungry, the unemployed, those without medical care—none of that mattered. Now in the abstract this would have consequences but might not be gut-wrenching. In practice it proved otherwise.

In 1990 I was forced to resign from the board of trustees of a Catholic women's high school, a school that I attended and at which I had given a commencement address several years earlier, because—as I was told—Archbishop John Whealon had said that my continued membership on the board would endanger the school's certification as a Catholic institution. If I remained on the board, the school would be decertified because of my position on choice. I was so pained by this decision that I wrote a three-page letter to the Sister who headed the school, quoting Kennedy on how he did not speak for his Church "and the church does not speak for me. . . . Whatever issue may come before me . . . I will make my decision in accordance with these views, in accordance with what my conscience tells me to be the national interest, and without regard to outside religious pressures or dictates. And no power or threat of punishment could cause me do decide otherwise." Catholic institutions, however, had gone in a different direction. I could not serve the high school I loved.

I was disinvited from a communion breakfast at a local parish. Incidents like these were hurtful, but also probably trivial in the grand scheme of things. Over time they became more troubling. We had entered an arena wherein good Catholics had pro-life voting records, and bad Catholics voted pro-choice. End of story. For me personally, who had been raised with passages from Catholic teaching that emphasized how Jesus favored the poor, this was jarring.

In 2000 I organized a forum called Public Voices. The forum addressed politics, religion, and values. Columnist Ron Brownstein moderated, and brilliant commentators like journalist Joe Klein, Will Marshall of the Progressive Policy Institute, political theorist Alan Wolfe, Michael Novak of the American Enterprise Institute, and the Reverend Jim Wallis all spoke on the role that faith played in all of their public commitments. It was one attempt to have a voice about religion and public life where the landscape was changing quickly.

Shortly before Christmas 2003 Representative Nick Lampson (D-Texas) and I got into a conversation about our Italian Catholic backgrounds. (The family name is Nicholas Lampisino, in case you were wondering about Lampson.) He felt a similar pride in being raised Catholic, and still held a yearly breakfast to celebrate the Feast of St. Joseph. We both believed religion had a role to play in government, and in that respect we were different from some of our colleagues on the political left who would prefer religion fade away entirely.

But Nick also felt keenly that as representatives we had to acknowledge that we lived in a pluralistic society. Knowing that abortion was the law of the land, and that we represented constituents who did not wish to change abortion law, how could we broaden the conversation? And how could we get the Church to, in effect, stop making things worse?

These conversations are how we began our unofficial Catholic working group, inviting many guests from the faith and political worlds to speak to us. I started hosting dinners at my house in Washington specifically for my Catholic colleagues to talk about these issues. Not many people showed up at first. We had a lot of empty seats, a lot of leftover pasta.

But we kept on meeting, and before long an incredible roster of serious thinkers on the subject took the time to join us. They delved into questions like: How to live out one's Christian faith? That question has been contested territory since the time of Jesus himself. The Gospels are full of stories of Jesus clashing with his followers, challenging them to think outside of established categories.

And we were not alone. Three Democratic groups were meeting to discuss faith and politics at this time. In addition to my group with Nick, there was Jim Clyburn's Democratic Faith Working Group. David Price—who taught at Yale at the same time as my husband Stan—assembled another.[1] Price was like a big brother to me in the early days of this effort, a steady source of advice and support.

The focus on browbeating Catholic pro-choice politicians, however, really amped up during the long months preceding the 2004 election. George W. Bush was in the White House. He had leaned heavily on religious expression throughout his first campaign and during his first term. Much to his credit, he did make a point of reaching out to American Muslim communities in the wake of September 11. But the overall drift was very much toward labeling pro-choice Catholic Democrats as a threat to the country.

In our meetings, we heard and shared stories. The Eucharist was now being used as a political weapon. Senator Dick Durbin said he would go around looking for a church to attend on Sunday. In February 2004 Cardinal Raymond Burke announced that if then Democratic nominee for president John Kerry ever presented himself at the altar for communion, he would deny him the sacrament. Threatening to deny Kerry communion? I was astounded when I first heard that. Here the church itself was making it difficult for a Catholic to run for president of the United States. All because of his record on a single issue. Burke had also let David Obey know that he would do well to change his votes on abortion, stem cell research, and the UN population programs or face excommunication.

Emotions ran high whenever we gathered to talk. Some people might not mind being called godless or irresponsible, but for us it was like being accused of betraying our own families. There was a real outpouring of hurt and pain. Nick Lampson, Anna Eshoo, Bill Pascrell . . . all of us were being pilloried. Some people were afraid to go to church. Obey was not at the meeting where we decided to go public with our concerns, but I knew that the talk of excommunication had rattled him to the core. Not only were our contributions to social justice largely ignored, we were being painted as dangers to the social fabric. To hear this from Republicans was old hat. That we were used to, that we could handle. But to hear it from our church was another level of pain.

As I learned from my parents: when upset, start making phone calls. I called Robert S. Bennett. Bob Bennett is a well-respected D.C. lawyer who is also Catholic, and has strong ties to Cardinal Theodore McCarrick. I asked Bennett if he would act as a go-between between our group of Catholic legislators and McCarrick. He agreed.

In May 2004 with Bennett's help we sent a letter to Cardinal McCarrick—about abortion, about the current political climate, about how our faith was being challenged. Forty-eight House Democrat signers—some pro-life, some pro-choice—wrote that "while some of us differ on this issue, each and every one of us is committed to the basic principles that are at the heart of Catholic social justice: helping the poor and underprivileged, protecting the most vulnerable among us, and ensuring that all Americans of every faith are given meaningful opportunities to share in the blessings of this great country."

Personally I was wrestling with other issues. The Church had spoken eloquently on the rush to war in Iraq. Bishops even wrote to the president as the pope beseeched him not to go to war. I voted against the Authorization for Use of Military Force Against

Iraq Resolution of 2002, ostensibly voting "with the church." I did not receive a call to commend me for that, only censure on my abortion votes. Had the bishops acted against the members who voted for the use of force in Iraq? They had not. On the matter of abortion, the bishops spoke of "cooperating with evil." So why did the Church's commitment to life not prompt them to be more activist on these other issues—like war, or like the death penalty? Why were Catholic legislators who were indifferent to the poor not being barred from communion breakfasts?

After sending our letter to underscore the point that we did not think the Church should encourage the use of religion as a divisive political strategy we met with Cardinal McCarrick. Few meetings I have been in can match that one for poignancy. People spoke not as politicians but as everyday vulnerable, wounded people. Members poured out their hearts about their faith, their values, their very sense of self. Catholicism was part of their DNA—and now they were being attacked. The cardinal listened to this outpouring with genuine sympathy. We were encouraged when, speaking at a meeting among bishops at a Denver conference, Cardinal Mc-Carrick expressed concern over how communion was being turned into a partisan political battleground. He said he could not recommend denying communion for political reasons. "We do not want to encourage confrontations at the altar rail with the body of the Lord Jesus in our hands." Talking together with respect and open hearts seemed to make a difference.

But the temperature could not be lowered. Politicizing Catholicism proved very effective throughout Bush's long 2004 campaign. In August the Catholic magazine *America* ran an op-ed that David Obey wrote in which he explained his record on abortion.[2] The editor who gave him space in the magazine to do so, Father Thomas Reese SJ, was promptly fired for letting him have his say.

Many Catholics defected to the Republican Party on election

night in 2004. Democrats lost the Catholic vote, 52 to 47 percent. Fourteen percent of white Catholics who voted for Bill Clinton in 1996 did not vote for John Kerry eight years later.

After Bush's re-election, we needed to define ourselves more fully. Ignoring these developments and remaining on the sidelines of these debates was not an option for us. If we could put more energy into publicly defining ourselves as Catholics, then perhaps we could not waste so much time on defense.

Some called what we did next a matter of political expediency, but it came out of a deeper reality. It came from a desire to try and rescue the Catholic faith, as we had lived it, from those who wanted to take it from us. I wanted my Church to be a moral force in the broadest sense, at a time when we were looking at growing numbers of Americans living in poverty and going without health insurance.

Our group took action where we could. We challenged the administration's budgets that proposed cutting programs for working families and the poor. We were seeing budget after budget that went after agencies like the Department of Health and Human Services—at the same time that they increased tax cuts for the wealthy to the tune of $106 billion, as the budget released in early 2005 did. That same budget took $10 billion from Medicaid.

Our informal caucus drafted a Statement of Principles. In five hundred words we tried to suggest that the way we saw it, reducing poverty, increasing access to healthcare, and taking care not to blunder into wars should also factor into church leaders' musings on who could call themselves a good Catholic. Using only abortion as the litmus test for someone's faith showed a lack of grace. And when we saw Congress pushing to repeal the estate tax while 13 million American children lived in poverty, we were just appalled and angry.

Here is an excerpt of the statement we Catholic Democrats released late February 2006:

We envision a world in which every child belongs to a loving family and agree with the Catholic church about the value of human life and the undesirability of abortion. . . . Each of us is committed to reducing the number of unwanted pregnancies and creating an environment with policies that encourage pregnancies to be carried to term. We believe this includes promoting alternatives to abortion, such as adoption, and improving access to children's healthcare and childcare, as well as policies that encourage paternal and maternal responsibility.

We hoped this document would raise awareness that decisions made by this Congress had clear social and moral implications that directly contradicted Catholic values. They include decisions that benefited the few at the expense of a larger community. They made it harder, in our view, for parents to raise their children and balance the pressures of work and family.

Response to the statement was swift, and our optimism was not immediately rewarded. Catholic League president William Donohue wasted no time in responding that "the most convincing evidence that this statement is a sham" was the fact that I was the point person. He cited my work for Emily's List as evidence that I could not be trusted to speak with integrity on the subject. He went on to say that the letter was not a statement of principles but a statement of politics.

The political strategist Patrick Hynes, calling me "virulently pro-abortion," proposed that I must not understand the principle of subsidiarity, a tenet of Catholic social teaching that maintains that government should intervene at the most local level possible.

I can only guess that putting assistance directly into the hands of poor people—as food stamps do, as the refundable Child Tax Credit does—does not count as local enough in Hynes's view.

In the spring of 2006, I spoke at a Pew Forum with E.J. Dionne, who had been sympathetic to our cause from the beginning. I remarked that things have become so politicized, you almost had to wear a hard hat going into most meetings on the Hill these days. Yet we were determined to have some constructive conversations.

Pro-life congressman Tim Ryan (D-Ohio) and I began working together to introduce the Reducing the Need for Abortion and Supporting Parents Act in September of that year. The bill proposed to increase support of pre- and post-natal care as well as early childhood support. We recognized that people wanted to see fewer abortions, and that the first step toward making that possible was helping women never to have to face that decision in the first place. Frances Kissling, president of Catholics for a Free Choice, welcomed the bill at first as a sign that policy makers who hold different views on aspects of sexuality and reproduction can work together to tackle a root cause—unintended and unwanted pregnancies. She later became hostile to the bill and impatient with the "common-ground" project.

The bill was no knee-jerk reaction. We worked on it for a long time, not least because we both knew we had to be very careful about how to approach groups on both sides. Again I would be surprised by the unintended consequences. Some women's groups were annoyed with me, to say the least. Lack of common ground on abortion would nearly derail the vote on healthcare reform—as I detail in the next chapter.

Two principles sustained me throughout: that people hunger for authentic leadership, and the Catholic teaching that our full human dignity is only realized in relationship with others.

In February 2012, I was called to Hartford along with the rest of the Connecticut congressional delegation to meet with Archbishop Henry Mansell, Bishop William Lori, and Bishop Michael Cote to explain why we were aiding and abetting the abortion cause. At the end of this meeting, the archbishop asked me to stay behind so he could speak to me alone. He proceeded to tell me I was married to a Jewish man, who was divorced, and therefore, he asked, how could I still present myself for communion on Sundays? I told him I would continue to receive the sacraments, and asked him a question: How could the church be so blind to the fact that healthcare reform could save millions of lives? How was *that* not a pro-life issue? And where were they when I voted against wars, or to grow programs for the poor? Where were they then? Meanwhile the pedophile scandal wherein senior church officials looked the other way as priests violated boys and girls—why had little been done about that? There was no rapprochement in this meeting. I arrived feeling on the defensive, I left pissed off.

In April of 2012 I was again taken aback by a Republican budget proposal. Paul Ryan is Catholic and also a fan of Ayn Rand; his Randian principles take over whenever he sits down to compile a budget. I wrote to Timothy Cardinal Dolan, archbishop of New York, to explain my dismay and ask the Catholic Church if they might join me in mobilizing against the budget. I did not want to let the House majority jettison most of our government's capacity to protect the common good.

"I write to urge you to call on Congress to give priority to the poor and the vulnerable in this year's federal budget written by Budget Committee chairman Paul Ryan and the House majority. I would also urge you to highlight the moral consequences of these budget priorities," I wrote.

I listed all of the things Ryan's new federal budget proposed to do—including getting 62 percent of its nondefense cuts from services that help poor families. I said I agreed with the bishops who had written to members of the House on this key point: that "a central moral measure of any budget proposal is how it affects 'the least of these'" (a reference to the Gospel of Matthew, chapter 25). Were we as Catholics not agreed that those who are hungry and homeless, without work or poor, should come first?

I asked Archbishop Dolan if he and other bishops could raise their voice on this issue of our social safety net, and make the case that the federal budget is a document that should advance the moral responsibilities of government. His response was warm, thoughtful, almost immediate. He replied within four days.

He thanked me for the letter and assured me that the U.S. bishops would continue to speak out, and that he wished more members of Congress would also affirm that the church had a role as moral voice in public life. Then he segued into abortion. All of the work Catholics did in the areas of service to the poor and disenfranchised rested, he wrote, on Catholic belief "in the dignity of each and every human life." Yes, the budget was critical, but so, too, was the right to life. Everything from upholding marriage as the union of one man and one woman to defense of the immigrant—all of this hung together. But protection of the unborn was bedrock. "A failure in one area to respect the dignity of *every* human life, and especially the weakest, undermines the principle in all other areas. And when the failure occurs in an area of foundational importance, the damage to the broader principle is especially severe."

He cited the bishops' use of a house metaphor. Direct attacks on human life (abortion, euthanasia) struck at the foundation. Other serious threats to human dignity (poverty, hunger, lack of employment, housing, healthcare) damaged the walls and crossbeams. He ended by saying that he would pray for me through the Easter season.

In turn I thanked him for his thoughtful response. I repeated my assertion that if the archbishop of New York were to make public his view that fiscal responsibility efforts couldn't be balanced on the backs of the poor, it could make a difference.

Then, because it was clear he was asking me to reconsider my pro-choice voting record, I replied that I disagreed with the foundation idea. A foundation is essential to a house, but without walls and crossbeams, the foundation would wash away in a storm. In other words, without healthcare, childcare, employment, housing, and anti-hunger and nutrition programs, many women would have a more difficult time bringing a child into the world and caring for it. For that reason alone, I wrote, I believed the House majority's budget did in fact jeopardize human life. So the cardinal archbishop and I differed on abortion, but perhaps we could work together on issues of social and economic justice.

His final reply to me reasserted his view that some issues of justice were so fundamental that to deny them was "to undermine justice in all other areas." Regardless of public opinion—whether views on abortion changed or not—he thought it important that members of Congress "take some responsibility" for the success or failure of laws that restricted access to abortion. Again, it all came back to abortion.

Then with the election of Pope Francis in 2013, a ray of light appeared. I went to St. Peter's Square for his installation, along with many of the Catholic members of Congress. Francis gave a stunning homily, one that reminded me of why I got into politics in the first place. "[He] must open his arms to protect all of God's people and embrace with tender affection the whole of humanity, especially the poorest, the weakest, the least important."

When Francis demoted Cardinal Burke, the one who had threatened David Obey, I called David. I would not call that phone call a celebration, exactly, but we did feel vindicated.

Voices raised in support of religious liberty grew louder. Sister Simone Campbell, long a champion of individual dignity, rightly pointed out that "in our pluralistic society the government is often called on to balance competing liberty interests—a difficult task requiring compromises that respect the freedom and dignity of all sides and, to the extent possible, provide everyone with the space necessary to exercise his or her own conscience."[3] It was possible, she argued, to protect people's religious liberty and assert an individual's freedom of conscience—to decide what was best for herself and her family—at the same time.

Pope Francis expressed his desire for expanding the scope of our conversation whenever we talked about "a culture of life" in stark, unmistakable terms in his first encyclical, *The Joy of the Gospel*:

> Just as the commandment "Thou shalt not kill" sets a clear limit in order to safeguard the value of human life, today we also have to say "thou shalt not" to an economy of exclusion and inequality. Such an economy kills. . . .
>
> Some people continue to defend trickle-down theories which assume that economic growth, encouraged by a free market, will inevitably succeed in bringing about greater justice and inclusiveness in the world. This opinion, which has never been confirmed by the facts, expresses a crude and naïve trust in the goodness of those wielding economic power and in the sacralized workings of the prevailing economic system. . . . Almost without being aware of it, we end up being incapable of feeling compassion at the outcry of the poor, weeping for other people's pain, and feeling a need to help them, as though all this were someone else's responsibility and not our own. The culture of prosperity deadens us.
>
> I beg the Lord to grant us more politicians who are genuinely disturbed by the state of society, the people, the lives of the poor! It is vital that government leaders and financial leaders take heed and broaden their horizons, working to ensure that all citizens have dignified work, education and healthcare.

Poverty and inequality are right-to-life issues. The way Pope Francis spoke about these issues felt like a homecoming. As a society we are to be measured by how we treat the least fortunate among us. There is a great deal at stake, for our nation's values, and for the lives of the families at risk. If we want a twenty-first century in which life in America gets better, not worse, we need to work hard to get more people enfranchised, fed, paid fairly, and protected from the worst vagaries of competition in an increasingly winner-take-all economy. And for some of us, this is not just good public policy but religious duty.

8

In Defense of People Who Get Sick

I've been asked a lot for my view on American healthcare. Well, it would be a good idea.

—Paul Farmer

BY THE TIME the Affordable Care Act (ACA) passed in 2010, awareness that something big had to be done about the United States healthcare system had been brewing for decades. In 1979, nearly 70 percent of people in the workforce had health insurance provided through their employer. In 1985, about two-thirds of companies employing a hundred or more workers paid their employees' health insurance premiums in full. Ten years later, only half that number did. By 2007, less than 55 percent of people received any health coverage at all through their employer. Health insurance premiums were rising faster than wages—four times as fast, by some accounts. Many worried that these rising costs threatened American economic competitiveness, never mind the pressure these expenses put on families. And digging into the details, like health insurance companies' discriminatory "gender rating" practices which had some women paying up to 48 percent more than men for similar policies, made me see red.

Helping to pass the Affordable Care Act at a life-and-death

moment stands as one of my proudest accomplishments as a leg-islator. It was a long time coming, and no legislative effort I had ever been involved in balanced so precariously on a knife edge for so long—or better represented, when the ink was dry, the value of persistence when giving up would have been both easier and politically expedient.

I came to Congress focused on healthcare because of my ex-perience with ovarian cancer. A plan for universal healthcare had been central in my first campaign. I initially sought out a seat on Energy and Commerce because of my interest in healthcare. In early 1994 I was asked by House Majority Leader Dick Gephardt to join the Democratic side in a televised Oxford-style debate about healthcare reform that Gingrich and Gephardt coordinated in a rare moment of seeing eye to eye. The idea was to have ninety min-utes of back-and-forth, after the close of regular House business for the day, broadcast by C-SPAN and NPR, and show the American public that some of us, at least, knew our stuff. On the Democratic side were Gephardt, Henry Waxman (D-California), Pete Stark (D-California), and myself; on the other side stood Gingrich's team of Bill Young (R-Florida), Nancy Johnson (R-Connecticut), and Thomas Bliley (R-Virginia). Gephardt probably was scared to death I would be a weak link in the debate and I was, too—joining a panel of people who had spent their whole careers involved in healthcare policy. When he asked, I immediately said yes, though when I looked at the lineup, I said to myself, "what have I done?" I went into full tutorial mode and prepared for it like a student cramming for finals.

I took every opportunity to focus on healthcare issues and sought to get the Labor, Health, Human Services, and Education slot on the Appropriations Committee. There, I found my platform and vehicle. I banded together with Nita Lowey and Nancy Pelosi on the subcommittee and we formed a bond in our battle to get more funding for women's healthcare. The three of us ganged up on Neal

Smith (D-Iowa), the Appropriations Committee chair, and told him the status quo was not acceptable. The three of us still laugh about that meeting.

Our focus was the National Institutes of Health, the premier health research organization on the earth, which had no women and no minorities in its clinical trials. In 1993, we passed a law that, for the first time ever, required NIH-funded researchers to "ensure that the trial is designed and carried out in a manner sufficient to provide for a valid analysis of whether the variables being studied in the trial affect women or members of minority groups, as the case may be, differently than other subjects in the trial." In other words, clinical trials had to make sure that conclusions drawn regarding health maintenance for white male subjects were not simply deemed true for everyone else.[1] This law proved critical to advancements in medical research for women and people of color.

This critical change happened with the enthusiastic collaboration of impressive Republican women, including Congresswomen Connie Morella, Marge Roukema, and Nancy Johnson. What an unusual idea! It was a time when bipartisanship was important to constructing our safety net, regulations, and healthcare investments.

I joined the push for a Patient's Bill of Rights under Clinton. I also worked on the Breast Cancer Patient Protection Act, which would guarantee a woman a forty-eight-hour hospital stay to recuperate from a mastectomy or lumpectomy should she and her doctor decide it was necessary. Many insurance companies were forcing women to have "drive-through" mastectomies on an outpatient basis, as if having one's breasts surgically removed was as low-impact as a wisdom tooth extraction. The bill never passed, however. Another bill I championed, the Scientific Fairness Act for Women, would prevent the FDA from putting corporate or ideological interests above the interests of women, as it did when it delayed a decision on over-the-counter sales of Plan B emergency contraception for three years, and then limited sales to women eighteen years or older, despite the fact that its own advisory panel recommended otherwise. Advocating for women's health has always been a priority for me, even when I am told I am tilting at windmills—as happened with the Scientific Fairness bill.

As first lady, Hillary Clinton took on healthcare with tremendous enthusiasm for change. She represented the administration's proposal for universal healthcare during several days of testimony in front of Congress—and she paid dearly for it. The insurance companies opposed it, and conservatives mobilized in force against it. Her popularity plummeted and the bill never got out of committee.

When President Obama took office in early 2009, we had a Democratic majority in the House and Senate. We were poised to take on healthcare in a comprehensive way, and it was Speaker Pelosi and committee chairs George Miller, Charlie Rangel, and Henry Waxman who did the historic work of shaping and driving the bill through the House. As proposed by President Obama, the healthcare reforms would build on the current private insurance system, though progressives in the House were agreed there would be a public option for insurance. That would keep the private companies honest and create competition. I was prepared for a fight for a public option, the highest priority of the Congressional Progressive Caucus. It was part of the healthcare reform law passed by the House, but conservative Democrats blocked it in the Senate.

What I was not prepared for, however, was another fight over abortion.

In early July 2009, when the healthcare reform bill was being worked on in committee, anti-abortion lawmakers were concerned that reform would force private insurance companies to cover abortions. The Catholic bishops were also fearful that the Affordable Care Act would mandate abortion coverage—and seemingly not impressed at all with its many provisions for women, the working poor, and the uninsured. Simultaneously, pro-choice lawmakers were threatening to vote no on the ACA if it strengthened or expanded existing restrictions on abortion access. Abortion had become the issue on which irreconcilable stands could actually defeat the reforms. And that was where I used all my energy, credibility, and networks to help bring the law over the finish line.

At this point I had more of a reputation as a coalition builder than I did during my early days in the House, and I used it to actually make progress. In September 2006 pro-life and Catholic congressman Tim Ryan (D-Ohio) and I introduced together the "Preventing Unintended Pregnancies, Reducing the Need for Abortion, and Supporting Parents Act."[2] It had provisions for teen pregnancy prevention education, after-school programs, and efforts to prevent unplanned pregnancies among community college students. It also made access to family planning services and supplies mandatory under Medicaid, and improved support for prenatal, labor, delivery, and postpartum care. The point of the act was to make it easier for women to choose to carry their pregnancies to term, but alongside that practical, immediate goal was another: to soften the dividing lines on the abortion issue. Too many pro-choicers over the years had been tarred as "pro-abortion" and too many pro-lifers as religious zealots who could not be reasoned with. I believed the bill would build common ground.

Ryan had worked with the Third Way, a group helping more ideologically moderate members of the Congress, and he reached out to me as a Catholic to work with him on the issue of reducing abortions.

Many people did not see the bill that way. Instead they saw it as a betrayal. The letters that flowed into my office in the aftermath of introducing the bill were very agitated. Cecile Richards of Planned Parenthood was a dear friend and a collaborator on so many issues, and she didn't like the proposal one bit. She felt it put pro-choice groups on the defensive, and its view of abortion was too negative.

Richards is a fierce and effective advocate for women's reproductive rights and in this moment, we were not seeing eye to eye.

My response to the blowback was that no one should underestimate how hard it was to get anti-abortion Congress members to support family planning and contraception. The bill Ryan and I drafted, I believed, was a step in that direction. We brought the bill up first in September 2006 and then again in February 2007 with forty Democratic co-sponsors, including several prominent moderates—Bart Stupak (D-Michigan), Stephanie Herseth (D-South Dakota), Marcy Kaptur (D-Ohio), Mike Doyle (D-Pennsylvania), and Jim Langevin (D-Rhode Island) among them. Eventually the bill's language found its way into candidate Obama's 2008 presidential campaign. Obey put the language in the Labor, Health and Human Services section of the Appropriations report, and ultimately it made its way into the 2008 Democratic Party platform. The ideas moved forward even if the bill did not.

Because of the outreach I had done to pro-life members of Congress in the preparation and aftermath of the bill with Ryan, Pelosi thought I would be the right person to help with the looming showdown over abortion in the Affordable Care Act—as long as no one knew. In order to pass the Affordable Care Act in the House, we had to figure out a way to deal with the convictions of those who opposed abortion without rolling back abortion rights. We were stepping into an arena with both intense beliefs and proprietorship. Members of Congress are territorial and resent what they see as encroachments on their turf. And here I was, not on Energy and Commerce, the committee with jurisdiction over the bill, and not a chair or co-chair of the Pro-Choice Caucus. The situation was extremely delicate.

Complicating the situation was the fact that long-term allies in women's advocacy work—some of those most upset with me over the Ryan bill—now wanted my help securing access to abortion in the Affordable Care Act. I rejected linking the two. Above all, I wanted healthcare reform to pass. Having pro-choice groups support a bill that explicitly affirmed fewer abortions as a policy goal could be seen as progress toward softening the cultural divide. Or so I hoped.

My staff got together with Tim Ryan and Laurie Rubiner of the Planned Parenthood Federation of America to discuss the common-ground bill to find a path forward. Later that day Rubiner called to say her organization could support the bill, and in fact she would speak at the press conference when we reintroduced it. This was huge. For the first time since we introduced the Reducing the Need for Abortion and Supporting Parents Act in 2006, all pro-choice groups were declaring their support for it. We called a press conference for July 23, 2009, and had the unusual satisfaction of seeing representatives from Planned Parenthood and NARAL speaking alongside religious leaders like anti-abortion pastors Derrick Harkins and Joel Hunter.[3] Rachel Laser from the Third Way was also present.

When President Obama sent the Affordable Care Act to the House of Representatives, portions were sent to the three committees with jurisdiction: Ways and Means, Energy and Commerce, and Education and Labor.

At a hearing of the Energy and Commerce Committee just a few days after the press conference on reducing the need for abortion, committee member Congresswoman Lois Capps (D-California) offered an amendment that she hoped would assure both sides that the Affordable Care Act does not represent a threat to the status quo regarding abortion. The status quo regarding federal funds and abortion in the United States is known as the Hyde Amendment. It dates back to 1976, and specifically prohibits funding of abortions through Medicaid and federal employee health plans except in the cases of rape, incest, or to save a woman's life. Under the Capps Amendment, insurers would not be required to cover abortion services in order to participate in the healthcare exchanges. However, as with the Hyde Amendment, those covered by Medicaid—abortions in the event of rape, incest, or danger to a woman's life—would be covered under the "public option" plan. Abortions under any other circumstances could be covered, but only if the insured party was paying for the coverage with their own money. The monies would be segregated, with insurers keeping premiums and co-payments for abortion coverage in a separate pool.

Abortion opponents protested that segregating the funds was utterly meaningless. The National Right to Life Committee argued that the government was still paying subsidies to people who were then able to obtain abortion coverage, and that was unacceptable.

Republican leaders were not much help. House Minority Leader John Boehner went on record saying that the health bill "will result in federally mandated coverage of abortion on demand" and make it "illegal for health-care providers nationwide—even Catholic and religious-based hospitals . . . to provide anything less than abortion on demand for anyone who seeks it." Ads from the Family Research Council showed older couples upset that Medicare would not cover their surgery yet they were "forced to pay for abortions."[4]

It seemed the common-ground project was done for now. The Capps Amendment passed the Energy and Commerce Committee in late July 2009, and in fact helped bring warring sides together in the process, but barely. Pelosi now wanted to get the bill to the House floor for a vote, despite the strong opposition of the pro-life coalition outside. The rhetoric from the Republican side, spurred on by the National Right to Life Committee, was growing more and more forceful. Still others could not see why issues that pertained mainly to women's health should be the cause of so much hand-wringing. In September 2009, during a hearing on the ACA, Senator Jon Kyl (R-Arizona) famously deemed insurance coverage of maternity care unimportant because, "I don't need maternity care." Senator Debbie Stabenow (D-Michigan) reminded him that his mother probably had.

In November, just before the House was scheduled to vote on the healthcare reform bill, my colleague Bart Stupak introduced an amendment that would require insurance companies that currently provided abortion coverage to choose between continuing that coverage *or* selling insurance to customers on the healthcare exchanges who received government subsidies. They could not do both. The effect would be to eliminate abortion coverage in most health insurance plans.

The Stupak Amendment was very problematic. It would prevent any plan in the exchange from receiving federal subsidies if it covered abortion. It compromised the option for women to purchase private plans that cover abortion if they paid for most of the premiums with their own money. It put an undue burden on women dealing with unplanned pregnancies. In effect, it would take away their freedom of choice. Nonetheless, many members respected Stupak, and the great majority of pro-life members would vote with him. Stupak threatened not to vote for the overall bill if his amendment was not put up for a vote, potentially killing the Affordable Care Act.

The U.S. Conference of Catholic Bishops liked Stupak's move. The bishops began threatening members of Congress that if they voted for the ACA bill, they could expect to be lambasted from the pulpit for abandoning their Catholicism. The nuns and Catholic hospitals, by and large, felt differently, but their voices were drowned out in the barrage of misinformation that was to come.

I huddled with Democrats in Energy and Commerce to try to lower the temperature and argued that abortion did not have to be so divisive. I first met privately with Tim Ryan, who had worked on the common-ground Reducing the Need for Abortion and Supporting Parents Act. We then met with other pro-life members in the evening and early mornings, and for obvious reasons, other members could not be aware these meetings were happening. I also attended countless Pro-Choice Caucus meetings, where they were saying they would never vote for the Affordable Care Act if it included Stupak's amendment. (Stupak's amendment was referred to as the "coat-hanger amendment" in some circles.) Pro-choice caucus members led by Diana DeGette and Louise Slaughter wrote Speaker Pelosi a letter to that effect; forty Democrats signed it. On the other side, pro-life Democrats threatened to sit the vote out if Stupak was *not* able to offer his amendment.

Matters were made dramatically worse when Stupak and the Catholic bishops began spreading confusion about whether the Capps Amendment would still allow federal funds to be used for abortion. The lies about the Capps Amendment were blatant. Some claimed the Treasury would be issuing checks to abortion clinics to reimburse for abortion on demand. Not true. The bishops' conference exhorted priests to encourage their congregations to contact their representatives and urge them to oppose any bill that did not contain Stupak's language. The Capps language was clear; the Capps Amendment did nothing to alter the decades-old Hyde Amendment that already prohibited federal money to be used for abortions. But paranoia and distrust were around every corner, spreading through the Capitol building like a toxic fog. The advocacy group Healthcare for America NOW! had promised to run ads for Democratic House members in the critical 2010 midterm elections if they supported health reform, but they switched and recanted—only those who voted "yes" on healthcare reform, "no" on the Stupak Amendment would receive their support. Diana DeGette (D-Colorado), co-chairwoman of the Pro-Choice Caucus, called it "the greatest restriction of a woman's right to choose to pass in our careers."[5]

Meanwhile Catholic bishops continued to spread misinformation about the bill. They claimed the Stupak Amendment was simply the Hyde Amendment updated, that under the Stupak ban, women could still purchase insurance that covers abortion with their own money. In fact, insurance experts had gone on record stating that the Stupak ban would create a system whereby women could not purchase a health benefits package that *included* abortion coverage in the exchange, but would instead have to buy abortion riders—abortion-only policies that undermined both the principles of insurance and privacy. They claimed there would be a mandatory "abortion surcharge" that would require pro-life purchasers to pay for other people's abortions. In truth there was simply no such thing in either the Capps Amendment or the Senate bill. The suggestion that conscience clauses would be weakened by the healthcare bill was equally off-base; the opposite was true. Speaker Pelosi had held several meetings with the Catholic bishops by this point, and they continued to ask for more meetings and always added further demands and always mischaracterized the law. My advice to her was to stop meeting with them. It was pointless.

It was so personally disheartening to see my church ready to kill the Affordable Care Act—a once-in-a-century opportunity to construct a healthcare system that would care for all people, not just a fortunate few. What had happened to their historic role as calling for us all to help all those "in sickness, old age, and distress"? It seemed they were now content to act as moral scolds on the abortion issue, and forget about everything else.

The pressure on Speaker Pelosi and Chairmen Miller, Rangel, and Waxman could not have been greater. They were driving the train to bring comprehensive healthcare reform to America, and its fate was always in the balance. The issue was all-consuming in October 2009, and there was not a moment during which supporters of the bill felt we were home-free.

Reva Price and Terri McCullough were extraordinarily skilled in dealing with healthcare policy from the speaker's office and were the point of contact as the Affordable Care Act moved fitfully ahead.

As the vote neared it became clear that Pelosi had to add the Stupak language in order to save the healthcare bill. On November 7, 2009, the House passed the Affordable Healthcare for America Act on a 220–215 vote. I voted for the rule that allowed the Stupak Amendment to come to the floor, and it passed 240–194, with 64 House Democrats voting yes.

I voted for the overall amended bill and gave a speech on the floor condemning the Stupak Amendment for going beyond current law to restrict access to abortion. My reason for doing so is probably best explained by my friend Phil Schiliro, who once described the three types of legislators. The first type gets so wrapped up in their issue that even if on balance a bill constitutes a net plus for their cause, they do not see it that way—because they are not getting 100 percent of what they want. The second type will accept a bad deal, even a net negative, because at least it looks like something is getting done. The third type fights to the bitter end, but when a clear-eyed assessment tells them they cannot get everything they have been fighting for, they accept that and choose a path forward. That is typically how I operate.

My goal was now to make sure the Senate version of the bill did not contain Stupak's language. Eventually, the House and Senate bills would have to be reconciled to produce a single bill to send to the president. I worked with Senator Barbara Boxer (D-California) to offer alternate language in hopes of stopping Senator Nelson from introducing Stupak's language in the Senate bill. The idea was a segregated payment system: insurers who wanted to cover abortion would collect two payments from every enrollee. One payment would go into the general fund, and the other into a fund that exclusively covered abortion. Pro-choice groups hated this fix.

Senator Dodd was chairman of the Banking Committee when Harkin took over the Health, Education, Labor and Pensions Committee after Ted Kennedy's death in August 2009. What a tragedy. This was Kennedy's life's work. Dodd and Kennedy were close;

they could have been brothers, and now, as chair of the healthcare subcommittee, Dodd emerged to succeed his friend as the central figure pushing the ACA forward in the Senate. The Senate passed its version of the Affordable Care Act on Christmas Eve 2009 with Dodd shepherding the law to final passage.

The Senate version passed without the Stupak Amendment but with new compromise language in place. States could prohibit exchange insurers from offering plans that covered abortion, and anyone receiving federal subsidies to buy insurance was on their own if they wanted abortion coverage. In January the special election in Massachusetts to fill the vacancy left by Ted Kennedy's death ushered in an another obstacle; the new Massachusetts senator, Scott Brown, was a Republican opposed to the ACA, and with his taking office the Democrats' filibuster-proof majority evaporated overnight. We faced some fateful choices on how to proceed.

Rahm Emanuel, who was White House chief of staff, proposed breaking up the Affordable Care Act into pieces so that at least some healthcare reforms could be enacted. The White House called Speaker Pelosi to propose that strategy in the face of the new situation. Pelosi rejected the idea of moving piecemeal, a decision President Obama supported. That meant finding a way to get the House to pass the Senate version without amendments. That is the only way comprehensive health reform could become law, and that decision set Speaker Pelosi's place in history.

One of the most difficult issues remained how to deal with women's health issues.

From January to March 2010, many pro-choice Democrats threatened the healthcare bill because of this compromise language (now known as the Nelson Amendment). I worked hard and was ultimately successful in getting the pro-choice advocates to accept the segregated payment system, but pro-life Democrats remained unconvinced. There was great anxiety that the revised bill would not pass again in the House.

Four days before the scheduled House vote on the Affordable Care Act, the debate reached a boiling point. Late one Wednesday afternoon in mid-March I got a call from Laurie Rubiner of Planned Parenthood. They had heard that we were six or seven votes short and were going to make a deal with Stupak. I assured them there was no deal.

Early the next morning Politico reported that the House was short seven votes, and that there was talk on Capitol Hill of an Executive Order that would please the pro-life Democrats. I had never seen such worry and paranoia wafting through the halls. Rumors that we were about to cut a deal with Stupak flew all morning. People wondered, is Henry Waxman, chair of Energy and Commerce, working with Stupak? What about Hoyer? At two p.m. that Thursday in March Stupak dropped a concurrent, i.e., non-binding, resolution that would reenact his amendment banning coverage and access to abortion. Would Waxman go for that? We did not know; he was hard to pin down.

At five p.m. we had a leadership meeting in Speaker Pelosi's office to discuss the abortion issue. The atmosphere in the room was charged and took on a men-versus-women tone. At one point some male members urged us women to give up on the "women's issues." At that point I was indeed emotional. Waxman, a friend, said to me, "Rosa, I'm not fighting with you but you're sure screaming a lot." He urged me to "not be so emotional." He wondered aloud if maybe we should just set the stuff regarding women and contraception to the side for the time being. The women said, "No!" Then there was silence.

Speaker Pelosi told the group that the pro-choice leaders needed to meet first, alone. Waxman wanted to come to the meeting but Pelosi said, "Henry, the girls need to huddle." At 6:30 p.m. with a slew of reporters outside, Pelosi, Lowey, Capps, DeGette, Shakowsky, Baldwin, Slaughter, and myself moved to the speaker's

ceremonial office adjacent to the House floor. We huddled, returned to the room, and said, "No."

When the meeting ended the path forward was clear. The White
House was proposing an Executive Order, and it had to reaffirm the
Hyde Amendment and include some language that applied Hyde
to Community Health Centers funding. The leadership could live
with that. I also talked to Rahm from the cloakroom phone booth
and told him it could not set back women's rights.

I was on the phone with the pro-choice group leaders Marcia
Greenberger, Judy Lichtman, Cecile Richards, and Nancy Keenan
of NARAL. I was also on the phone with my colleague Mike Doyle,
who had been the liaison with the pro-life faction this whole time.
He and Stupak were roommates in Washington, which greased the
wheels, but Doyle was also the perfect person for this particular
job; he was neither lightning rod nor ideologue, but a world-class
listener. That night the last calls from my office were made around
10:30 p.m.

I met Stan and Margharita Mascola, our friend interning in my
congressional office from Italy, for a late dinner at Jaleo, a tapas
restaurant in D.C. I was very distraught and said, "I fear we could
lose the Affordable Care Act."

Saturday morning, at 9:00 a.m., we were back in Speaker Pelosi's
office, going through whip lists. Each person took an assignment.
Outside in the hall we were met by a colleague, Rob Andrews
(D-New Jersey), who again suggested—as if we had not heard
this enough times—that the women were being irrational and we
should let Stupak's resolution go forward since it would be easy to
kill the resolution in the Senate.

At one p.m. the speaker's office received the first draft language
from the White House for a possible Executive Order. It looked
fine—at the least it was consistent with the Senate bill. I was on
the phone with Ruth Katz and Tim Westmorland of Waxman's staff

to confirm the language was right, since they were the ones who really knew the fine points of the law. And within the hour the press was all over the news that pro-choice Democratic women were giving Obama the green light to reaffirm that no federal money could be used for abortion.

I called Doyle and he sent me the new Executive Order language drafted by Stupak that I then circulated to all of our offices and the pro-choice group leaders. Stupak was remaining firm on the application of Hyde to Community Health Centers funding. We were being updated by the White House staff, including Dana Sangiser and others. The White House was meeting later with Stupak's allies. Stupak was also meeting with the bishops and Speaker Pelosi in the Capitol.

We all promised to keep one another informed. Several drafts of the Executive Order were circulating, and if we did not have a consensus by the next morning, the Affordable Care Act would go down in flames. All of these drafts had to be reconciled, and everyone involved reconciled to what the final language contained.

I left the Capitol at 8:30 that night and got a ride to Rahm Emanuel's house, where the Emanuel family was in the midst of celebrating his son Zach's bar mitzvah. In situations like this, entering into an hours-long phoneathon late at night, it helps to know your colleagues very well—in fact it is not possible to know someone too well. Rahm and I had known each other for thirty years. Many years ago, my husband Stan and I, Rahm, and our friend Doug Sosnik met for dinner every Wednesday night. When Rahm came to Congress, Stan did polling for him. He even lived in the basement of our house before it was turned over to the grandchildren for a play area. Rahm and I could yell at one another but always come to productive conclusions. Once upstairs, the din of the celebration below, we started the phone calls, which lasted the whole of the evening. Rahm missed a lot of the celebration and me more. I was on the phone with Dan Turton, the White House congressional liaison who was married to Ashley Turton, my former chief of staff. I was sharing draft language with Pelosi all along the way. Minutes after eleven p.m. I received word from Doyle that the White House's meeting with the Stupak bloc had gone well. They just had a few changes that they would send first thing in the morning. How about now, we asked.

Around midnight we got Stupak's new language. It read heavily pro-life and we would have liked to see a few small changes, but aside from that, there was nothing in it not already in the bill. It was decided that the speaker would convene the pro-choice leaders in the morning and run it by them.

At 7:00 a.m. on Sunday, March 21, the day of the vote, I called Letty Mederos, my Catholic legislative director, and said, "Instead of going to church, I need to meet you in the office as early as possible to pass the Affordable Care Act and stick it to the bishops."

I called a meeting in my office by 8 a.m. with my staff and members of the speaker's staff, Reva and Terri. We went over the Executive Order language and planned the day's conversations with pro-choice members and groups. Like at other key points, early morning or very late at night, I would call through to all the groups so they were up on the ongoing deliberations.

Then we called the White House with our suggested edits to Stupak's last draft. They emailed back what would be the final version minus technical corrections. We tried to get in touch with Nita Lowey, who had led the pro-choice caucus and many members looked to on legislative issues, but she was on a plane and would not be back in Washington until 11:45 a.m. The meeting with pro-choice leaders still had not happened, and time was running short. Finally Lowey arrived around 12:30 p.m., the White House congressional affairs house liaison Dan Turton read her the final version of the Executive Order, and we waited for the reaction. It was not the first time I had heard the Executive Order. The order prompted questions, some negative reactions, and then

Lowey said, "I can live with this." The mood in the room changed in an instant.

Then Turton met with Leader Pelosi and the pro-choice members and read the language of the Executive Order and answered questions. And then he met with Stupak and the pro-life caucus.

At four p.m. Stupak held a press conference to say that the final language of Executive Order 13535 was enough to satisfy his concerns. He and his allies would vote "yes" on the Affordable Care Act. We had the votes we needed. Tears started pouring down staffers' faces; Letty Mederos, Amy Rosenbaum, Ruth Katz, Reva Price, and Terri McCullough—women who had worked tirelessly for this cause—had the look of people who'd summited a mountain, both exhausted and elated. People started hugging.

The Affordable Care Act passed the House that night, 219–212, at 10:48 p.m. The Republicans attempted to pass a motion to recommit the bill back to committee. Stupak spoke against the motion, calling it "a last-ditch effort of 98 years of denying Americans healthcare. The motion to recommit does not promote life. . . . This motion is really to politicize life, not prioritize life." It was defeated and by 11:18 p.m. we were done. Universal healthcare was President Obama's signature away from being the law of the land. At the signing ceremony in the Oval Office, Vice President Joe Biden was overheard by a member of the press saying, "This is a big fucking deal." He was right.

What did the Affordable Care Act accomplish? It eliminated all pre-existing conditions. Before healthcare reform, 45 million Americans were uninsured. Everyone not poor enough for Medicaid, and not old enough for Medicare, who did not have a job that provided health insurance, was at risk of financial collapse should they ever encounter serious health problems. Diabetic twenty-two-year-olds who had graduated from college got kicked off their parents' plans. Cancer survivors could not find policies that covered them, or if they did, they would have to pay astronomical premiums.

The Affordable Care Act increased health security overall. It gave the uninsured subsidies to assist in purchasing insurance. It expanded Medicaid for the working poor. Now, insurance companies cannot arbitrarily hike up rates beyond the rate of inflation. There are no more lifetime caps, and annual caps are being phased out.

The benefits for women are especially noteworthy. The discriminatory practice of gender rating is no longer allowed. Women and men pay the same premiums. Millions of women are now eligible for recommended preventive services with no out-of-pocket costs. Before the Affordable Care Act, having a child, or having had a caesarean section, or even being a victim of domestic violence were all too often treated as "pre-existing conditions" by health insurance companies. That is over. Maternity care is covered.

Everyone can receive free recommended preventive healthcare services with no out-of-pocket costs—services like annual check-ups and preventive screenings like colonoscopies and mammograms. The ACA is an extraordinary achievement for all Americans.

Stupak paid for his ability to sway people to vote for the healthcare bill. One Republican congressman yelled "baby killer" at him from the House floor (then later amended his comments to say he was referring to the bill as a whole, not Stupak himself). People thought he capitulated. Stupak knew he would not be able to run for office after it passed, and he did not.

For six years, the Republicans in Congress and Republican presidential candidates battled tirelessly to repeal, defund, and derail the Affordable Care Act. In 2013, twenty days before Americans could start shopping for insurance on the marketplaces, we on Capitol Hill saw our forty-first vote to undermine the Affordable Care Act. Republicans introduced a bill that would have prevented millions of Americans from getting the tax credits they needed to buy insurance. In spite of what the bill's sponsors alleged, we already had procedures in place to ensure the tax credits only went to eligible parties. They were determined to show their base how committed they were to overturning "Obamacare" and to keep the ACA from winning broader public support.

In early 2015 we saw the fifty-sixth vote to repeal or undermine the Affordable Care Act. As I remarked on the House floor at the time, these ideological gestures were getting old in the chamber. But as will soon be evident, these gestures were animating the Republicans' base to defeat Democrats and overturn the Affordable Care Act.

Never during the debate—what little there was of it—did any Republican come forward with a plan to replace the Affordable Care Act. In the meantime, many millions got health insurance for the first time, healthcare inflation slowed, women got equal treatment with men, insurance companies could no longer discriminate because of pre-existing conditions, and people no longer faced lifetime limits.

We are a better country because of the Affordable Care Act.

Donald Trump won the presidency with a promise to "repeal and replace Obamacare." We will see whether he can repeal or unravel these reforms, but I also expect to see Americans rise up to demand healthcare that is affordable for all. We have work to do.

9

In Defense Of Children

A family, like a house, can withstand only as much wind and weather as its construction and maintenance allow; the storms that rage around the poor would test the resilience of any structure.

—David K. Shipler, *The Working Poor: Invisible in America*

THE UNITED STATES HAS TWO tax credits that together lift more children out of poverty than any other federal government policy. They are the Earned Income Tax Credit (EITC) and the Child Tax Credit (CTC). The Earned Income Tax Credit was enacted in 1975, and expanded in 1986, 1990, 1993, and 2001. As a cursory glance at those dates tells you, both Democratic and Republican administrations have championed it, because it is effective and because it uses the tax code, rather than creating new programs. In 2010, the Census Bureau reported that 5.4 million people had been lifted above the poverty line thanks to the EITC and CTC together.

One can also argue that programs like these tax credits are hallmarks of advanced democracies; similar programs exist in the United Kingdom, Canada, New Zealand, the Netherlands, Belgium, Denmark, Sweden, Finland, France, and Austria.

The mechanism for receiving either the Earned Income Tax Credit or the Child Tax Credit is not complicated: if you have earnings, you file a tax return and receive a credit back based on the amount of your earnings and the number of kids under seventeen you have. The credit rises along with your earned income until a set limit, then phases out at higher income levels. The CTC phases out at a much higher income level than the EITC, allowing families to keep their tax credits as their earnings rise well into the middle class. Wealthier families do not qualify for the CTC, as they presumably have sufficient resources to take care of their families' needs. Yet many low-income families are left out, too, since eligibility is based in part on a family's earnings, not need.

The fight over the Child Tax Credit has been different from others because the biggest obstacle has not been lies or obstructionism or direct opposition, but indifference to the condition of children, particularly poor children. In the past many Republicans felt the CTC was the right thing to do to buttress both families and family values, and it was effective. Most Democrats liked the program. Still, overcoming the general attitude that improving the CTC was not worth losing political capital kept it in the background for many years, despite the fact that it constitutes a real opportunity to lift people out of poverty. The Child Tax Credit ought to be a flagship issue for both parties and the country.

Why? The United States is exceptional in the extent to which it does *not* invest in children. Today, approximately a sixth of American children live in poverty and two-fifths live in low-income households. Child poverty rates in the United States are high compared to other countries.[1] That is not merely because we have a lot of kids born into single-parent homes; our poverty rate for dual-earner families is high, too. In late 2010 UNICEF released an international assessment of children's well-being in twenty-four countries; the United States ranked twenty-second in overall children's health, nineteenth in educational well-being, and twenty-third in material well-being. With our tremendous wealth and resources, we should be near the top of these measures. Sadly we only spend about 0.7 percent of GDP on family benefits.[2] This is one of the clearest examples where law betrays our true social priorities and values.

Senator Chris Dodd created the Children's Caucus to advocate for children in 1983, and it was long overdue—even commodities like steel had caucuses that put spotlights on their special needs. In the House, George Miller had founded the Select Committee on Children, Youth, and Families in 1983. Dodd was devoted to winning bipartisan support for children's issues like childcare and family leave, and it was as Dodd's chief of staff that I started my professional career in Congress.

In 1989 two plans to offer families who paid for childcare a tax break circulated. President George H.W. Bush's proposal would have given working families who made up to $13,000 a year up to $1,000 as a tax credit for each child under the age of four.[3] A Senate plan targeted three out of four dollars directly to working families, but would also have been available to higher-earning families, covered kids up to the age of fifteen, and included provisions to ensure that the money was actually spent on childcare. It also set federal minimum safety standards for day care centers.

The Senate plan was sponsored by Senator Dodd but was a bipartisan effort. The conservative senator Orrin Hatch (R-Utah) was a prominent co-sponsor, and he testified at the Senate hearing that he did not think the increasingly treacherous economics of child rearing in the United States was "a Democrat problem or a Republican problem; this is a bipartisan problem of families that we really have to solve." When a reporter asked Dodd what he thought about the president's plan, he replied that it was too stingy and did not cover enough families. Nonetheless, he said, "the good news is we are beyond the threshold question about whether we ought to be doing anything."[4] Neither his bill nor the president's proposal became law, however.

The strange thing is that for some conservative supporters of tax credits for working families, the stinginess of Bush's plan was partly the point. Republicans, Bush Senior, and conservatives supported the EITC, but a person only qualified if they had taxable income above $10,000, and they knew that this threshold meant that the very poorest working families did not benefit. That was deemed acceptable because for them the program was mainly about promoting "family values," not about helping those most in need. Efforts to lower the threshold were attacked as bringing back welfare. Some even worried that subsidizing childcare would have the effect of undermining traditional family arrangements, even the role of grandparents.

The Republicans try to help working families with a top up in income, again, because they are trying to support the values of family and childbearing and reward hard work. For many conservatives, however, a per-child tax credit was seen as a family-friendly, small-government policy—a good way to keep money out of Washington's hands.

Gingrich's "Contract with America" promised to bring before the House for a vote a $500 partially "refundable" per-child tax credit. So, if you did not have enough income, the government would give a small payment to help families with the cost of raising children. This was a very important principle, and it was established by Gingrich in his "Contract with America." The amount was half of what Senator Jay Rockefeller's (D-West Virginia) bipartisan National Commission on Children report had proposed, and it left out the poorest children, but it was a start. Democrats, including President Clinton and his administration, were also starting to show interest, as it could help lower-income and poorer families. A consensus on how to help the working poor and the poorest seemed within reach.

The terrain for the Child Tax Credit soon got rockier, however. President Clinton put a $300 to $500 per child tax credit in his fiscal year 1997 budget proposal. But it was "non-refundable." Non-refundable tax credits are subtracted from your total income tax liability, and can effectively drop the amount you owe down to zero dollars. But if your income is below a certain level you get nothing and no help.

"Refundable" tax credits work differently. A refundable tax credit is subtracted from the amount of income taxes that you owe, and if the amount of the credit exceeds your total income tax liability, the IRS sends you the balance as a refund. This is obviously a huge plus for the neediest families; they could conceivably not only not owe income taxes, but still get money back from the government. Since most families pay more in payroll taxes for Social Security than they do in income taxes, it spreads the benefit to additional taxpayers. Contrary to what some critics allege, these families *are* paying taxes—payroll, state and local, sales taxes, and so on—and a refundable credit implicitly acknowledges the significant taxes that families face outside of our income tax system. Why would a policy maker choose one over the other? In this case, the Clinton administration had already helped achieve a significant expansion of the EITC, and its proposals for welfare-to-work had not yet passed. Adding a refundable child tax credit to the mix might have been seen as politically risky—one too many programs for our vulnerable populations.

Negotiations over a later budget now crystallized the sides and flipped the main political players. Now Clinton wanted some refundability and Gingrich was calling that "welfare." A deal was made and the Budget Reconciliation Taxpayer Relief Act that passed in late summer 1997 included a $500 Children's Tax Credit, to start in 1998. The age of eligibility was dropped from children under the age of nineteen to children under seventeen to keep costs down. The new Child Tax Credit was non-refundable for most families, though there was a small refundability provision for families with three or more kids. It left out about one-fourth of all kids in families too poor to pay income taxes, the vast majority of whom pay payroll taxes. That is to say, there would be no credit for virtually all low-income working families.

In 2001, President George W. Bush passed his first big tax cut, estimated to cost $1.3 trillion over ten years. Among the tax provisions to be phased in over a decade were a doubling of the Child Tax Credit to $1,000 per child. Very importantly, he offered partial refundability regardless of family size. The Senate wanted to make sure that only parents working close to full-time were eligible, so they passed an eligibility threshold of $10,000, indexed to inflation. If a family earned less than $10,000 they got nothing. As it happened, stagnant wages meant that indexing the eligibility threshold had the perverse effect of shrinking the CTC for some families, and bumping others off the rolls entirely.

In November of 2002 the father-and-son team of Bill and David Harris came to D.C. to talk to Stan and my stepdaughter Anna Greenberg about asking questions about the Child Tax Credit in a national survey. I was privy to these conversations and started to look more closely at the data and what it said about these issues. Stan would later circulate an article that he wrote, "Kids as Politics," that used some of these findings.

I got to know the Harrises very well when they began meeting with Senator Dodd after he created the Senate's first children's caucus. Dodd was deeply focused on children and that is why he was the Senate sponsor of the Family and Medical Leave Act, the first bill signed by President Clinton. In the process, I turned to the Harrises regularly and we became close friends. Stan and I were at their family weddings and Bill was there election night when I squeaked in and got elected to Congress. Bill has devoted most of his working life to promoting the welfare of children, and he advocates before the Congress and administrations on how budgets and legislation affect children. David Harris devotes himself full-time to this effort as well and is incredibly imaginative legislatively. He wrote about the Child Tax Credit for his PhD dissertation. They get nothing in return, except seeing the benefits for the poorest kids. Amazing.

The Harrises worked with a number of senators and members of Congress and their staffs, and I began to take their analysis and policy recommendations very seriously. The overwhelming evidence is that, as a society, we all benefit when all families with young children have the resources they need to thrive. First of all, we know now that a child's earliest experiences have a long-lasting impact on his or her whole life. These first few years are the optimum window for investing in human capital. Child development experts have been saying for years that what happens to a kid before age three is critically important. Eighty percent of brain development occurs by that age.

What do children need during that time?[5] When children are very young, they need more time with parents. They also need more financial support. Children are much better off in households where their caregiver is not chronically stressed over how to pay for food, diapers, and utility bills.

The scientific research on money's effects on a child's development is astounding. Ample research in biology, neuroscience, and social science tells us that added income means healthier babies and greater scholastic abilities. An extra $1,000 added to the yearly income of a low-income family with a young child can increase that child's math and reading scores significantly. These kids are more likely to stay in school and attend college. Kids whose families experience a boost in income will also earn more as adults. For every additional $3,000 that flows into that kid's household, their average earnings when they are between the ages of twenty-five and thirty-seven will increase by a whopping 17 percent.[6]

There is even evidence that family income is a stronger predictor of a child's achievement outcomes than the levels of schooling their parents obtained. This is fantastic news for parents with ample resources to lavish on their little kids. But if you are two years old and your parents are jobless, it's terrible news.

I started having conversations with Janice Mays, chief counsel for the Democrats on the Ways and Means Committee, who would become Democratic staff director when Rangel was chairman. Mays is brilliant and became my go-to person on Ways and Means for all the activities on the Child Tax Credit. She told me when we had difficulty, and when we were OK, she'd say, "You are in your mother's arms."

I decided to take this issue to the House. At this point, I had become the most outspoken voice in the Congress continually advocating for the Child Tax Credit, primarily because I saw it needed to be done and so did it. I wanted to lower the threshold to zero, so that the CTC would be available to parents without earnings. I also wanted to make it fully refundable, permanent, and indexed to inflation.

It is not unusual for me to take up an issue that is not part of my "committee of jurisdiction." I simply took on pay equity, paid family leave, food stamps, an infrastructure bank, and the Trans-Pacific Partnership Agreement. In each of those cases, the issue was propelled by social and political forces, and I worked with advocacy groups to keep up pressure and make progress. But though I sensed similar levels of injustice and unfairness on the matter of child tax credits, tax credits are fairly arcane and not greatly understood by voters. Nobody had run for office carrying this issue on their banner. So the action on tax credits tends to remain in the committees of jurisdiction: Ways and Means in the House and Finance in the Senate, or the White House economic team or Treasury. I would use my position as an appropriator to horn in on the discussions of any omnibus funding bill or tax package. I moved the ball on the

Child Tax Credit by constantly looking for opportunities to make progress.

The bipartisan history of the Child Tax Credit gave me hope that it might happen. If fellow House members Pelosi, Rangel, and Levin, who all cared deeply about the CTC, and I joined forces, we would be within striking distance. When another Bush tax cut loomed in 2003, I thought we might have another opportunity to expand it. The Jobs and Growth Tax Relief Reconciliation Act of 2003 was projected to cost $350 billion. This time Bush's focus was on cutting taxes on dividends and accelerating all of the personal income tax cut provisions in his 2001 bill, except for the estate tax cut (controversially set to disappear altogether in 2010) and the two tax cuts that would directly help poor families: the EITC and the refundable portion of the CTC. President Bush proposed accelerating the CTC tax break for everyone except those who most needed it—low-income working families. His version was particularly hard on African American and Hispanic children, leaving out half of the former and more than 40 percent of the latter.[7] Meanwhile the dividend tax cut would have given nearly two-thirds of its benefits to the top 5 percent of the population—people pulling in about $350,000 a year on average.

Bush's economic team said they believed that rebates sent to poorer families would be used to pay down credit card debt and not stimulate the economy. I knew this not to be true; the refundable Child Tax Credit puts money in the hands of families living paycheck to paycheck who are most likely to spend it soon in their own neighborhoods. As economist Mark Zandi said when the financial crash took down the economy, refundable tax credits, like the CTC, are among the most stimulative of tax cuts. Later estimates from the Tax Policy Center and Moody's would confirm my beliefs. But at the time there was no national debate about it—absolutely none.

I began my legislative journey on the Child Tax Credit in March 2003, as a member of the Committee on the Budget. Working with Ranking Member John Spratt (D-South Carolina), I ventured into uncharted territory and introduced an amendment to accelerate the increase of the tax credit to $1,000 per child, starting immediately, and to make it fully refundable. It would be available to all families, including those who did not pay enough in income taxes to receive the CTC under Bush's plan—even those with no earnings. To pay for it, the amendment would reduce other tax cuts assumed in the budget resolution. I pointed out that my proposal would stimulate our economy—only one-quarter of the $300 rebates in the last tax cut had been put back into the economy, and the rest had been stashed in savings. I argued that it was mind-boggling that we were willing to decimate all manner of opportunities for American families, whether it be school lunch, child nutrition programs, Pell Grants, student loans, or veterans services, all to provide an enormous tax cut to our country's wealthiest. I knew my Republican colleagues would not be comfortable severing the Child Tax Credit's tie to work.

My amendment proposal was defeated on a party-line vote, which I had expected—but at least we had started the conversation, allowing me to begin an aggressive campaign to promote the Child Tax Credit. Unfortunately some of my Republican colleagues preferred to change the subject. Sitting at that table, I had to listen to men who wanted to bring up how prisoners were receiving the Earned Income Tax Credit, and that billions in EITC monies were paid out in error. And that was it—conversation over. Twenty-four nos to nineteen ayes for the amendment.

My friends Bill and David Harris advocated for months to expand the number of families eligible for the refundable Child Tax Credit and also to speed up the clock on when changes would become effective.

As Bush's second tax bill moved through committee, it became clear that they would need every Republican vote on the Senate Finance Committee. Senator Olympia Snowe (R-Maine) was the lone holdout because she objected to the dividend tax cut. She and Senator Blanche Lincoln (D-Arkansas) took the lead in the Senate on the CTC. I had forged a relationship with Senator Lincoln. We had been House members together, and we regularly conferred on this issue. They offered an amendment that sped up when the Child Tax Credit would be refundable. Their yes votes were secured and Chairman Chuck Grassley moved the Senate bill to the floor.

The bill that came out of House-Senate conference cut both capital gains and dividend rates to 15 percent. The provision speeding up when the Child Tax Credit would be refundable was dropped, leaving the families of 11.9 million children out of the bill. Vice President Cheney was called in to provide the tie-breaking vote, and the bill was signed into law on May 28, 2003. The cost of accelerating the low-income portion of the CTC would have come to $3.5 billion, only 1 percent of the final $350 billion package.

David Firestone of the *New York Times* picked up the story and it became part of the news cycle. For over a month the major networks and national papers wrote about how the new tax law cut out the Child Tax Credit for lower-income children and families. *USA Today* highlighted how it left out one million children from military and veteran families.

Now even some Republican senators said they were willing to revisit the issue. Compromise language was drafted that contained the $3.5 billion to speed up when the Child Tax Credit would be refundable. GOP senators even proposed moving the phaseout level from $110,000 to $150,000. They did not include one additional kid in a low-income family.

The full Senate approved the restoration of the Child Tax Credit benefits by a vote of 94–2. The Senate Majority Leader was seen pretending to stick his finger down his throat after taking the vote as he walked away from the Senate floor. The GOP majority in the House did not want the Child Tax Credit to be refundable, however, and the debate on the House floor got uglier. One Republican representative said that the main source of contention was that Republicans "like paychecks, jobs, and opportunities," while Democrats "seem to like unemployment checks and government handouts," plus "welfare and low expectations."

GOP Majority Whip Tom DeLay of Texas, aka "The Hammer," did not let the Senate bill come to the House floor, calling the supporters of speeding up refundability of the Child Tax Credit "shamable." This tax credit was wealth redistribution, in his eyes, and therefore an anathema. DeLay further claimed Democrats were only angry because they did not get to pass a spending increase. He wasn't alone. The *Wall Street Journal* editorial page referred to families too poor to pay income taxes, who were thus eligible for the low-income part of the tax credit, as "lucky duckies."

To memorialize those observations, the Harrises gave me a set of rubber duckies that are in my office today.

The House Republicans then brought to the floor a proposal that sped up low-income families receiving a refundable tax credit, though only temporarily, and for good measure made all better-off families, including the wealthy, eligible permanently. The total cost was more than $3.5 billion and the costs for the best-off far exceeded the marginal benefits to lower-income families. So pay attention. I was incensed: they proposed to help low-income families a little bit, and temporarily, in exchange for permanently helping wealthier families. There was no way such an expensive bill was going to pass.

In October of 2004, with our unrelenting pressure, the expansion of the Child Tax Credit was finally accelerated, like the other tax provisions had been the year before. Ironically the vehicle was the 2004 Jobs Bill—a bill largely driven by multinational corporations. Multinationals that had parked overseas profits in overseas accounts wanted to "repatriate" these profits but at a lower tax rate. If they could do that, they argued, they could create more jobs in the United States. So the Senate picked up the tax credit bill that passed the House in June of 2003 and used that as a shell. Their new bill lowered the tax rate at a lower rate than the regular U.S. corporate tax rate for repatriated corporate profits to 5 percent— and tucked in a one-year speeding up of the refundable CTC in order to get the sixty votes needed to pass.[8]

The final cost of speeding up the expansion of the Child Tax Credit was $2.4 billion, and that allowed over 10 million low-income families to benefit. That is de minimus. One company, General Electric, received a $2 billion tax cut in the same bill. But 10 million people is a lot of families. Imagine how many people and families we can help as a country with a safety net that includes tax credits with the right priorities.

Hurricane Katrina devastated New Orleans and the Gulf Coast and exposed how families and children face some of the same catastrophic risks as farmers and businesses in a natural disaster. Here is the problem. Eligibility for both the Child Tax Credit and the Earned Income Tax Credit depends on your earnings, but if a natural disaster flattens your home and place of work, your income drops precipitously, and perversely, you're now at risk of losing your tax credits as well.

I knew the tax code allows farmers and businesses to "smooth out" their taxes, precisely because of such unforeseen, unpreventable events. So I had conversations with the Ways and Means staff to see if the Katrina relief bill could include a "Look Back" provision that would allow families affected by Katrina to use a previous year's earnings for calculating their refundable Child Tax and Earned Income Tax Credits. That provision was included in the Katrina Emergency Tax Relief Act of 2005 and became law for those affected by Hurricanes Katrina, Rita, and Wilma.[9]

The 2006 midterms saw the Democrats taking back the House,

and Pelosi elected speaker. On the eve of assuming the speaker's gavel, at the Women's Tea highlighting the fact that she would be the first woman speaker of the House, Pelosi announced that she would dedicate the 110th Congress to women and children. In advance of a National Summit on Children, held in May 2007, a series of meetings leading up to it had members of Congress, including committee chairs, and their most senior staff members, all gathered to discuss various child policies. I asked the speaker to hold pre-meetings leading up to the Summit, and the one on economic policy included the Child Tax Credit. I asked David Harris to do the presentation, and he did. All of the leadership, the chairs of the major committees, and their staff directors attended.

I became the point person for the Child Tax Credit. At any meeting with colleagues when conversation turned to taxes, everyone expected me to bring it up and ask how any proposal would affect the CTC. And I did.

Meanwhile, evidence that working families were feeling the pinch kept piling up. The first quarter of 2007 marked the eighth consecutive quarter with a negative personal savings rate. The economy was growing, but little of that growth reached working families. In six years, weekly wages had crept up a measly 2.1 percent. Millions of people were going without health insurance.

Representative Rangel, now chairman of Ways and Means after decades in Congress, offered a revenue-neutral tax reform bill that would repeal the Alternative Minimum Tax. He was proposing to take the extra dollars in revenue and apply them toward reducing the Child Tax Credit earnings threshold from an annual income of $11,000 to $8,500. Eligibility for the CTC would no longer be linked to inflation to keep the threshold from climbing higher each year. I was chair of Agriculture Appropriations, and I was pressing to lower the threshold. Rangel supported it, also knowing the speaker wanted it to happen.

This bill never became law—it had no chance, and we knew it—but Democrats got the idea on the table.

A "tax extenders" bill that came at the end of session gave us another opportunity to lower the threshold of the Child Tax Credit to $8,500, for one year only. Attached to the extension of imminently expiring popular tax breaks, it would be more likely to be included. Senate Republicans stripped this tax credit expansion out of the bill before passing it.

When the economy began to falter in late 2007, House Speaker Pelosi saw an opportunity to reach a compromise with Minority Leader John Boehner. Democrats were pushing for extending unemployment insurance and food stamps to help stimulate the economy. Most Republicans were dead set against that. Speaker Pelosi, Boehner, and Treasury Secretary Paulson then negotiated in Pelosi's Capitol hideaway. Boehner said he could not do food stamps or unemployment benefits. But knowing Democrats wanted more refundability of the Child Tax Credit, he agreed to that. It was a "tax cut" after all. Pelosi pushed and got a more generous benefit for families, lowering the threshold for the first time to $3,000. The resulting bipartisan House bill made the CTC refundable for families that earned between $3,000 and $25,000 a year for one year. Over six million children were made newly eligible. This was big. Refundable tax credits were put into a stimulus bill for the first time in history. Checks went out in the mail for $300 per child for up to two children in each family, on top of the $600 per parent tax credit in the Economic Stimulus Act of 2008. These provisions gave money to families who could spend the money on behalf of their families in their communities, as I had argued years earlier, and this would stimulate the economy.

In October 2008, the House voted down President Bush's first attempt to pass TARP, the Troubled Assets Relief Program, widely seen as a bailout for banks. Stock indexes plummeted. With new urgency, the U.S. Senate then took the initiative, added sweeteners to the bailout bill, including Chairman Rangel's 2008 package of tax cuts and, critically for me, a provision that lowered the threshold for the Child Tax Credit to $8,500. This version of the bailout passed the Senate and then the House. TARP spared the United States a financial collapse. I was pleased that the CTC threshold was lowered to $8,500 for one year.

In February 2009, the American Recovery and Reinvestment Act (ARRA) provided another opportunity to move on the Child Tax Credit—but getting the monies to families in need would prove complicated. The House passed a version of the economic recovery program that lowered the refundable Child Tax Credit threshold to $0 for two years, but the Senate, while supporting expansion of the tax credit's eligibility, chose not to be as generous. Pelosi negotiated the back-and-forth, and I badgered Pelosi about the Child Tax Credit daily. After a tense few weeks of negotiating, she reported back in the leadership meeting, "She couldn't get the threshold down to $8,500." I was loaded for bear. "Damn it," I said. She smiled and said, "I got it to $3,000 for 2009 and 2010." "Yes," I said. "A real triumph." This meant that most families who worked full-time, for a full year, at the minimum wage would get nearly a full tax credit for up to two children. A single earner in the same work circumstances and two or more children would get $1,515 instead of $82.50. The families of 15.9 million children would receive an increased tax credit up to $1,432.50. This tremendous swing toward caring for our country's kids would be the law of the land, at least for the next two years.

Confirming what I had been arguing for years, researchers at the nonpartisan Urban-Brookings Tax Policy Center graded this expansion of the Child Tax Credit an "A-"—tied as the most stimulative of all tax measures included in the recovery package. It would have been an A, in their minds, if it could have gotten out the door sooner.[10]

But now we faced a near crisis. As people lost work, hours, and income in the Great Recession, a growing number of families earned less than the $3,000 threshold and were no longer eligible to receive the Child Tax Credit.

I proposed to Speaker Pelosi that something more needed to be done. Unemployment insurance didn't take into account family size. The child poverty rate was considered to be the worst in years. My preferred answer was to lower the eligibility threshold to $0, still conditioning eligibility on work. This would provide an additional $450 to the lowest-income underemployed families. Since the House had already pushed for this in the economic recovery program, both the House and Senate as well as the administration knew the policy. Unfortunately it would do nothing for those families who lost all earnings due to unemployment. With Dave Obey's help, I got the zero threshold into our December Jobs bill but the Senate would not go for it. Sixteen million kids would be helped by the House bill, but that was not incentive enough for Republican senators to support it.

This was worrying. The original expiration date for the Bush tax cuts was the end of 2010. The economic recovery program's expansion of the Child Tax Credit would also expire at the end of 2010. This dramatic drop in income from the tax credit would be devastating for these families and affect them for a lifetime.

In the lame-duck Congress at the end of 2010, President Obama and the Republican leadership cut a deal. The president agreed to extend the tax cuts, including the Child Tax Credit extension that was part of the economic recovery program and a one-year payroll tax cut, and the Republicans agreed to extend unemployment insurance.

The Democratic leadership was called to the White House to talk about the deal. We didn't know whether the deal had already been made and agreed to. In fact, as we would discover, it had. Vice President Biden briefed us, and I asked specifically about the status of the estate tax and the Child Tax Credit. The vice president told the room that the dollar floor for the estate tax would be raised to $5 million, $10 million per family, so it affected even fewer estates, made permanent and indexed to inflation to protect the richest against further erosion of their wealth. I gasped. It can't be. The Child Tax Credit was extended for five years. I thought we squandered the opportunity to get the most for the people we represent at our maximum period of leverage. Others in the room felt the same way.

That same deal with the White House eliminated the Bush tax cuts above $450,000—not the $250,000 that we all ran on and fought for. Most Democrats supported it because they feared an expiration of all the Bush taxes might end up raising taxes even for those earning under $250,000. I was one of only sixteen Democrats who voted against the deal because we gave away the revenue from many top earners, and because it only temporarily extended the Child Tax Credit, the Earned Income Tax Credit, and the education tax credit through 2017. It allowed the payroll tax cut for working people to expire. Worst of all, it reduced the estate tax for the wealthiest families and indexed it to inflation. The package represented an unbalanced approach to the challenges we face as a nation. Opposing it was one of my proudest votes.

The fight continued. In 2012, the $1,000 per child tax credit was made permanent for all middle-class families—but only temporarily extended for low-income families. Then the next year, we had to fight for the $3,000 income threshold all over again.

In 2014, House Republicans voted for the Child Tax Credit Improvement Act. It would increase the income threshold from $110,000 to $150,000 and allowed an inflation adjustment to the threshold amounts. The catch was that taxpayers had to put a Social Security number on their tax return in order to claim the refundable portion of the credit, designed to exclude undocumented immigrants. The effect would be to make some five million children and their parents ineligible for the credit, 80 percent of them Latino. Thankfully the Senate did not take this measure up.

In late 2015, I viewed the prospective tax extenders bill as another opportunity to boost the Child Tax Credit, but not everyone viewed it as the top priority or best way to help kids. There was no meeting where I wouldn't vigorously fight for it. The White House, Pelosi, and Levin were strongly for indexing, but came to believe that the Republicans would not accept it. I asked Sandy Levin, in one of our many meetings, whether indexing the child tax credit was gone. He just looked at me and said nothing, so I knew it was gone.

In the final weeks of 2015 the $3,000 Child Tax Credit threshold enacted in 2009 was made permanent, however. Pelosi did not like the overall tax package because it was not paid for, and she wanted Democrats to vote against it—and she did not like the fact that I and others voted for the bill. But I could not vote against making the CTC permanent, regardless of what else that win came saddled with. After eighteen years the Child Tax Credit would finally join the ranks of other permanent taxes, like the estate tax. This was a big change.

While not many journalists focused on it, the 2015 permanency of the Child Tax Credit and (smaller) EITC expansions were part of the largest anti-poverty legislation in decades, after the Affordable Care Act. Now, together, the EITC and CTC lift more children out of poverty than any other federal provision. And the CTC alone now lifts nearly one out of every eight children out of poverty. The 2015 changes did not, though, index the Child Tax Credit to inflation, so we will keep fighting on that front.[13]

Families with young children receive the smallest CTCs, in spite of the fact that the economic literature suggests that these credits have particularly beneficial effects for families with young children.[14] With staggering inequality and poverty too high, I have introduced a bill with Pelosi and Levin to directly address this problem: the Young Child Tax Credit. The new Young Child Tax Credit will be built on top of the current CTC, adding an additional tax credit of $1,500 for all children under the age of three. Because of the critical importance of these early years, it will include all children except those whose families earn too much to be eligible for the current CTC. There will be no income threshold, so the poorest of the poor will qualify for it. And it will end $2-a-day poverty in America for nearly all families with young kids.

Providing additional economic support to families with young children just makes economic sense. I hope the Young Child Tax Credit will not take eighteen years to be enshrined in law like the CTC did. Imagine if the United States reached the top of international indexes of child welfare, instead of languishing near the bottom as it does now. I cannot imagine a prouder legacy for any legislator who helps make that happen.

10

In Defense of the Unemployed

You might think of what is happening in the economy—and thereby to you and your family—in terms of a professional hockey game, a sport renowned for its physical violence. Imagine how the game would be played if the old rules were repealed, if the referees were removed. That, in essence, is what is happening to the American economy. Someone changed the rules. And there is no referee.

—Donald L. Bartlett and James B. Steele,
America: What Went Wrong?

IN THE EARLY YEARS of the Great Depression, my father helped compile a study of industrial workers laid off from the L. Candee Rubber Company. Candee had a factory in New Haven that employed about eight hundred people, and on April 6, 1929, they all lost their jobs when the factory was completely and permanently shut down. No one had much time to prepare—the announcement of this shutdown was made just a few weeks earlier. At the time, the Candee factory was the second oldest rubber manufacturing plant in the world; it had been in operation since 1842. When Candee shut down their Rubber Works in the city of Hartford,

Connecticut, later that year, another fourteen hundred people were suddenly without a job.

I think about this story whenever I encounter the argument that employees should not be surprised when their employer decides to outsource jobs or cut staff, especially if their employer is part of a dying industry or one that stands to profit from shipping jobs overseas. Very rarely are employers that transparent about their strategic plans with workers.

The findings of the Candee study were published in a 1934 book called *After the Shutdown*. The author's conclusions were unambiguous: the people who were laid off suffered a multi-year decline in wages and working time, even those who were able to find other jobs. "That employable workers can, in three years after a lay-off, secure work on the average only two-thirds of the time and earn little more than half of their former full time wages is an indication of the [impact of unemployment] . . . outside of the workers' control." This lesson remains relevant today.

The Great Recession cost 8.7 to 15 million Americans their jobs, depending on who's counting. From the end of 2007, the ranks of the long-term unemployed—those jobless for six months or longer—surged 400 percent, exceeding six million by early 2011.[1] Sixty percent of the unemployed received no notice that their jobs were being terminated; 84 percent received no severance pay. Half subsequently cut back on medical treatment, and half had to borrow money from friends and relatives.[2] It was brutal and the pain was protracted. Recovery took a long time, and in many senses continues as I write this.

I hear from my constituents all the time: being out of a job is very painful. They are embarrassed, often ashamed. They want to work. They are also well aware that the chance of reentering the employed ranks dims the longer they are unemployed, especially for those aged fifty and up. You hear stories of men who worked for

IBM for thirty years and then find themselves stocking the holiday shelves at Macy's.

Former director of the National Economic Council Gene Sperling reported in the *Financial Times* in December 2014 that while the number of long-term unemployed workers had fallen by nearly 60 percent since its post-recession high, long-term unemployment was still higher than at any time between World War II and the 2008 financial crisis. After previous recessions, many people who had been laid off eventually found jobs similar to their old ones in salary and benefits once recovery was underway. Now the average person without a job remains so for 50 percent longer than was the case even thirty years ago. They are discriminated against by prospective employers. If a job candidate has been out of work for more than six months, many companies are not interested in hiring them.

It is a self-reinforcing bias: employers' screening practices discriminate against the long-term unemployed. Being out of work and financially strained for an extended period damages people's morale, which in turn makes finding a job and excelling at it that much harder. As Sperling concluded, "If we do not take this problem seriously now, we could soon be talking about a new class of the structurally unemployed."

For many, their status as unemployed cannot be laid at their feet as proof that they did not play the game correctly. In most instances, these people did nothing "wrong." As Princeton economist Judd Cramer put it, "They were in the wrong place at the wrong time as the economy continued to go on and there weren't job opportunities for them."

Today, most everyone has some sense of where these jobs go. Some go overseas. Others go to robots. Some of these jobs are never coming back, even as the economy grows, for the simple reason that companies—thanks to automation and digital technologies—are doing more with fewer people. A recent report puts this in historical perspective. In 2014 Google (now Alphabet) was valued at $370 billion. At the time it had fifty-five thousand employees. Fifty-five thousand is only a tenth of what AT&T's workforce was in the 1960s.[3]

So what good can legislation do in the face of the forces of automation and globalization? Mark Zandi's recommendation is that one of the best ways to stimulate the economy is via unemployment benefits. Extending and enhancing unemployment benefits is good for people—and for the economy.

First, some logistical concerns. Most work on unemployment insurance is done in the Ways and Means Committee. Anyone outside of that committee—that includes me—does not have much influence there. Second, historically, unemployment insurance was often supported in a bipartisan way. Dating back to Dwight Eisenhower's presidency, extending unemployment benefits was routine when jobs were scarce. Now Democrats tend to rally around the unemployed during recessions, while Republicans largely prefer inaction. Another problem is that debates over strengthening unemployment insurance occur *after* a recession hits, and rarely in good economic times. By the time Congress moves on the unemployment insurance system, American workers have been left waiting instead of immediately getting the support they need during a recession.

Conversations on Capitol Hill surrounding unemployment benefits in the wake of the Great Recession took on a surreal cast. We had people walking the plank as our nation's economic structure was changing, and the total indifference of some of my colleagues was a thing to behold. For them, the unemployed were essentially roadkill. The attitude seemed to be, well, it is very unfortunate what happened to them but best to sweep them to the side of the road and keep moving.

For legislators who did not want to do that, there were only a few public policy options to pursue. Speaker Pelosi asked Rob Andrews (D-New Jersey) and I to use Steering and Policy Committee hearings to open the discussion about why and what is really happening in the country. What can be done? We found people whose state unemployment benefits had expired and were saved from bankruptcy and foreclosure by federal unemployment benefits. We looked for people with stories of hardship in hopes of swinging some Republicans to take action on long-term unemployment insurance. We heard from Dave, a construction worker sixty-seven years young, "capable, fully able, and more than eager to work. I need to work. I love to work. It's who I am," he said. His savings were depleted, and even with unemployment insurance he was barely scraping by during a tough winter. We heard from Sarah, laid off from her job in cancer research, who had completed over eighty job applications for jobs at all levels, even ones she was vastly overqualified for. Her husband's small business was in the pits but he couldn't collect unemployment because he was self-employed. The end of federal unemployment insurance spelled foreclosure on their house, their cars repossessed, and further cutting back on already meager food expenses. "I applied for everything and anything," another woman testified, even jobs that paid nearly half of her earlier salary. Unemployment insurance had helped her keep her home, her sanity, and her pride as she got back on her feet.

With unemployment benefits expiring or getting reduced in high unemployment states, my Democratic colleagues in both chambers kept chanting, "Have a vote!" on extending benefits.

Some of my Republican colleagues said $26 billion for another year of long-term unemployment benefits was too expensive. Others said that extending unemployment insurance decreased the incentive to get out and find a job. I reject that argument entirely. I find it downright bizarre. Unemployment insurance is simply a bridge that keeps people sane and healthy while they are between jobs. It keeps their kids from suffering, too. As we heard over and over again from constituents, it is not a disincentive to finding work but a lifeline.

In summer of 2011 I pushed for the Fair Employment Opportunity Act to protect people who were being discriminated against for being long-term unemployed. We were hearing reports of people being told that if they were currently out of work, not to bother applying for the job. In short, the law would outlaw hiring policies that stated that applicants "must be currently employed" to be considered for a job. Research was telling us that this practice was becoming pervasive, with devastating results. At the time we were working on this legislation, unemployment was still hovering at 9.2 percent, and nearly half of the unemployed—44 percent—had been without a job for over six months.

Most members of the public agreed with our proposed legislation. They thought it was unjust to discriminate against people who were out of work. Eight of ten poll respondents characterized it as "very unfair," while another one in ten would only go as far as calling it "unfair."[4] The bill was referred to the Subcommittee on Health, Employment, Labor, and Pensions and stalled out there. In 2014 Obama—looking at numbers showing that among the millions still unemployed, many had been jobless for longer than twenty-six weeks—issued a memo to federal agencies stating that unfavorable determination with respect to the suitability, fitness, or qualifications of an applicant for federal employment because that applicant is or was unemployed was not acceptable. Obama also got companies to pledge to help the long-term unemployed.[5]

The same year Senator Jack Reed and I had championed the Layoff Prevention Extension Act, which would provide federal support for states to develop work-sharing programs that give employers the flexibility they need to maintain their workforce. This is known as the German model: don't lay people off if you can help it, just cut back people's hours. Struggling companies reduce hours instead of their workforce, which helps them on rehiring costs, while employees keep their jobs and receive a portion of unemployment insurance benefits to make up for lost wages. It was enacted in 2012 as a provision in a related bill and as a result of that effort twenty-two states and the District of Columbia implemented similar programs, saving more than 570,000 jobs.[6]

On other fronts we were less successful. In December of 2013 I refused to vote for a $1.04 trillion budget deal that averted a government shutdown and eliminated across-the-board federal spending cuts.[7] I did so because it failed to fund federal long-term unemployment benefits for people out of work for more than twenty-six weeks.

In 2014 the House Ways and Means Committee published a report that claimed employment had grown faster since the Emergency Unemployment Compensation Program expired in late 2013. Republican leadership interpreted this as evidence that unemployment checks *create* high unemployment levels. I have never believed that, nor do I think that the Republican argument makes sense from a business perspective. Unemployment checks do not have the power to discourage employers from staffing their businesses. All the growth in employment numbers meant was that the economy was improving—slowly. In fact, the research is pretty clear: cutting off Emergency Unemployment did not encourage more job-searching; what happened was that by this time a portion of people who had been looking for work for a long, long time simply dropped out of the workforce. The rest found jobs at roughly the same rate they had while receiving Emergency Unemployment, only without the lifeline that unemployment benefits had provided them and their families.[8]

I am impressed with initiatives like Platform to Employment (P2E), a program to assist people that have run out of unemployment benefits and are still without a job. Joseph Carbone, CEO of The WorkPlace and founder of P2E, remembers one eight-month stretch of being unemployed as a dark moment in his life he did not really talk about for years because he was so ashamed. He also remembers how as late as 2010, it was hard to get people to take the problem of long-term unemployment seriously. "Nobody cared, coast-to-coast, nobody cared."

How does P2E work? First, career development training helps get people up to speed with changing expectations in today's workplace. Then participants effectively take on a paid internship. For eight weeks, P2E covers their wages so prospective employers can see how well they work and how well they fit into the organization, risk-free. If they do well, they are offered full-time employment, and most people do well. Eighty percent of participants who start the program are offered internship positions, and 90 percent of those remain at those organizations after P2E stops subsidizing their salaries.

These programs are realistic, remarkably effective, and especially helpful at reducing the pain and stigma of unemployment for older workers. Moreover, they take a gross injustice and turn it into a program that gives people hope. Government has a role to play in our changing economy, whether that is extending and enhancing unemployment benefits or subsidizing employment programs. All workers deserve a fair shake. They deserve opportunities to reinvent themselves in a game often rigged in favor of business. Government is a vital referee.

But a properly functioning economy and society shouldn't need to rely so heavily on the safety net. Building a good life for oneself starts with a job. My parents were always helping someone find a job. Of course at that time there were plenty of jobs to be had—if you were out of work, all you needed was training, a work ethic, and somebody willing to give you a break.

Early on in my time serving in the Congress, I began to focus on ways government could play a bigger role in growing American jobs and accelerating economic growth—in ways that had been successful in the past. I asked my staff to develop legislation that would allow much more public investment in infrastructure. The rationale was simple: there had to be a way to solve infrastructure problems and help people at the same time.

That infrastructure projects can create jobs we have known for centuries. Throughout the 1800s and 1900s, infrastructure investment allowed the U.S. economy to grow and compete, particularly in the manufacturing sector, and set the conditions for long-term prosperity. Massive infrastructure investment gave us canals, railroads, and public highways, making life better and commerce easier for millions of people.

Not only that. Jobs generated by infrastructure projects pay well and cannot be offshored. They are jobs that get America building things again, not just consuming. Finally, there is a huge multiplier effect, as infrastructure is the lifeblood of any economy.

And yet spending on infrastructure in the United States is abysmal. That was true in the early 1990s, and it was truer by the time of the Great Recession. For too long we have been lax in maintaining infrastructure investments already made. We spend about 2 percent of total GDP on infrastructure. The American Society of Civil Engineers gives our infrastructure a D+ rating and estimates that we need to spend $2.2 trillion just to bring our infrastructure up to a good condition. China, meanwhile, invests 9 percent. India invests 5 percent and plans to increase that number.

As per usual, I had no committee jurisdiction in this area. When I asked my staff to draft my first infrastructure bill in 1994, they did so knowing it would be an uphill battle. The plan we drafted included a proposal for innovative public-private financing, a so-called infrastructure bank. Federal funding for infrastructure projects typically comes through fees, formula funding, and grants to states, and in the case of highways and roads, via a gas tax—in other words, public money. The idea behind the infrastructure bank idea was to leverage private investment and create public-private partnerships to significantly increase the investment we are able to make in a wide range of infrastructure: transportation, water, energy, and telecommunications.

I took the idea to Robert Reich, who was labor secretary at the time. He supported me in private but could not come out in favor of an infrastructure bank publicly because of internal politics and jurisdiction issues. I then spoke with the secretary of the treasury, Robert Rubin. His response was: Why do you want to increase the deficit? Why would you want President Clinton to increase the deficit? And he would not allow me to speak with the president on the issue. I was able to speak with others in the administration, and I was heard. But at every point I met opposition because the infrastructure bank meant more public borrowing. Then we lost the 1994 midterm elections and could not do anything further on the bank for years.

And then in 2007 the catastrophic collapse of the I-35 W bridge across the Mississippi River in Minneapolis got people thinking.

With the help of experts who had given a lot of thought to the concept, such as Felix Rohatyn and Bernard Schwartz, in 2008 we revamped the infrastructure bill I had championed since 1994. The revamped infrastructure bank bill was modeled after development banks around the world, such as the European Investment Bank. In this model, the bank is a government-owned corporation, run by an independent board, that issues insured federal "public benefit bonds" to institutional investors, attracting private dollars to the bank and its projects. It then considers applications for transportation (bridges, airports, high-speed rail), water (drinking water and wastewater systems), energy (clean energy distribution, energy efficient housing) and telecommunications projects (expanding broadband to rural and urban communities). This merit-based system would then provide financing, loans, and loan guarantees to projects that have regional and national significance, as well as clear economic, environmental, and social benefits. No pork barrel earmarks or short-term thinking allowed. Along with the federal support, infrastructure projects must have financing from other entities, public and private. Approved projects would be required to have an identifiable, reliable revenue stream (such as tolls on bridges or water/energy user fees) to repay loans, making the bank self-sustaining.

Chris Dodd was a strong supporter of infrastructure investment and as the chair of the Senate Banking Committee, he had jurisdiction over transit and housing funding. He too championed an infrastructure bank and included the concept in his economic plan when he ran for president. When Dodd dropped out of the race, then Senator Obama incorporated the bank concept into his economic plan and then ultimately into his first budget as president: five billion a year for five years. This number was later winnowed down to two billion.

The first real opportunity to enact legislation to establish an infrastructure bank was in the economic stimulus plan that became law as the American Recovery and Reinvestment Act in early 2009. I pushed for it in meetings convened by Speaker Pelosi, including with economists like Larry Summers and Alan S. Blinder. It didn't happen, even as we had the majority in the House and the bill garnered around a hundred Democratic co-sponsors.

Some of the problem was jurisdictional. Due to the complex nature of the bill, it was referred to three committees: Transportation and Infrastructure, Finance, and Ways and Means. I had a good relationship with Jim Oberstar (D-Minnesota), then chair of Transportation, but he never fully embraced the concept. My friend Charlie Rangel at Ways and Means liked the proposal but the bank never got high on his radar screen. On the Finance Committee, Barney Frank (D-Massachusetts) was strongly supportive but that support was not enough. According to some of my colleagues, only a Republican co-sponsor in the Senate would do. But that meant limiting the infrastructure bank proposal both in scope and ambition.

It also did not happen in 2009 because we knew we had to pump money into the economy quickly to avoid turning the Great Recession into another Great Depression, and to do that meant funding existing programs. We did spend $150 billion on infrastructure: roads, bridges, dams, ports, rail, transit, water, broadband, public housing, high-speed rail, and renewable energy.[9] We could have gone bigger but for the beginnings of what would be unflinching objection from House Republicans to anything President Obama sought to accomplish for the American people (though it should be noted the House Republicans' alternative stimulus included heavy spending on infrastructure).[10]

That said, considering that infrastructure bank legislation had otherwise laid dormant since the Republicans took over the House in 1994, the issue did gain real traction inside and outside of Congress. The bill garnered the support of unions such as the Steelworkers, who favored the provision requiring the use of American-made steel in infrastructure projects, as well as their environmental advocates in the BlueGreen Alliance, who supported investment in clean-energy projects. The SEIU supported it, seeing it as a means for building badly needed stable, long-term pension fund investments. The concept also had the support of the Chamber of Commerce, which recognizes how infrastructure spending supports American business, as well as the need to leverage private funds to make that investment. It was also supported by prominent investors such as Bernard Schwartz and Felix Rohatyn.

Think tanks such as the New America Foundation and Brookings Institution wrote papers and held events supporting the concept. Prominent columnists in the *New York Times*, the *Washington Post*, and elsewhere wrote favorably about the legislation.[11] Critically, the infrastructure bank has bipartisan support from state and local politicians, led by the Building America's Future coalition started by Governors Ed Rendell (D-Pennsylvania) and Arnold Schwarzenegger (R-California), as well as Mayor Bloomberg in New York City. In fact, Governor Rendell invited me in 2009 to speak on the topic at a National Governors Association session in Biloxi, Mississippi, at the time headed by Republican Haley Barbour.[12]

Still, this was one of the hardest areas to navigate in the ongoing policy discussion. Speaker Pelosi recognized the role I was playing but there were also proposals from other House members, and they competed for the oxygen in the room. Earl Blumenauer (D-Oregon) led on green infrastructure and revenue issues from his seat on the Ways and Means Committee. Chris Van Hollen (D-Maryland) championed a green bank—also, a viable vehicle. Mine was the most comprehensive but also the most difficult to achieve.

After we lost the House majority in 2010, and with the Republicans continuing to refuse to do anything economically for the American people, much of the push for stronger economic policy came from the Senate. With Senator Dodd retired, Senator John Kerry joined Texas Senator Kay Bailey Hutchison to introduce an infrastructure bank bill that was significantly scaled down from what I was proposing. President Obama made another big push on infrastructure spending in 2010, proposing $50 billion in spending, including financing for an infrastructure bank.[13] That push continued after the midterms, but went nowhere in either the Senate or the House as Republicans refused to act.

Much of the conversation surrounding the infrastructure bank has since focused on how to pay for it. One idea that was popular for a while was to pursue a "repatriation" tax holiday, which would allow U.S. multinational corporations to bring overseas profits home at a tax rate lower than the usual 35 percent, and to use those proceeds to capitalize the bank. I looked carefully at the idea, but determined it would not work for a number of reasons, including the fact that when repatriation was tried by the Bush administration in 2004, it didn't produce the promised domestic investment. In fact, companies benefiting from the holiday used the repatriated funds to line the pockets of shareholders while some actually laid off workers. The Joint Committee on Taxation also said the policy would increase deficits as more companies shifted money overseas in expectation of the next tax holiday.[14]

Whether through a financial transaction tax on Wall Street or by asking the highest-income earners to pay their fair share, we must find a way to establish a national infrastructure bank. We have already squandered years of historically low interest rates when we should have been heavily investing in infrastructure. Infrastructure investment is crucial to creating middle-class jobs that cannot be outsourced and critical to ensuring that our businesses, small and large, have access to world-class infrastructure that helps them compete in a globalized economy.

But support for thinking this big has to come from the top. There is tremendous historical precedent for this type of bold, visionary thinking. During the Civil War, President Lincoln built the Transcontinental Railroad. FDR ushered in rural electrification. In the 1950s Dwight Eisenhower built the Interstate Highway system. And in 1961 John F. Kennedy announced that we would be going to the moon within ten years. Meanwhile we cannot get Congress to fund an increase in transportation funding from the gas tax. Obama always has a strong budget for infrastructure but never fights for it—and it is the first thing Republicans cut.

One of the biggest surprises in the 2016 election was that Hillary Clinton promised an infrastructure bank as a high priority and that Donald Trump promised to spend more than Clinton and to build big projects to create jobs.

There is also a great appetite in the private sector to get involved.

Over the past five years, the private funds available for infrastructure have quadrupled to approximately $250 billion. There are over
sixty infrastructure funds ready to invest in the U.S. market with a
leveraged purchasing power of $625 billion. If put to use, this could
mean approximately 1.9 million jobs. Across partisan divides, the
American public wants to see this happen. It is high time we got
it done.[15]

11

In Defense of Fair Trade

IN EARLY 2015 THE PRESS began reporting that I was on "a collision course with President Obama and some of Connecticut's largest companies" over the Trans-Pacific Partnership (TPP), a proposed trade deal with twelve Pacific Rim countries, including Australia, Brunei, Canada, Chile, Japan, Malaysia, Mexico, New Zealand, Peru, Singapore, the United States, and Vietnam.[1] Together those twelve countries, including the United States, make up approximately 40 percent of the global economy.

Taking a different position from someone you agree with 98 percent of the time is challenging. Being at odds with President Obama was not on my agenda, but the Trans-Pacific Partnership was worth a *battle royal* because it constitutes an agreement that would grant new powers to foreign corporations, push down wages and lose jobs, and jeopardize the health and safety of Americans. The push to pass it was suffused with favoritism toward investors, plus arrogance on the part of both the Bush and Obama administrations respectively. Those of us who had grave questions about the TPP were energized to fight bad trade agreements like never before and we would have to sustain a formidable coalition for years to stop it.

At 5,600 pages long, including the many "side letters" that clarify certain bilateral and multilateral sub-agreements, the TPP's provisions are hard to summarize. Like most of today's "trade" agreements, it does not mainly focus on traditional trade matters, such as cutting border taxes, called tariffs. Indeed only six of the TPP's thirty chapters cover trade matters. Many people may not realize how broad the subjects covered by deals like the TPP are. They establish rules and principles governing the quality of our food supply, drug prices, and our nation's ability to enforce our own laws and regulations. The TPP also has rules related to labor standards, patents and copyrights, land use, agriculture and product standards, the environment, professional licensing, e-commerce, service sector regulation, and much more. At the heart is regulatory harmonization to make sure the rules in Country A are the same as rules in Country B so that it is easier for companies to produce in one country and sell in many without being impeded by country-specific regulations.

The effect on food safety regulations got my attention first. The TPP's provisions will affect the quality of our food supply—both food safety standards and inspection protocols, one of my main areas where I focus in the Congress. It also regulates drug prices and our nation's ability to create and enforce our own laws and regulations.

How could extensive negotiations result in such a raw deal for the American people? Why wouldn't it? The TPP was negotiated with five hundred U.S. companies and lobbyists serving as official trade advisors with special access to the process and the texts while the public, press, and, to a large degree, Congress were shut out.[2] Among the official U.S. trade advisors were Connecticut's own United Technologies, General Electric, and Pfizer, the Distilled Spirits Council of the United States, the Securities Industry and Financial Markets Association, Dow Chemical, the American Petroleum Institute, and many more.

For progressives, the test for any such deal, regardless of who is writing it, is whether the agreement creates or costs jobs and whether it raises or pushes down wages. And whether the rules we put into trade agreements will promote public health and protect the environment or if they will winnow our regulatory apparatus to the lowest common denominator and erode labor standards here while doing nothing to improve the lives of exploited workers abroad.

If the economists who have reviewed the TPP are correct, the agreement will also deepen inequality in our country. That current trade policies widen income disparities in developed countries has been the academic consensus view for decades.

Some historical background helps explain how: trade affects what types of jobs are available and what they pay. The last time we had a trade surplus was around 1975. That means 1975 was the last time we exported more than we imported. Since then, we have lost millions of the manufacturing jobs—more than one out of every four—that had provided the 70 percent of Americans without college degrees opportunities for well-paying middle-class livelihoods.

Trade deals like NAFTA and the TPP include the legal and financial protections that make it cheaper and safer for companies to export our jobs to low-wage countries. American companies that used to hire U.S. workers relocated for cheaper overseas labor instead to become more profitable, leaving their American workers to suffer. While new jobs were created, those available to the majority of Americans, including many in the service sector, paid considerably less. Middle- and lower-class workers in developed countries have to compete for paychecks with labor forces in countries where wages are much lower.

This outcome was not the invisible hand of the market at play. Rather, agreements like NAFTA and the TPP provide special protections for certain interests, such as the pharmaceutical industry, and contain incentives to offshore American jobs.

Free trade's loudest advocates argue that people laid off from their jobs because of trade can switch sectors and find new jobs, but history shows us that workers who lose jobs to trade will often be poorer for it. According to data from the U.S. Bureau of Labor Statistics compiled by Public Citizen, 60 percent of manufacturing workers who lost a job to trade and were rehired in 2014 experienced a wage reduction. About one-third took a pay cut of 20 percent or more. Even those in jobs that can't be offshored are affected, because competition pushes down wages as those who lose their jobs continue to look for work.

Thus, during this forty-plus years of a trade deficit, wage levels have remained flat. The median weekly wage in 1979 was $749 (in today's dollars). By 2014, thirty-five years later, that number had crept up to just $753 per week. No one can argue that this wage stagnation is due to declining productivity—in fact, U.S. workers' productivity doubled during this period. But middle-class incomes have not budged much in forty years.

What did rise, and dramatically, is the share of national income enjoyed by the richest Americans, especially after 1980. From 1981 until 1994, the richest 10 percent increased their share of national income by 1.3 percent each year. From 1994 to 2000 the top 10 percent gained 2.6 percent more of the national income share each year. The disparity between the rich and the poor in our country continues to grow.

What happened after 1994? The North American Free Trade Agreement went into effect in January 1995. That too is when the World Trade Organization began to operate. The WTO replaced an earlier global trade agreement—the General Agreement on Tariffs and Trade—that had been in place since just after World War II. Its focus had been limited to real trade matters such as eliminating quotas and tariffs.

This new generation of "free trade" trade agreements like NAFTA and organizations like the WTO that enforce more than a dozen agreements often conflate "trade liberalization" with the interests of global corporations and industries looking for new ways to grow and raise profits. Those corporations are using their money and lobbyists to write the rules of the economy in their interest: yes, to rig the economy so it works for them.

I voted against NAFTA. It was not a comfortable decision. President Bill Clinton called people who voted against NAFTA "thugs." My husband Stan was pollster for the president and for NAFTA. We had some of the biggest arguments in our marriage over this issue, and one evening, our daughter Anna was embarrassed by our loud exchanges while having dinner at the Bombay Club near the White House.

Vice President Al Gore debated NAFTA with a seemingly underprepared Ross Perot on CNN and won handily. The campaign to get the American people on board with NAFTA was well-executed, leaving those of us who were skeptical of the claims made for NAFTA looking foolish, even naive.

David Bonior and Dick Gephardt led the charge against NAFTA. Bonior organized weekly meetings providing members with information about the potential devastating effects of the agreement. He led a substantial whip operation to garner the votes against NAFTA. And it was the model that I adopted in our fight against the TPP. While the arguments against NAFTA were on balance on our side, at the end of the process we watched the vote slip through our fingers. The pressure, the arm-twisting and deals by the Clinton administration—promises made, most not kept—we lost the vote. I cried when we lost.

Years later I can honestly say that I did not get any satisfaction from having been right. NAFTA dramatically sped the loss of manufacturing jobs in my home state of Connecticut and many hundreds of thousands more jobs nationwide.[3] One of the small businesses that fell victim to our failed trade policy was Ansonia Specialty Metals. The manufacturer was a Connecticut institution since 1847, employing hundreds of men and women for generations. I first visited Ansonia Specialty Metals in July 2002, when I met

John Barto, who was then serving as the company's vice president. At that time, nearly four hundred people worked at the Ansonia plant. I frequently stopped in to visit with the employees and tour facilities. Over the course of the next decade unfair trade practices emanating from Mexico, Germany, and Korea caused the small firm to bleed jobs. The final nail in the coffin was driven when the Korea Free Trade Agreement went into effect in 2012. Ansonia Specialty Metals closed its doors in 2013. Subsequently, I invited John to the State of the Union address in 2015 to speak to the press about what happened to those jobs in Antonia and Waterbury.[4] I still continue to visit the site of the former plant to highlight the damage that unfair trade policy is doing to our communities.

Every time a trade deal is before Congress, the same arguments are made by its supporters:

1) Earlier trade deals might have been a bad deal, but this time is different. Unlike last time, when we walked into a scenario that left us unable to uphold environmental and labor standards, now we are determined to do it right.

2) The opponents haven't read the agreement, don't understand what it means, and are ill-informed.

3) People who do not agree with this trade deal are on the wrong side of history.

4) This is going to help the middle class.

5) Those who oppose it are in denial about the demands of globalization, or somehow opposed to progress in general.

6) If we fail to do this deal, fill-in-the-blank competing nation will clean our clocks.[5]

7) Rejecting this agreement will undermine our national security, and that should trump all other considerations.

A lot of money is at stake in trade deals. Whenever there is potential for making a lot of money, a lot of money gets spent. Quid pro quo offers emerge on the Hill—vote for this bill and I will support you on that. In the run-up to the vote on NAFTA, members of Congress were offered rides on Air Force One. They were offered a presidential visit for a fund-raiser or a bridge to be built in their district, or protection for their commodities, if the member was in a farming district.

Negotiations for the TPP did not start under Obama but in 2008, during George W. Bush's presidency. After campaigning against NAFTA and promising a new approach on trade, initially the Obama administration seemed cool on anything that looked like a NAFTA-style trade deal, but announced that it would resume talks on the TPP in late 2009.

I started tracking the TPP in 2011, when I realized that it could require the United States to permit imports of meat, poultry, and possibly seafood products that do not meet U.S. food safety standards. Relaxed safety standards for imported seafood in particular worried me. In 1994, the year Congress voted for membership in the WTO, half of the seafood consumed by Americans was imported; by 2011 that figure had risen to 84 percent. Under existing laws, we can refuse two-hundred-ton fish shipments from Vietnam because they do not meet our consumer safety standards. In 2011, the FDA issued twenty-five import alerts for Vietnam, with Vietnamese seafood detained for misbranding, E. coli, unusually high levels of antibiotic residues, and microbial contamination. There was already reason to believe that Chinese shrimp—flagged by the FDA in 2007—was being rerouted through Malaysia to avoid U.S. anti-dumping duties. The problem has not improved over time. In total, nearly four hundred shipments of Vietnamese shrimp were rejected at the border in 2015, a record. An April 2015 study by *Consumer Reports* found that 60 percent of global frozen shrimp imports were contaminated with Salmonella, Vibrio, Listeria, or E. coli. The superbug *Staphylococcus aureus* was found on 2 percent of tested shrimp.

The issue is not limited to just shrimp. Since the U.S. Department of Agriculture began inspections of Vietnamese catfish imports in May 2016, 39,000 pounds have been rejected for contamination with illegal drugs, along with an additional 28,000 in June for failure to follow inspection protocol and another 40,000 in August for malachite green.[6]

We fought hard to pass a new law to protect consumers from unsafe imported food. We cannot allow trade agreements to undermine these protections. But were TPP implemented, we would have even less control over our food safety.

I first wrote to the U.S. trade representative's office in September 2011 about my food safety concerns. I never heard back from them. In 2013, I wrote again, this time a bipartisan letter with my House colleague Walter Jones (R-North Carolina) and my Senate colleague Mary Landrieu (D-Louisiana).[7] The Southern Shrimp Alliance was very engaged in this issue.[8] Again, no response. This silence was frustrating, but also made no sense. The White House had just made a big deal of the Healthy Hunger-Free Kids Act. Why not also work toward guaranteeing kids food that doesn't kill them?

In a 2013 Agriculture Committee hearing, I asked Secretary of Agriculture Tom Vilsack what the USDA could do to stop dangerous food imports under the TPP. He had no answer.

That goes to the crux of the problem. Countries like Vietnam and Malaysia with a long history of exporting contaminated seafood (farmed by fishermen often working in deplorable conditions) will easily see their food safety system deemed to be "equivalent to the U.S." I have been fighting the same challenge for years for poultry imported from China as the USDA keeps moving closer to allowing chickens slaughtered in China, a country with as checkered a food safety history as one will find, into our grocery stores and onto our kids' school lunch plates because they find the Chinese food system "equivalent" to ours.

Negotiations surrounding the TPP were conducted in extreme secrecy. "Think of the TPP as a stealthy delivery mechanism for policies that could not survive public scrutiny," as my friend Lori Wallach, the director of Public Citizen's Global Trade Watch, put it.[9]

My objections to the TPP were pretty straightforward: it would cost American jobs and suppress wages. It would grant new rights to thousands of foreign corporations to sue the U.S. government before a panel of three corporate lawyers. These lawyers can award the corporations unlimited sums to be paid by America's taxpayers, including for the loss of expected future profits. These foreign corporations need only convince the lawyers that a U.S. law or safety regulation violates their TPP rights. Their decisions are not subject to appeal, and the amount awarded has no limit. It would waive Buy American and other Buy Local procurement preferences. It would threaten environmental regulations and consumer protections we have worked hard to uphold.

The threat to the safety of our food supply bothered me most of all. The TPP would require the United States to allow food imports even if the exporting country's safety regimen did not measure up to our own. Any U.S. rule regarding pesticides, bacterial contamination, labeling, or additives could be considered an illegal trade barrier if our standard was higher than international standards. And the TPP requires us to certify that other countries' food safety systems with standards different from ours provide an "equivalent" level of protection, and then allow in any and all food produced under that system. The TPP, in other words, would let other countries do our food inspections for us. We would have more unsafe seafood on our tables and at restaurants.

This concern is not paranoia on trade watchers' part. Labels like "dolphin-safe" on cans of tuna fish, as well as labels on meat that tell consumers where the livestock was raised, have already been successfully challenged under WTO rules that, while problematic, are less constraining than those in the TPP. Even after U.S. inspectors found horrifying safety problems in Chinese facilities, the WTO ruled that the U.S. ban on chicken processed in China was illegal. Under TPP, such encroachments on consumer protections and consumer labeling would only increase, yet while campaigning for TPP at a Nike facility in Oregon, President Obama said: "Critics warn that parts of this deal would undermine American regulation—food safety, worker safety, even financial regulations. They're making this stuff up. This is just not true. No trade agreement is going to force us to change our laws."

Except trade agreements already have done that. I had a significant role in enacting country-of-origin labeling for meat sold in the United States. A bipartisan effort in Congress resulted in a Farm Bill including provisions that required that packages of chicken, beef, and pork sold in American grocery stores had to bear a label showing where the meat was raised, slaughtered, and processed. This law withstood a U.S. court challenge by the U.S. meatpacking industry. But then Canada and Mexico challenged our law at the World Trade Organization. Even after changing the law to fix specific problems identified by the WTO, we lost every WTO appeal and the WTO authorized one billion dollars of trade sanctions to be charged against us annually unless and until we eliminated the law. The result: Congress repealed the U.S. law on country-of-origin labeling of beef and pork in 2015.

At the same time, the results were coming in from the U.S.-Korea Free Trade Agreement, which went into effect in 2012. The administration promised that this agreement had fixed the problems of pacts like NAFTA, and that it would mean "more exports, more jobs." Many Democrats relied on those promises to support the pact. But the agreement was causing a jump in our trade deficit with Korea, and America had lost more than 95,000 jobs in a little over four years.[10]

So, skepticism about trade agreements and TPP was growing in the Congress, though the trade working group waxed and waned and had not yet galvanized the opponents into an effective force. They had not been able to win against the powerful forces pushing for further agreements. That has always been the unhappy story and ending for those fighting the agreements. And now the TPP, the biggest of all of these agreements, was scheduled to be completed in 2011.

My friend Lori Wallach, probably the leading expert on the pluses and minuses of these trade agreements, knew of my earlier opposition, and came to see me in my office and asked whether I would lead the congressional opposition. I said yes. But I have learned some things about organization, and I was also determined that the coalition of advocacy groups and unions raise its game to a new level.

And quickly, as the first test was looming: the administration announced it would ask Congress to enact trade promotion authority or "Fast Track" for the TPP. TPA or Fast Track allows a president to sign and enter into an agreement before Congress approves its contents and then be guaranteed an expedited vote with all congressional amendments prohibited and debate limited.

The coalition of labor and progressive advocacy groups that came together to strategize surrounding the TPP was unprecedented. In the past, it was viewed that labor unions were always opposed to trade agreements and called "protectionists." But now it was not only labor but environmental, consumer, faith, seniors, health, human rights, and some farm groups plus an array of other non-profits. I visited personally with all the major labor leaders making the case that with an organized campaign, well-funded, we could win the Fast Track vote. Given many of the countries involved in TPP negotiations were skeptical that Congress would approve the deal absent this constraint on Congress, winning this vote was likely to derail the TPP negotiations altogether. They agreed and supported my efforts.

I had not witnessed such unity of purpose from such a diverse array of interests in decades. We designed our opposition like a campaign. The outside groups hired a campaign manager, Karin Johanson, who had run political and grassroots campaigns with great success and created a communications apparatus. They conducted polls and activated an external field operation. Karin operated out of the AFL-CIO. And I set up an internal whip operation. Lloyd Doggett, a whip-smart lawyer who had served on the Texas Supreme Court, became a main policy protagonist in the caucus. With a laser-like focus on issues he understood like no other, he could challenge the merits of the administration's case. Louise Slaughter was relentless. George Miller was critical to getting off the ground. And Jan Schakowsky, Debbie Dingell, Mark Pocan, Barbara Lee, Peter DeFazio, Donna Edwards, Marcy Kaptur, and Paul Tonko joined the battle at every point and Keith Ellison mustered the full force of the Congressional Progressive Caucus. In all, there was a thirty-person whip team.

We engaged with Democrats who wanted to support the administration on principle, and give Obama a win, but had serious doubts about how the TPP would affect people in their district.

Initially, we held meetings every couple of weeks, then every Wednesday, with a smaller sub-group meeting Fridays as well. Every Sunday I held a conference call with the campaign.

We provided materials and organized meetings with academics, economists, and national security experts who were concerned about the direction of TPP negotiations and alarmed about those texts we were able to view thanks to leaks. We created forums at various congressional retreats and the caucus. We organized renowned economists who had supported past pacts but opposed the TPP, including Joseph Stiglitz, Jeffrey Sachs, and Jared Bernstein, to share their concerns with the caucus. We were creating the intellectual foundation for opposition to the specifics of the TPP and Fast Track, not knee-jerk opposition to a trade agreement.

The fight over TPP would have been grueling enough but the personal and political dynamics were made vastly more complicated because the Obama administration asked for Fast Track authority very late in the game. Usually Fast Track is set up *before* a trade agreement is negotiated, and it gives Congress some say over the deal's objectives and who gets invited to the negotiating table. After five years of negotiations, the TPP, however, was nearly complete when the White House asked Congress to grant them fast track to seal the deal.

A key argument for Fast Track is that foreign governments won't sign on the bottom line without assurances that Congress can't change the deal. If Congress would hand over its constitutional role in regulating foreign commerce to the executive branch, there would be less drawn-out debate, and less time wasted. Expanded opportunities in the fastest growing markets in the world would materialize faster. Most of the parties making the argument for Fast Track are those who stand to benefit most from shortened debate: pharmaceutical firms, agribusiness, and Wall Street among them.

My job in protesting Fast Track authority for President Obama was easier because I had a record of opposing Fast Track deals for presidents both Democratic and Republican. In 1998, the House of Representatives voted down Fast Track for President Clinton; I was among the 171 House Democrats (and 71 GOP members) voting no. I also had opposed the Trade Act of 2002, which included a Fast Track grant, this time for President George W. Bush. I also voted no on the 1991 Fast Track extension for NAFTA.[11]

In November 2013, George Miller, Louise Slaughter, and I got 151 Democratic members to sign on to a letter to the administration saying the Fast Track mechanism and its broad delegation of congressional authority was not appropriate for twenty-first-century agreements. I was tenacious in getting members on the House floor to sign, leaving it open for many weeks so advocates could press them in their districts. Before the administration could even begin its lobbying on Fast Track, we got many past proponents of past trade deals and key ranking members to go on the record in opposition. We also noted that the United States could not afford another trade deal that replicated past mistakes. But we didn't simply oppose the old Fast Track process. We offered principles for a new trade authority system that would include meaningful congressional input in the formative stages of a trade agreement and principles that would allow trade deals to win acceptance in the Congress. We were ignored. Our ideas fell on deaf ears. It was pure arrogance from the White House.

There was enough churning in the caucus that Leader Pelosi thought it would be wise to bring in the administration and opposition together. In January 2015, Leader Pelosi called a meeting in her conference room on TPP and Fast Track. Included in the meeting were Jeffrey Zients, director of the National Economic Council and assistant to the president for economic policy, and Secretary of Labor Tom Perez, Donna Edwards, and myself. The leader wanted to give the administration the opportunity to make its case and hear those who were opposed. I like and admire Secretary Perez—he is a friend and I know that he was doing his job—but the evidence did not support the pro-TPP claims.

Leader Pelosi was neutral. She had a record of supporting some trade agreements and opposing others and vehemently opposed most-favored-nation status for China. She was determined that the administration be able to make its case and that the opposition could get heard, too.

It was at this meeting that administration officials first realized they had a serious problem with passing Fast Track authority and TPP. We countered their premises and demonstrated a serious knowledge of the agreement and Fast Track principles. They needed to take the opposition seriously, yet they still didn't. Why weren't they able to make a turn? Not sure.

The White House put a tremendous amount of pressure on

members of Congress to approve Fast Track for the TPP. Some received calls from White House staffers every night. Some received calls from every single cabinet member. This level of attention from the Obama White House was a new experience for many congressional members. This sudden flurry of attention was not as effective as it might have been had the attention been spread out over time. Some members complained that they had not heard from the Obama administration in five years, not a single word. Now because of the need to pass Fast Track, they received a barrage of phone calls. To receive so much attention only because your vote is needed is hardly gratifying. Other members complained of the escalating pressure. They were promised campaign support if they voted for Fast Track, or a deafening silence from the White House when they were up for re-election if they didn't. The deal-making had begun.

The campaign for and against Fast Track had dragged on for eighteen months. Draft negotiating texts for TPP were still not released to the public, though. Even Senator Ron Wyden (D-Oregon), who had been chair of major Senate committees with jurisdiction over trade, was denied access to U.S. proposals to the negotiations at key points. (At the same time, the European Union was releasing its proposed text for the Transatlantic Trade and Investment Partnership to the public.)

The administration claimed it was being transparent and noted it had held over a thousand informational meetings. Anyone in Congress who wanted to look at documents could, they said. In fact, until the summer of 2012, members did not have access to text—not even the U.S. proposals. Indeed, the extent to which TPP was kept under wraps was unprecedented. What the administration claimed was transparency involved congressional briefings and meetings that featured a slew of generalities that did not address the main concerns people had. And once the administration finally allowed members of Congress access to the text, it was under

extremely limited terms. Congressional staffers were not allowed
to look at the TPP draft document unless they had security clearance, and most do not, save for the few who deal with the Defense,
Intelligence, and Foreign Affairs committees. Initially, in fact, they
did not make a copy of the text available for congressional members
to read at the Capitol. We wrote letters and emailed the U.S. trade
representatives numerous times, demanding access. They tried to
stall and tell us that they could not bring in the entire text for
members to read, so my office set up a system whereby we booked
rooms across the Capitol complex for certain times and dates over
the course of several months. Then we coordinated with the USTR
and asked for only certain chapters to be brought in at specific
times and days, and invited members of the whip team to review
those chapters that were of greatest concern. Chapters were only
available for an hour or two at maximum before USTR staff would
haul the documents back across town. Frequently, TPP "reading
sessions" were interrupted by votes, and I would only get fifteen
minutes to read through as much as I could. After doing this for a
couple of months, the USTR relented and made a copy of the draft
text available in the Capitol full-time, in a room in the basement
designated as classified.

I often went to read TPP chapters with Lloyd Doggett, who had a
cleared staffer. We had to hand over our cell phones. Then we had
to tell the trade representative's office which chapters we wanted
to read. We could not remove the documents, and at the outset we
could take no notes. Staff of the trade representative were there
and we could ask questions, but never got answers. We also could
not rely on the text to be the latest draft of the document following
each round of negotiations. Ultimately we came to rely upon leaks
to know what the administration had most recently negotiated.

Trade agreements are very complex, packed with arcane legal
language, and include many references to prior or future chapters
or other past trade agreements. Reading the TPP text out of context

was very difficult and being unable to take notes or have staff help us put members of Congress at great disadvantage. It was a way of controlling the process and making us look uninformed. (Congressman Sandy Levin, ranking Democrat on Ways and Means, made his staff available to talk with members since they had clearance to accompany us to the classified room.)

In my first encounter, I was handed the chapter on food safety. I began looking at the issues I had discussed with my staff. What I was not prepared for was what I read on the cover sheet of the chapter. It stated, "This document must be protected from unauthorized disclosure, but may be transmitted over unclassified email or fax, discussed over unsecured phone line, and stored in unclassified computer systems. It must be stored in a locked or secured building, room, and container." I asked myself, then, why is this "classified" and why am I in this room? I asked the trade representative staff at what level this document was classified—top secret, or secret. He told me it was classified as "confidential," close to the lowest level. Members and staff read confidential documents all the time. This process was an attempt to keep members of Congress in the dark.

I was trying to read the text in the midst of a normal congressional day, which included committee hearings, votes, and constituent meetings, without being able to take notes or take the document to read overnight. It was another way to hamstring the Congress.

Why would the White House risk the fallout from being so secretive? I believe the administration knew this unprecedented level of secrecy would damage their cause, but they must have thought it was a price worth paying.

When President Obama came to speak at the Democratic Issues retreat in Baltimore in January 2016, Maryland, Leader Pelosi invited a small group of us to have dinner with President Obama. I was there, along with Steve Israel, Joe Crowley, Jim Clyburn, Xavier Becerra, Donna Edwards, and Chris Van Hollen. The president brought up TPP. He said this is the most progressive trade agreement ever, and that it contained strong labor and environmental standards that would be enforceable. He said we could design enforcement mechanisms that reflected our national values. I respectfully but forcefully disagreed and we went back and forth for a while to no avail, each of us holding on to our strong positions. I said the text did not support his assertions. I said it includes ISDS, corporate protections that can undermine U.S. laws. He said it wasn't true. The exchange wasn't angry, but it was contentious. I know my colleagues were very uncomfortable. A few tried to raise other issues to lower the temperature, to no avail. I haven't been invited to dinner with the president again.

The battle with the administration on Fast Track was joined. The administration, knowing that most Democratic members were opposed, worked actively with the Republicans, as had previous Democratic administrations wanting to pass these agreements. Sandy Levin headed up Ways and Means, the committee of jurisdiction. He is known as someone respected by his colleagues on trade, writing provisions that included strong labor, environmental, and human rights protections, an important voice on trade who has voted in favor a number of past agreements. He was trying to get to yes on Fast Track and TPP. And in a hearing of the Ways and Means Committee, he tried to offer amendments that would strengthen the congressional role in Fast Track and allow us to hold treaty partners accountable. But the Republicans and the administration worked together to block any consideration of his amendments.

Trying to marginalize Sandy Levin, who was so respected, was a major error. It shifted some votes against Fast Track. It was also an error for the president to publicly attack Senator Elizabeth Warren, responding to her substantive critique of the TPP's ISDS regime and provisions that would roll back financial regulation. The president declared that she was "absolutely wrong" and a "politician like everybody else."

With most Democrats opposed to Fast Track and a growing bloc of House Republicans announcing opposition, the Republican leadership focused on me as the face of the opposition. Signs were circulated around the Republican conference meetings with two photographs side by side: Paul Ryan's face and mine. "Who are you going to go with?" it asked. Ryan was leader of the free-trade bloc and chaired the Ways and Means Committee, which has official jurisdiction over trade agreements in the House. He had repeatedly gone on the record warning America would lose market access to other countries if we did not pass Fast Track, and thereby lose jobs. I had become the face of the anti–Fast Track and anti-TPP campaigns.

The campaign was in full swing nationwide. Congressional offices were being visited daily. The phones were ringing off the hook, with most calls by far from constituents opposing Fast Track. An intensive field operation was doing its work. Numerous organizations were engaged and working hard, including the Communication Workers of America's Larry Cohen and Shane Larson, the AFL-CIO's Bill Samuel, the Sierra Club's Ilana Solomon, and the Teamsters' Nicole Brener-Schmitz. They were joined by the Machinists, Steelworkers, AFSCME, and National Farmers Union. After it became it clear that the administration was only giving lip service to the concerns of organized labor, President Richard Trumka put the full weight and force of the AFL-CIO against Fast Track. Soon, the entire union movement was solidly unified in opposition.

If a member of Congress had a technical question, or wanted to know how past agreements had affected their districts, a detailed memo was prepared and handed to them directly in an operation coordinated by Peter Chandler. Peter had previously served as chief of staff to fair trade champion Mike Michaud and was now helping to coordinate Hill operations as the congressional strategy director. We had a full-scale communications operation with at least one press event and usually several organized every week and members on the radio and TV. Experts were conducting member briefings and holding press conferences. Democrats and increasingly Republicans were announcing their intention to oppose Fast Track. The momentum was now on the side of the opposition.

In an attempt to create more discussion with members, Leader Pelosi organized forums, again, classified, but open to members who wanted to attend. Michael Froman, the trade representative, was present, as well as some cabinet members and administration staff. I went to all of the meetings. Most members would describe them as a waste of time. Again, no answers to questions. But the sessions did demonstrate the paucity of information available to us on what was in the agreement. Anti-TPP members dominated the conversation and that angered the supporters and the leadership at times. But we were determined to ask for more information. Congressman Lloyd Doggett was a chief questioner in holding the administration's feet to the fire.

To the end, the trade representative was arrogant and showed a lack of respect for the opponents. It was as if we were speaking different languages. As a result, the White House never made a turn that took the opponents and the questions they raised about trade seriously.

The morning of the vote, I organized a meeting in the Capitol office of Congresswomen Louise Slaughter, the ranking member of the Rules Committee. The whip team—several dozen members— was gathered with bagels and cream cheese and whip lists to solidify people we were sure of and shore up those that were shaky. The key was an accurate count. What did we know about Republicans? I received a call from Leader Pelosi and took the call in Louise's private office. The leader told me that the president had requested a meeting with the Democratic Caucus. He was coming in just an hour or so to speak about the Fast Track vote. I was nervous. My leadership of the opposition was well known. I kept a low profile. I did not, as I usually do, stand and circulate around the meeting.

President Obama asked Democrats to approve Fast Track. It was a short speech and a condescending one, and he did not take questions. It did not go over well. People with real standing in the House, people with extensive knowledge of the issue, felt snubbed.

Ultimately the fight came down to unique tactical maneuvering as the vote approached. The traditional way of getting a trade measure passed is to sweeten the deal with something to help workers who will be adversely affected, enhanced job training for workers, called Trade Adjustment Assistance. Even staunch free-traders have generally signed off on this approach, as no one with any intellectual or political integrity can rightly argue that trade deals benefit *everyone*—there are always losers. But by the time Fast Track was headed to a vote, Republican leaders found themselves in a strange situation. Republicans in the House detest Trade Adjustment Assistance both because they view it as welfare and had become so unwilling to compromise on TAA that they would not accept the usual bargain.

But the White House had structured a Senate bill that combined Fast Track and Trade Adjustment Assistance. To try to gain momentum for the much more difficult House vote, the Senate had acted first and the bill they passed was sent to the House. Speaker John Boehner soon discovered that the Republicans would oppose the Senate bill because it contained TAA as well. They were willing to lose on something they wanted (Fast Track) to make sure that Democrats didn't get what they wanted (some measure of relief for affected workers). The White House and the Republican leaders then came up with a new plan: separate the bill into two parts and hold votes on each part separately under a procedural rule that would reunite the pieces once each part was passed and thus approve the Senate-passed bill in two steps. Republicans would pass the trade part, Democrats the assistance portion, and done deal. With this plan they inadvertently handed control of the process over to those of us challenging Fast Track (and TPP).

I figured that if we could convince enough House Democrats to vote against Trade Adjustment Assistance, we could bring down Fast Track as well. Under the tricky procedural rule the administration and Republican leaders had cooked up, if only one half of the bill passed, it would be dead in the water. No one was expecting us to go that route, even some members of our own party.

At a late-night meeting a week before the vote, going through the whip list, I saw an extraordinary level of coordination. We had a thirty-member whip team. I would call out a member's name, and someone else would say they knew which way he was going to vote: "I talked to him thirty minutes ago." And "I talked to him fifteen minutes ago," someone else would pipe up.

Speaker Pelosi called me the night before the vote with what I assumed was the White House's list of who would vote with them. I got nervous that she wanted to give the White House more time. "Do you have the votes?" she asked. At this point Pelosi had been remarkably even-handed, both publicly and privately supportive of the administration's goals of getting a full hearing with the members but also making sure our objections got heard. I went through the list of Democrats. I assured her we had the votes.

And something else unprecedented put us in this strong position. Not only did I have a count of all the Democratic votes, I had the vote count for the Republican side as well, thanks to a friendly Deep Throat figure from across the aisle, someone whom if it were known he was talking to me would be frozen out at best, ostracized at worst.

In a speech in the well of the House the Leader came out in opposition and voted no on Fast Track. The White House was surprised.

Trade Adjustment Assistance sank, with 303 votes against.[12] Trade Promotion Authority passed by a narrow margin—219–211— immediately thereafter, but it was a moot point. The way the legislation was bundled, Fast Track would not advance to the president's desk without the trade assistance half.[13] The White House had lost, and they were stunned. They had to come up with a new strategy.

Our victory was short-lived because the administration didn't give it a second thought to work with the Republicans to change the rules of the game. This is what they did in the Senate. They separated the two pieces of legislation, willing to risk killing trade adjustment assistance altogether to pass Fast Track. They would be voted on separately the following week.

The next week both were again on the House floor. On the second vote, Fast Track passed by a vote of 218 to 208. But 160 House Democrats never wavered from their opposition to it; 158 were present on voting day to vote against. Eighty-five percent of House Democrats voted "No" and all of the Democratic leadership did. This was unprecedented Democratic unity.

Twenty-eight Democrats voted for it. Who's to say if the 28 Democrats might have been swayed with more effort? And who knows whether those 28 votes would be there for TPP itself had the treaty ever come up for a vote.

The Senate sent Trade Promotion Authority to the president, and Trade Adjustment Assistance back to the House, where it passed.

Some spoke about defeating Trade Adjustment Assistance to put pressure on the White House not to sign a Fast Track bill, but it was clear they were going to sign it with or without help for workers. I talked with Rich Trumka and other labor leaders. Given the White House's determination to win Fast Track, I believed it made no sense to try to defeat trade adjustment. They agreed. And so I worked to get other Democrats to vote for trade assistance.[14] Charlie Rangel asked at the caucus meeting what the Democrats' plan was. I happened to be at the mic, and I said, "I am voting for trade adjustment assistance and it's the right thing to do." I didn't want to hurt workers.

Several months after the president signed Fast Track into law, and in October a final deal was announced on the TPP.

But our success in delaying consideration of TPP and the shift in momentum carried this whole debate into the presidential election year, and that would prove fateful. It also presented a unique opportunity to force a major, long overdue debate about our country's trade policy.

The TPP's full text was finally released in November 2015. Its contents were even worse than expected. It contains monopoly protections that will likely increase drug prices. (Doctors Without Borders called it "the most harmful trade agreement ever for access to medicines.") It will let unsafe food enter our supermarkets, and jettison six out of seven multilateral environmental agreements whose enforcement had been required in the last trade agreements George W. Bush had signed. Its "Investor-State Dispute Resolution System" was copied from NAFTA and expanded in ways that would make it easier for corporate interests to challenge U.S. laws and regulations that stood in the way of a company making as much money as it desired. In other words, TPP gives companies the right to sue governments over policies they do not like in front of industry-friendly arbitration panels that sit outside of any court system. These three-person international tribunals can then direct governments to pay damages to these corporations. Taxpayers end up writing checks to multinational corporations—and this happens with no appeals process. If it were not true, it would be almost impossible to believe.

And think about this dramatic political change. The Republican and Democratic Party platforms opposed or raised fundamental questions about TPP—the exact opposite of what they said four years earlier. Both Donald Trump and Hillary Clinton opposed TPP and the special corporate protections that allowed U.S. laws to be overturned. And President Trump announced the United States' withdrawal from the agreement.

What principles a President Trump brings to our trade agreements will soon be clear.

Remember though, it was the powerful campaign in and outside of the Congress that defeated TPP, and we must battle to ensure our values matter going forward. Trump seems more interested in contracting trade, but that is not our vision. We want to harvest the benefits of expanded trade to ensure that our citizenry, consumers, and workers, not just corporate interests or particular industries, are the primary beneficiaries. We must write new rules of the road.

12

Paul Ryan's Assault on the Poor

The right to suffer is one of the joys of a free economy.
—Howard Pyle, aide to President Dwight D. Eisenhower,
arguing against unemployment benefits

WHAT BOTHERS ME ABOUT Speaker Paul Ryan's vision and agenda is what it portends for the vulnerable in our society. Ryan brings to it a belief about human nature and an ideology that argues these cuts in support are for the poor's own benefit, but that does not lessen the consequences. What he believes can "solve" the problem of poverty would actually make it worse. He believes that the best way to help the poor is by pulling away the social safety net so they will be motivated to take up work opportunities. When the poor get less government support, they will benefit morally and materially. And when government gets out of the poverty business charities, church groups, and philanthropists will play a much bigger role.

That is a huge risk, never mind that those charities depend on the government, too.

Speaker Ryan starts with the premise that the United States has spent trillions of dollars on poverty since the War on Poverty and that little has been achieved with the official poverty rate unchanged over fifty years. That is flat-out false and deceptive.

The official poverty rate doesn't take into account all America does to fight poverty. It doesn't count the Earned Income Tax Credit or the Child Tax Credit. It doesn't even count food stamps, all the things I've been battling to expand. When you do count them, you see a country that cut poverty by 40 percent over the last fifty years and child poverty by 35 percent.

Ryan believes he is helping the poor, but he is making the poverty problem worse. That puts him among the leaders with the biggest gap between his public image and the reality, between his decent personal style and the harsh effects of his plans for the poor, and between his expressed morality and the morality of our shared Catholic Church.

Let me be clear. I like Speaker Ryan. When he was mired in the Appropriations quagmire after making many promises to his caucus, I made "welcome to the NFL" jokes, and he rolled his eyes. When we were on the floor during the debate about Fast Track and the TPP, he said, "You are a worthy adversary." And when my granddaughter Rigby was writing a paper on D.C. statehood, he readily agreed to an interview at the White House congressional picnic on how Congress could justify "taxation without representation." That is when I learned that Ryan described himself as a conservative in the tradition of Jack Kemp and had voted to allow D.C. representatives a vote in committees, as Democrats had supported.

That is the rub. When he was chairman of the House Budget Committee, the budgets Ryan put forth routinely achieved two-thirds of their savings from cutting programs designed to help working families and the poor.[1] That is why Network, the organization of Catholic nuns headed up by Sister Simone Campbell, decided to organize a national bus tour to mobilize opposition to the Ryan budget and highlight how badly it would hurt the poor. She is a remarkable woman who was fearless in the face of the bishops who pilloried her for focusing on the poor and social justice and now leads the fight on immigration and poverty. The Paul Ryan budget gave us "Nuns on the Bus," calling into question the morality of his plans at a time when the Catholic Church was increasingly vocal about the effects of social policy on life and the most vulnerable.

In his first major policy speech as speaker of the house, Ryan said that the 45 million Americans living in poverty were "stuck in neutral," and we needed to get them "off the sidelines." The speech reprised many of the themes he had explored in "The War on Poverty: 50 Years Later," a report issued while he was chair of the House Budget Committee. The gist of both speech and report was this: our social safety net hindered poor people from seeking work and reaching their full potential. In its place we should usher in "a true opportunity agenda" in contrast to what Ryan felt were failed liberal and progressive policies. He created a task force on "Poverty, Opportunity, and Upward Mobility" that was limited to Republican members. Everyone on this task force had voting records that had slashed funding to food stamps, Pell Grants, housing assistance, childcare, Head Start, and Medicaid. In Ryan's view, this was all good. Democrats wanted to "take care" of the poor, whereas he wanted to "empower" them—and taking away benefits was his preferred way of doing that.[2] In Ryan's worldview, you solve the poverty problem by increasing poverty.

To get to his optimistic prediction on how this will turn out for the poor, Ryan is pretty blind to evidence that would force him to go back to the drawing board. He fails to include government assistance in calculating people's incomes—such as food stamps, the Earned Income Tax Credit, and the Child Tax Credit—which allows him to declare that poverty programs are failing and require a fresh approach, but it all adds up to an assault on the poor. Blinding himself to the facts allows him to assert that the best way to respond to a hungry child is to deny her parents aid that would allow them to buy a meal—and in so doing bring home the importance of them working more hours to put food on the table. Nothing could be further from the truth.

Paul Ryan's problem with facts is multi-faceted. First, he is wrong about how much our existing social safety net has done to lift people out of poverty. Ryan has repeatedly claimed that the poverty rate remains flat despite our social safety net. Yet according to the Brookings Institution, the poverty rate declined 26.4 percentage points between 1960 and 2010. While there is more work to do regarding poverty in our nation, we must not turn away from our progress.

Ryan is also wrong to say that programs like food stamps are "trapping people in poverty." He says food stamps are riddled with fraud and ineffective at improving the prospects of people receiving benefits, even though SNAP has one of the lowest error rates of any federal program. Less than 1 percent of SNAP benefits are issued to households that do not meet the program's eligibility requirements. In fact, the Council of Economic Advisers found that the food stamp program *alone* kept almost five million people out of poverty in 2014, two million of them children.[3]

SNAP functioned exactly as it was designed to during the Great Recession. Participation expanded to meet increased need, and then contracted as economic conditions improved—just as predicted. About 1.2 fewer million people participated in SNAP in January 2014 than had in January 2013. Along the way food stamps did what they were intended to do: they kept people from facing hunger, so that they were fit enough to seek and find work, and so their kids could concentrate in school. Contrary to the Republican conception of someone on food stamps as a lazy layabout who eschews all responsibility, 72 percent of food stamp recipients live in households with children. Who are the food stamp participants after all? Children, the elderly, and the disabled.

And lacking initiative? About half of all new SNAP participants leave the program within ten months, and 74 percent within two years. According to the CBPP, SNAP spending fell for the second consecutive year in 2015, and is projected to keep falling.[4]

Still, Ryan's budget for 2015 proposed to cut $125 billion from food stamps over ten years. That was on top of the $8.7 billion cut that had been enacted through the Farm Bill and the $12 billion from the economic recovery program.

Ryan is also mistaken, or at least conflicted, about the societal benefits of the Child Tax Credit. He supports the CTC in theory, but when debate on Capitol Hill turned to indexing the value of the CTC to inflation—merely to ensure that the CTC kept up with the cost of living—he and his Republican colleagues would not hear of it. But the fact remains that because the value of the CTC is not tied to inflation, families have seen its value erode by $360 in real terms since 2001.

On Medicaid, Ryan seems content to reprise the moves made by predecessors like Newt Gingrich. Ryan wants to turn Medicaid into a block grant program wherein states would receive a fixed dollar amount, which would not adjust for increased need, particularly in an economic downturn. Why does he want to do this? He says this would improve the healthcare situation for low-income Americans. The Congressional Budget Office, however, does not see it that way. They concluded that unless states increase their Medicaid funding by a wide margin to make up for Ryan's proposed cuts, they would have to cut eligibility, cut covered services, or cut the payment rates to healthcare providers, which are already low. All in all, more people would be uninsured and underinsured. How many? Up to 20.5 million people, by some estimates.[5]

In 2015, when looking at yet another Ryan budget plan that would devastate the social safety net, I tried to raise attention among my colleagues that Labor, Health, and Education spending was already $17.1 billion below 2010 levels when adjusted for inflation.[6] The budget Ryan was proposing for 2016 would cut yet another $18.2 billion. My staff and I worked out what Ryan's budgets would

mean for an array of critical programs that develop the next generation of Americans: for the NIH, one thousand fewer research
grants.[7] (Even though every dollar of NIH spending generates two
dollars of economic activity.) For Head Start, 150,000 fewer children served. (Though research shows that kids who attend quality
preschool programs are four times more likely to earn a college degree and earn a living wage.) Federally supported childcare would
reach 68,000 fewer children. Senior nutrition programs would be
cut, resulting in 25,000,000 fewer meals. (This at a time when
one in six seniors faces the threat of hunger.) Among students
covered by Title I, 2.6 million would see a reduction in education
services, and 16,000 fewer Special Education students would be
served. About 7,000 older kids who rely on Job Corps centers for
help earning their GED or learning career skills would be out of
luck. For workers, employed or unemployed, cuts to Training and
Employment State Grants would mean 600,000 adults seeking job
training would be left out in the cold.

Perhaps Ryan's way of thinking about poverty made sense in the
1990s. One could at least see how he might have arrived at the idea
that imposing a number of damning policies on our most effective
social safety net programs would help America's poor. In the 1990s,
the U.S. economy was going gangbusters, and wages were rising
even for less-skilled workers. The EITC had been expanded. If you
wanted a full-time job, you had a great chance of getting one, even
one that would pay you enough to keep you above the poverty level.
With that much economic opportunity, one could come to think
of poverty as the result of bad choices and unhealthy habits. You
could more credibly point to a person's laziness, or broken families,
or substance abuse, instead of broader structural shifts.

You would have a hard time arguing that poverty today is a lifestyle choice. In 2009, states and local governments laid off more
than half a million workers. Many of those jobs are not coming
back. The net wealth that many Americans lost during the Great

Recession is not coming back for most people, either. To assume that everyone who receives food stamps is doing so out of reluctance to take life and their responsibilities seriously is grossly insulting to millions of working Americans.

Nothing is more revealing of conservatives' worldview than their refusal to renew unemployment benefits nationally, and their push to cut benefits as soon as possible in Republican-governed states. They describe unemployment benefits as "welfare." This is a far cry from the time when we ended the welfare program under President Clinton. We are talking about working people who contributed to an unemployment fund, and who are looking for the right job. Even then, conservatives are trapped into viewing any government benefit as increasing dependency.

Ryan also finds it difficult to critique the social safety net without making demeaning statements about the people who in difficult times rely on it. For him, poor people are not people with limited resources; they are people who have stopped believing that upward mobility is possible for them. They live "lives of deficiency" in a "dependent culture."[8] If we do not address this state of affairs by cutting them off, Ryan says, "we risk hitting a tipping point in our society where we have more takers than makers in society. Where we will have turned our safety net into a hammock that lulls able-bodied people to lives of dependency and complacency, which drains them of their will and incentive to make the most of their lives."[9]

Ryan's view of poor people sits alongside a more traditional conservative worldview that simply argues that the federal government should stay out of helping regular people. Ryan has put forth a plan for what he terms the Opportunity Grant, and it is a strange brew of anti-poverty doubletalk and conservative paternalism. The Opportunity Grant would bundle the funding for eleven federal anti-poverty programs and establish a mega-block grant, and pay for what Ryan calls "opportunity contracts."[10] All means-tested programs would be redesigned so that everyone who receives benefits would be assigned a social-service provider who would essentially act as their social worker. Having entered into an "opportunity contract" with the state, someone who received food stamps, for instance, would be required to work with this provider on solving their life problems. This social-service provider would set goals for them, like getting a GED. The provider would set time limits for meeting those goals. They would also be empowered to offer rewards for good behavior and to punish noncompliance.

Experience suggests that many of the dollars plowed into the Opportunity Grant would never reach people in need. Broad, bulky block grants inevitably replace state dollars, so the total amount of money allocated to assisting vulnerable populations drops. It is also worth pointing out that SNAP, if handled in the Opportunity Grant way, would no longer work as an immediate income stabilizer when people lose their jobs.

I do not want to imagine what would happen if Ryan's proposals were put in place and a recession hit. Would people be put on waiting lists until their service provider could hire enough caseworkers? To me it sounds like precisely the kind of "nanny state" program that many Republicans say they abhor.

In June 2016 Ryan released another report, "A Better Way," in which he proposed to tackle poverty with more recycled Republican proposals repackaged with a poverty theme. He wants to force everyone who receives benefits from safety-net programs to work, even people who are really in no position (mentally or physically) to hold down a job; roll back Pell Grants; and cut Head Start and school nutrition programs.

Speaker Ryan's idea of making government aid onerous enough, and humiliating enough, will be tested when President Trump gives him free rein to enact his terrible plan. The human cost will be very high.

That is a slap in the face to the millions who do everything right and still cannot get by. It is a betrayal of a legacy of good government in the United States. This legacy is what I have worked to defend for twenty-six years. It is a vision for America that I want to expand so that all Americans can support one another in difficult times and share in prosperity.

Conclusion: Ten Policies for an American Twenty-First Century

TRAVELING TO SEE POPE FRANCIS'S installation in 2013 was a transformative experience. Standing in St. Peter's Square, alongside many of my Catholic colleagues, listening to his homily, I felt a clarity and optimism about the path forward. Francis's words were an affirmation that working to protect the poor and the vulnerable was a proper vocation, essential to a life lived to the fullest. He evoked Saint Joseph, the protector of the holy family, and called upon leaders in economic, political, and social life to emulate him, and how he exercised his role with "unfailing presence and utter fidelity." The vocation of protector, Francis said, "means protecting people, showing loving concern for each and every person, especially children, the elderly, those in need, who are often the last we think about. . . . It means building sincere friendships in which we protect one another in trust, respect, and goodness. In the end, everything has been entrusted to our protection, and all of us are responsible for it."

I was sitting next to Anna Eshoo and Loretta Sanchez, who knows Italian, and helped to translate. Our hearts swelled: our church was affirming our social values, which we thought they had abandoned. *Everything has been entrusted to our protection, and all of us are responsible for it*—what a beautiful idea. For me, Francis was taking us back to a time when elected leaders and the Catholic Church had a shared purpose.

Francis reminds us to be patient and determined and remember that our vocation to protect people will gather force.

The experience also underscored the fact that fighting for the vulnerable is bigger than Congress and any election. Perhaps we are being tried so we can remember what we share. The battle involves us all. It requires reawakening, both political and personal. It forces us to forgo complacency and mindless consumerism and to examine our individual consciences—and to stop justifying inequality, ignorance, and excluding others from our circle of concern because they do not look, behave, or believe as we do.

As I see it, ensuring that we have a genuine "culture of life" in the twenty-first-century United States will take a multi-faceted approach. Federal policy has a role to play but I look forward to collaborating with leaders in all sectors—public and private, national and local—to lift up all Americans.

We have to move beyond ideology and return to a time where all parties and leaders accepted the need for a safety net for the vulnerable. That safety net includes a minimum wage that rises with the cost of living, and unemployment insurance financed by employee and employer. It includes raising Social Security benefits regularly. It includes food stamps and a robust web of nutrition programs. And perhaps in the future it must include everyone having access to affordable health insurance.

Remember, we have had divided government for most of the post–World War II era, and for most of those years we did not have constant gridlock, government shutdowns, and threatened default on the national debt. Look at the history and you will see that the minimum wage has been raised nearly twenty times since World War II. Social Security benefits were raised regularly and in 1975 put on an automatic cost-of-living basis, under a Republican president. Food stamps were created and expanded on a bipartisan basis.

The two parties still had fundamental disagreements on how big the government should be, and on regulation, taxes, discrimination, equal rights, and abortion. But there was a level of consensus on a strong military, building infrastructure and highways, investing in research and development, and the social safety net. For post–World War II America, these were givens. In terms of the safety net, our programs were seen as part and parcel of our commitment to do the right thing. For many people serving in Congress, that was because we came to Washington informed by our faith and values, with a passion for making government work for everyone.

This was wrecked by Newt Gingrich and the Gingrich Revolution that took control of the Congress in 1995. I fought a life-and-death battle to defeat their destructive agenda. Speaker Gingrich set loose forces and people that do not believe in government, do not believe in the Congress of the United States, and do not believe in finding common ground.

The Tea Party–dominated Congress today hates the consensus, the sense of community and values, that allowed government to do important things, even with a divided government. They want to see government fail. These people will not pass a transportation bill; they explore every possible tactic to kill nutrition programs, food stamps, and unemployment insurance, not to mention support for the Centers for Disease Control and the NIH. No wonder only 20 percent "trust the government in Washington" always or most of the time. In 1960, about three-quarters did.

We are at a moment where I hope I can appeal to people to re-discover our common commitments. That is more important now than ever because we need to get a President Donald Trump and Republican-controlled Congress to agree to protect the vulnerable or pay a high price. And think back. How many years did it take?

How many setbacks did we face before our passion, persistence, and battles paid off? The expanded safety net of food stamps, tax credits, and the Affordable Care Act lifted millions out of poverty. We defeated a major trade agreement backed by all the elites.

How will this play out in the short term? The front line will be the fight to save food stamps and nutrition programs. Conservative Republicans will try to rip food stamps out of the Agriculture Department and bundle it with "human service" programs that they view as undermining people's self-reliance. They will propose dramatic cuts, intrusive oversight to root out waste, and drug testing for recipients—alone among federal beneficiaries to be treated so distrustfully. All efforts to ensure school lunches are healthy and school vending machines don't worsen our obesity problems will be at risk. With industry lobbyists over their shoulders, they are lowering nutrition standards and introducing paperwork to make fewer children eligible for school lunches. When you hear they want to experiment with state control over the school lunch program, be warned: they are trying to eliminate the federal guarantee that every child in America has a chance of at least one healthy meal a day.

Also on the chopping block will be healthcare. The Republicans won control nationally promising to "repeal and replace Obamacare" and to do it in a special session of Congress if necessary. Repealing Obamacare could be done quickly; replacing it may take years. Meanwhile the millions of people who buy insurance on the exchanges and are covered by the Medicaid expansion will live in a desperate limbo, and insurance companies will continue to withdraw from the exchanges. Expect the Republicans to turn Medicaid into block grants to the states, who will be encouraged to experiment in how they deliver health services to the poor. The new Republican budget will every year provide less money for Medicaid, at great personal cost to millions of Americans.

Will the Republicans then go on to attack the biggest and most universal elements of our safety net, Social Security and Medicare? Candidate Donald Trump repeatedly said no. But the Ryan budgets have repeatedly included a program of premium supports for future retirees to buy private insurance at the expense of Medicare, our current system of government health insurance for all seniors. With big tax cuts for the richest and big defense spending increases looming, Medicare may be too big a target to resist. This kind of slash-and-burn "reform" is what brought Paul Ryan to national attention, and this could be his day.

These radical plans will produce a popular revolt in the country and a battle royal in the Congress. The country will have to wait for a "New Deal" for working parents. We will also have to wait for paid sick days; paid family leave that cover mothers, fathers, and adoptive parents; and care for a child or sick relative. Trump has proposed that by expanding benefits under the already underfunded unemployment insurance system, we will be able to grant mothers six weeks of paid maternity leave. I say mothers, don't hold your breath. I expect a lot of talk here, but not much action.

There are some areas, however, where progress might be possible if we keep our values and principles front and center. We will get through these battles, as we have so many times in the past. And with the support of the American people, I am confident that momentum will build for a return to the basic policies that are key to our common future.

The following ten policy areas are critical for creating the kinds of jobs and opportunities that America needs now:

1) The Child Tax Credit as a central income support for families. We know the Child Tax Credit is a principal vehicle in Western democracies for having healthy children and equalizing opportunity. In the United States, it is a vehicle for raising children and families out of poverty, and it was conceived and supported on a bipartisan basis.

As currently structured, the Child Tax Credit helps families less each year as it is eroded through inflation and as the cost of raising a family rises. Going forward, we must index the value of the Child Tax Credit with inflation to stem these losses. The current credit also leaves the poorest and most needy families behind. Children should not have to live in poverty because their family cannot earn enough income to receive government benefits. This is why the Child Tax Credit needs to be universal for lower- and middle-income families.

We need to eliminate the phase-in and income threshold, which currently deny lower-income children access to the credit.

We also need to do more to help families with children under age three. That means we must expand the Child Tax Credit to provide additional support for families with the youngest children. I have proposed the Young Child Tax Credit, which would be a universal and fully refundable $1,500-per-child boost to the existing child tax credit for children under age three. Helping these young, most vulnerable families has to be our mission as a country.

The role of the Child Tax Credit is closer to being understood because national Democrats strongly supported it, and many Republican candidates advocated various expansions of it. Just as the Child Tax Credit has been regularly expanded in the "tax extender" deals, it must become part of a new deal in the future.

When people ask why I stay with these battles against such odds, I say it is because I see changes benefiting so many people coming at some point. And it is the right thing to do.

2) Quality care and education for all, starting zero to three.
If our country is to live by our professed values, our attention to children has to start with the first years of life.

Hillary Clinton was right when she declared in her campaign that "getting off to a good start should be our children's birthright, part of the basic bargain that we have with each as a nation." That is our shared vision for the country, and must become the moral center of our work ahead.

When my stepdaughter Kathryn Greenberg left New York University, she took her first job at a national program headquartered in New York City, HIPPY, or "Home Instruction for Parents of Preschool Youngsters." It helped parents teach their own children, and one of the program's chief advocates was the first lady of Arkansas, Hillary Clinton. Kathryn got me excited about the possibilities to do so much better with children, particularly at a time when more and more kids were raised by a single, often working parent.

It is so important that our country renews its focus on children, especially those aged zero to three. During the first three years, babies' brains develop at their most rapid pace, laying the foundation—either strong or fragile—for all learning and relationships that follow. Close relationships with parents and other caregivers shape this brain development.

We have to start at the beginning, and make sure all babies have the support they need to thrive. A concerted, comprehensive approach would include: broad support for parents as they take on this toughest, most rewarding job, with child development help through pediatric offices and home visits; ensuring the best early learning experiences through a major investment to improve infant-toddler childcare and expanding Early Head Start; and improving the way we identify and treat mental and behavioral health issues in our children. The consequences of not addressing the mental health needs of our youngest children are costly and sometimes even deadly. These things should not be an afterthought. They must be a major priority if we are to build a strong workforce for the future.

With respect to time, we need to move forward on paid family leave, to allow the parent of a young child to have the resources to opt to stay home and care for their child at that early time when it matters so much. With respect to money, we need to move forward on a young child tax credit, to provide a floor on earnings to families with young kids so that they can provide for their young children during this critical window.

And with only half of three- and four-year-olds in preschool or Head Start, our goal as a society has to be universal access to quality early childhood education.

We must build on the success of Head Start, Early Head Start, and the recent improvements to the federally supported childcare programs. We should double our investment in Early Head Start—assuring comprehensive, full-day high-quality services to low-income families.

The more seriously we take early childhood education and behavioral health issues for struggling families, the stronger our communities will be, and the more resilient our kids—and future workforce—will be.

3) A whole New Deal for the modern working family. America's social policies are still set in a Mad Men era, where one spouse generally stays at home to deal with family responsibilities. American families are stressed like few others in the developed world.[1] But we can achieve a literal "New Deal" for working families, and the change we need starts with the passage of the Paycheck Fairness Act, ensuring equal pay for women.

Also critical to the New Deal are paid family leave and paid sick days. America will soon join the league of nations that includes such benefits as part of the universal offer. We should guarantee up to twelve weeks of paid leave and ensure those taking leave can earn two-thirds of their current wages. We must ensure that hardworking men and women are able to secure paid leave when they have to suspend work because of illness, or to care for their families, and not just in times of illness but to welcome new life into the world.

We also need to pass the Schedules That Work Act, so that companies cannot unreasonably burden their employees with erratic scheduling practices that essentially make the employee bear the cost of last-minute shifts in staffing needs.

We simply must ensure that all families have access to quality affordable childcare. Our childcare subsidies and tax credits are dismal, and we don't invest enough in improving quality. There is no denying it: women are full participants in our workforce. They are also overwhelmingly still the primary caregivers in their families. Parents in the United States are left to scramble to make this work. We need to stop penalizing families whose mothers work, and find ways to prevent situations wherein quality childcare eats up the majority of one parent's take-home pay.

No family should have to pay more than 10 percent of their income for childcare, which will mean tax relief and credits for most working families. Our childcare workers need to be well-trained and well-compensated for their crucial role in supporting the growth and development of our nation's children. We also need expanded childcare services on our campuses, where many working parents are desperate for help.

Support for working families should also recognize that more and more families are caring for not only children but also the elderly. I support the care of my 103-year-old mother, and many, many families also support their elderly parents. This can place enormous financial and psychological burdens on working families that go unsupported in our society today. We need to fix that through our tax system, and by strengthening our caregiver support system on campuses and for the elderly.

4) Affordable and quality healthcare for all. Because of the Affordable Care Act, more than 20 million Americans gained access to healthcare. Consumers can no longer be denied coverage for pre-existing conditions. Preventive screenings, maternity care, and pediatric care are all now covered. Seniors enjoy some relief from high drug costs. Millions of low-income children have healthcare through CHIP. Women's health has been put on an even footing with men's. Insurers can no longer subject families to lifetime caps on coverage, and annual caps were completely phased out. We have to protect those gains with every ounce of energy.

The public must demand Medicaid work in all fifty states so the working poor have access to affordable healthcare. And to ensure all have it, we need to fight for a public option nationally and in the states.

Democrats in their national campaigns and platform had focused on unacceptably high co-pays and proposed reforms, including more sick visits without copay and a new refundable tax credit of $5,000 per family to effectively end these expenses for many low- and moderate-income families.

Even if we protect some of the gains of the Affordable Care Act, we have just begun to address our healthcare challenges.

Consumers in many states do not have enough choices in the health insurance marketplaces, and we need to tackle the pharmaceutical companies and prescription drug prices.

Corporate greed put the issue back on the table: first, it was Daraprim, then it was the Epipen. These outrageous price hikes put life-saving drugs beyond the reach of those who need them the most. The United States needs to join the rest of the industrialized world and institute price controls on excessive drug prices. We need to create a new government board to review drug and medical device prices and penalize corporations that gouge consumers.

Many pharmaceutical firms spend more on marketing then they do on R&D. What we need instead is to deny drug companies tax breaks for direct-to-consumer advertising. We need to get generics on the market faster. We also need to demand that drug companies stop charging American consumers more than they charge people abroad, and we need to let Americans import drugs from countries that share our regulatory and safety standards.

Early on I joined the fight to increase our investment in

biomedical research. I was part of a concerted effort to double the NIH's budget. Since that historic doubling, funding has eroded. We need to get NIH back on track, first by restoring the NIH's lost researching power, and then double its budget again. The NIH supports scientists in every state who are pursuing treatments and cures for the diseases that impact our mothers, our fathers, and our children. We must do everything we can to support it.

5) Long-term bold investments in rebuilding and renewing America. America has finally begun to recognize how much we were enriched by President Lincoln's building of the Transcontinental Railroad, President Teddy Roosevelt's establishing of the National Park System, President Franklin Roosevelt's building the Hoover Dam and TVA, and President Eisenhower's building of the Interstate Highway system.

Today, we need to renew America through innovative public and private partnerships that reflect American ingenuity and vision for the common good. We need to think on a grand scale here.

The European Union has already created a successful Infrastructure Bank that has raised private-sector capital from around the globe to leverage infrastructure investment. It has worked wonders for them, and it could work wonders for us. For every $1 billion spent on transportation projects, 13,000 jobs that cannot be outsourced are created and as much as $3 billion in economic activity is generated.

The bills are mounting for our failure to maintain and build. The American Society of Civil Engineers' last report card in 2013 gave America's infrastructure a D+ and suggests that a $3.6 trillion investment is needed in the next five years just to bring our infrastructure systems up to adequate conditions. Making this investment will create new jobs and modernize our infrastructure for the twenty-first century.

Candidate Trump promised something different on infrastructure investment. His $1 trillion dollar plan amounts to massive tax credits for contractors and construction-sector investors who will end up owning the resulting roads, bridges, and facilities. That is not how historically we have built great things, like the Interstate Highway system, in our country. His infrastructure plan is simply a disguised path to privatization. The cost would be covered by a onetime tax holiday for corporate profits kept overseas and anticipated revenue from promised growth. We have seen that trick before.

We also know that privately funded infrastructure projects do not have a great success rate. According to a Congressional Budget Office report, of the thirty-six privately financed road projects, fourteen were completed, three declared bankruptcy, and one needed a public bailout. I expect many voters in the Rust Belt who hoped to find jobs on these projects will be disappointed.

America needs to be even more ambitious than Presidents Barack Obama and Donald Trump. The country is ready to embrace a leader who has the vision of a Lincoln, the Roosevelts, or Eisenhower.

6) New framework for trade. And trade agreements that prioritize shared prosperity. Today, we are on the cusp of a new epoch in the history of globalization. Tomorrow's economy cannot run on yesterday's rules. As Nobel Prize–winning economist Joseph Stiglitz has argued, we must rewrite the rules for a globalizing and automating world. In my view, we must write rules that respect human dignity, environmentalism, anti-monopolistic competition, consumer safety, and the principles of transparency and inclusivity.

A new way forward will only be achievable when we reform the process for creating agreements. With the TPP, five hundred corporate lawyers sat at the drafting table for almost five years without meaningful input by civil society and the elected representatives of the people. Continuing in that vein will only produce deals that strengthen the affluent and exploit the disadvantaged at home and abroad.

I was encouraged that both Bernie Sanders and Donald Trump raised their voices against the TPP in the 2016 primaries, and both Clinton and Trump opposed it in the General Election. Now, the TPP is dead, but it was not killed by Donald Trump. A strong, progressive coalition stopped a vote on the TPP under President Obama, and it was a great victory for people tired of the job losses, lower incomes, and allied corporate interests getting special standing with government. Candidate Trump famously committed to renegotiate NAFTA—something I favor in principle. But the devil is in the details.

This break in the passage of a succession of trade agreements is a moment to set out clear principles going forward, as set out by Jared Bernstein and Lori Wallach in "The New Rules of the Road: A Progressive Approach to Globalization."[3] We must have trade agreements that reduce the monopoly power of corporate interests, promote U.S. exports, and, most important, create good paying jobs here in the United States. To achieve this, we need enforceable currency disciplines, enforceable labor and environmental standards, clear rules of origin, and trading partners that are selected based on their respect for the rule of law and compliance with international norms. A rigged process will only produce a rigged outcome. The process for creating trade deals must be transparent and include input from civil society and policy makers. We must end fast track.

Purging the archaic Investor–State Dispute Settlement system from our international trade deals must be a top priority. While strong investment is critical to the health of any modern society, ISDS is a tool increasingly used by financial investors to game international trade rules outside of democratic institutions. It ends up overriding our own laws, and it must go.

The agreements of tomorrow must respect human dignity by

encouraging innovation through competition, not by sustaining and reinforcing monopolies. Extending patent terms and data exclusivity for innovative treatments in our trade agreements is not fundamentally about promoting trade; it's about increasing profits for big pharma.

Standards for consumer protections and food safety should only ever go up, not down. Many consumer safety standards are put in place only after years or even decades of public pressure and activism against corporate obstructionism and convoluted government bureaucracy—only to have those standards voided in one fell swoop by way of an international trade agreement. This must stop.

We must also include enforceable standards with regard to currency manipulation by our free trade partners. Manipulation is not a comparative advantage; it is cheating.

Finally, we must use common sense when implementing trade deals so that the benefits of the agreement are phased in as reward for active, ongoing on-the-ground compliance with high labor and environmental standards. I am energized by the recent protests among men and women worldwide who are resisting the ongoing attempts by business interests to suppress their voices when it comes to shaping international trade agreements. Trade does not have to be exploitative. People are not widgets. Together, we will demand an inclusive, fair, and sustainable path for twenty-first-century globalization.

7) A dramatically reformed higher education system that is free and leaves graduates debt-free. Millennials are weighed down by debt. Average student debt at graduation has more than tripled over the last twenty years. Young people with good jobs are struggling to make the first big investments in their lives, such as buying a home, because of the student debt they hold.

This issue finally got the attention it demands due to the primary campaign between Hillary Clinton and Bernie Sanders. They were right—we need to make a college degree accessible and debt-free. For us to compete in the age of accelerating globalization, our economy demands a highly educated labor force.

We need to significantly increase federal support of higher education by increasing funding for and year-round access to Pell Grants. Low-income students need both funding and the flexibility to complete their degree on a schedule that works for them. We also need to hold states and colleges accountable for tuition increases. State budgets should not be balanced on the backs of students. We need to make it possible to get a four-year degree without debt if you come from a middle-class family. In-state tuition at public colleges and universities should be free for families who earn less than $125,000 a year.

We also need to promote the aspirations and dreams of those who are not seeking a four-year college degree and who will turn to community colleges and vocational and technical schools.

8) A living wage. A national minimum wage of $15 an hour is a good place to start the fight. The fight for $15 has already started in the states and our big cities, but we need to pass it nationally and index it to inflation.

Just as important, we need to remember the role unions played in securing widespread American prosperity. Unions raised wages and standards of living for millions of people throughout the twentieth century. We need to reject proposals that make it harder for workers to unionize, and we need to roll back the restrictions on collective bargaining that have already been passed in some of the states. We also need to give the National Labor Relations Board the resources it needs to protect workers' right to organize.

We need to tip the balance in favor of working people. That would be greatly helped by a growing, full-employment economy.

9) Enhanced Social Security benefits. Social Security is not in financial trouble because it is underfunded. Underfunding can be solved by people paying Social Security taxes on all of their income. The problem is that most people do not retire with a private pension, so they depend on Social Security for an increasing share of their retirement income.

We need to start by increasing monthly benefits by 2 percent, and stop penalizing workers who took time out of the paid workforce to care for dependents. Right now the annual Social Security cost-of-living adjustment (COLA) is too stingy, and takes money away from seniors who need it the most, robbing them of dignity and independence. We can adjust the COLA so it more accurately accounts for seniors' living expenses, including the rising cost of medicine.

We also need to reform the way Social Security treats stay-at-home parents. Historically, most women, and now some men, spend time at home taking care of children, an aging parent, or a sick family member, which means they spend less time in the workforce. When they retire they should not be penalized for having worked in the home. That leaves retired women with smaller benefits. Addressing this unfairness is hugely important.

How can we pay for expanded Social Security benefits? We can ask wealthy Americans to contribute more; as is, they do not pay any more into the system on incomes above $118,500. Given today's skewed wealth distribution, raising that ceiling to $400,000 makes more sense. Extending the Social Security "payroll tax" to investment income would boost Social Security so it can cover more robust benefits and allow us to stop raising the retirement age.

10) America without poverty. America is the wealthiest country in the world, yet millions of Americans live in poverty each year. Our social safety net has reduced poverty, but the poor are surely with us. That leads me to recall Robert Kennedy's call to action: "I believe that, as long as there is plenty, poverty is evil. Government belongs wherever evil needs an adversary and there are people in distress who cannot help themselves."

My dream is of an American future where all are agreed that anyone's poverty is all of our business.

Acknowledgments

I want to thank The New Press for embracing this book and be-lieving in its mission and my role in this story. Ellen Adler, the publisher, championed my book, and it would not have happened without her. I was introduced to The New Press by Megan Hustad, who became my collaborator in writing this book. We interviewed each other at a New York hotel in 2014, sizing each other up, and she helped me develop the book proposal, win over publishing peo-ple, and carry off a huge amount of primary research central to the book. She mastered the Congress in the process and helped me tell the very complicated story of passing and defeating laws. Our professional relationship became personal, too. Megan had a baby, Arlo James, while helping to write this book, more than she bargained for but the happiest possible reason for a temporary work stoppage. My editors at The New Press, Marc Favreau and Julie Enszer, were great champions, accommodating the congressional calendar and the mess of a presidential election to produce a book we are all proud of.

    I want to thank Google. When I decided to write this book, I knew I had to draw nearly entirely on my public speeches and tes-timony and the recollections of former staff and members, plus the interviews conducted by Megan and myself. Arjun Malhotra agreed to use his graduate school break to oversee the research and threw himself into this book project with such professionalism. Ryann Kinney eagerly gave her personal time to help with everything because she was so excited about the book and cheering for its success.

Leticia (Letty) Mederos went above and beyond. She kept unbelievable notes. Her memory of the events, emotional exchanges, and meetings was unequaled. She brought the story to life. She stayed engaged in every phase of the book, giving so many hours. If this book tells a story, it is because Letty dug into every draft to make sure the book was right.

I want to start by thanking all of those people who agreed to be interviewed for this book. They are doing such important work, particularly now, and yet each gave many hours to sharing their take on the battle for the vulnerable: Sister Simone Campbell, Joseph Carbone, Melinda Cep, Sarah Dash, Stacy Dean, Chris Dodd, Mike Doyle, Martha Foley, Fatima Goss Graves, Stan Greenberg, Marcia Greenberger, Bill Harris, David Harris, Maura Keefe, Miles Lackey, Lilly Ledbetter, Judy Lichtman, Lisa Maatz, Janice Mays, Leticia Mederos, George Miller, Ellen Nissenbaum, David Obey, Tom O'Donnell, Jim Papa, Collin Peterson, Beverly Pheto, Brian Ronholm, Becky Salay, Phil Schiliro, Vicki Shabo, Lori Wallach, and Dan Zeitlin.

People took the time to read the book proposal, individual chapters, or the full manuscript in draft. They all needed a lot of work, and I even listened to the advice. I want to thank Elizabeth Albertine, Eric Anthony, Chris Dodd, Martha Foley, William Frucht, Anna Greenberg, Kathryn Greenberg, Stan Greenberg, Marcia Greenberger, Pat Griffin, Jacob Hacker, Marcia Hale, Bill Harris, David Harris, Robie Harris, Brandon Honore, Maura Keefe, Philip Kremen, Miles Lackey, Jennifer Lamb, Judy Lichtman, Lisa Maatz, Arjun Malhotra, Janice Mays, Letitia Mederos, Tom O'Donnell, Beverly Pheto, Neil Proto, Cecile Richards, Marla Romash, Brian

Ronholm, Becky Salay, Phil Schilero, Theda Skocpol, Doug Sosnik, Lori Wallach, Dan Zeitlin, and Ari Zentner.

I am blessed to have worked with giants—U.S. senators and members of Congress—who mentored me, showed great loyalty, and ultimately worked arm in arm with me. That starts with Senator Chris Dodd, who hired me as his campaign manager and chief of staff in Washington, campaigned for me, and stood by my side when I was sworn in to the House of Representatives. I want to acknowledge him and his role in fighting for kids, working families, and health care. He made me understand that in the Congress, as he declared in his final speech in the U.S. Senate, "It is not your idea or mine. It is about the people beyond the walls of this chamber who are counting on us to get a job done for them."

I want to thank Senator Ted Kennedy, Congressman David Bonior, Congressman Dick Gephardt, and Congressman David Obey. I have such respect for them as historic legislators who knew why they served and who changed the world—and took time to collaborate with me.

I was the master of ceremonies for the tea when Nancy Pelosi became the first women speaker of the House of Representatives, and one of the most effective ever in our country's history. She was grounded in her Italian Catholic household and its values, and we became close friends and allies in moving a progressive agenda. She is focused, smart, politically savvy, and strategic. She is responsible for the Affordable Care Act and, as part of the Democratic leadership, responsible for my being empowered to be in the room to influence so many issues.

The election of Newt Gingrich as speaker changed my trajectory in the Congress. That was true for so many of my Democratic colleagues and I want to acknowledge my brothers and sisters who formed the message group: Lloyd Doggett, Dick Durbin, John Lewis, George Miller, Frank Pallone, Pat Schroeder, and Chuck Schumer.

In the defense of working families, it was my good fortune to work together with Senator Kirsten Gillibrand and Mayor Bill de Blasio.

In defense of the hungry, I was joined by leaders who have their own history of fighting on nutrition issues, including Michelle Obama in the White House; Dick Durbin, Tom Harkin, and Debbie Stabenow in the U.S. Senate; and Sam Farr, Marcia Fudge, Wayne Gilchrist, Bob Goodlatte, Marcy Kaptur, Barbara Lee, Jim McGovern, George Miller, David Obey, Collin Peterson, Earl Pomeroy, and Charlie Rangel in the House of Representatives.

In defense of women, I had as partners Valerie Jarrett and Tina Chen in the White House; and Hillary Clinton, Tom Daschle, Chris Dodd, Tom Harkin, Barbara Mikulski, and, of course, Harry Reid in the U.S. Senate. In the House, my partners included Joyce Beatty, John Dingell, Donna Edwards, and Doris Matsui (co-chairs of the Democratic Women's Working Group); as well as Rahm Emanuel, Carolyn Maloney, George Miller, Eleanor Holmes Norton, Nancy Pelosi, and Lynn Woolsey.

In the politics of faith, so many people anguished through and led on this struggle, including Senators Chris Dodd and Dick Durbin and Representatives Jim Clyburn, Anna Eshoo, Nick Lampson, David Obey, Bill Pascrell, David Price, Tim Ryan, Bart Stupak, and the forty-eight pro-choice and pro-life members of the Democrats' Catholic Working Group.

In defense of people who get sick, so many members have played heroic roles in changing how this country treats women's health. Early on, I was proud to work with Nancy Johnson, Nita Lowey, Connie Morella, Nancy Pelosi, Marge Roukema, Pat Schroeder, and Neil Smith. That seems like ancient history now. With the real prospect of losing on the Affordable Care Act, my colleagues worked to make sure women's health was treated properly in the new law. I want to acknowledge the key work of Rahm Emanuel in the White House; Barbara Boxer, Chris Dodd, Tom Harkin, and Barbara Mikulski in the Senate; and Rob Andrews, Tammy Baldwin, Lois Capps, Kathy Dahlkemper, Diana DeGette, Mike Doyle, Stephanie Herseth, Marcy Kaptur, Jim Langevin, Barbara Lee, Sandy Levin, Nita Lowey, George Miller, Jerry Nadler, Frank Pallone, Mike Quigley, Charlie Rangel, Jan Shakowsky, Louise Slaughter, Bart Stupak, and Henry Waxman in the House. Speaker Pelosi brought it home.

In defense of children, I did everything possible to make the Child Tax Credit encompass the most vulnerable and become part of our safety net. In the Senate my allies were Sherrod Brown, Blanche Lincoln, and Ron Wyden, and in the House, I could not have made an ounce of progress without Sandy Levin, Richard Neal, Nancy Pelosi, Charlie Rangel, and John Spratt.

In defense of the unemployed and creating a platform for long-term investment in infrastructure, I want to recognize Senators Chris Dodd, Tom Harkin, John Kerry, and Jack Reed, who championed these innovative policies. In the House, I need to acknowledge the work and thank Rob Andrews, Earl Blumenauer, Keith Ellison, Peter DeFazio, Barney Frank, Chris Van Hollen, Steve Israel, Hank Johnson, Sandy Levin, George Miller, Jim Oberstar, and Charlie Rangel.

In defense of fair trade, I want to acknowledge the heroic efforts of the leaders who worked over many years to produce the historic defeat of the Trans-Pacific Partnership. In the Senate, Sherrod Brown, Mary Landrieu, Bernie Sanders, and Elizabeth Warren put the proponents on their heels. In the House, I want to personally thank Xavier Becerra, David Cicilline, Elijah Cummings, Peter DeFazio, Mark DeSaulnier, Debbie Dingell, Lloyd Doggett, Donna Edwards, Keith Ellison, Tulsi Gabbard, Ruben Gallego, Alan Grayson, Gene Green, Raúl Grijalva, Walter Jones, Marcy Kaptur, Dan Kildee, Barbara Lee, Sandy Levin, Dan Lipinski, Steve Lynch, Sean Patrick Maloney, Michael Michaud, George Miller, Jerry Nadler, Rick Nolan, Don Norcross, Bill Pascrell,

Mark Pocan, Tim Ryan, Jan Schakowsky, Bobby Scott, Brad Sherman, Louise Slaughter, Paul Tonko, and Nydia Velázquez.

And I want to thank my Republican colleague, the "Deep Throat" of this battle, and the fifty-four Republican House members who voted with the opposition.

As should be apparent by now, getting government to work for "the least among us" cannot get done without visionary leaders brave enough to challenge convention, without outside advocacy and membership groups and philanthropists determined to press for a better society, and without rigorous and respected think tanks developing innovative policies. Across every one of these areas, I turned over and over again to a handful of very special people. For that, I want to thank Heather Boushey and the Washington Center for Equitable Growth, Sister Simone Campbell and Network, Marcia Greenberger and the National Women's Law Center, Bob Greenstein and Ellen Nissenbaum at the Center on Budget and Policy Priorities, Bill and David Harris, Judy Lichtman and Deborah Ness of the National Partnership for Women and Families, Lisa Maatz and the American Association of University Women, John Podesta and Neera Tanden and the Center for American Progress, and Cecile Richards and Planned Parenthood.

In making progress for working families on paid sick days and paid leave, I also want to acknowledge Family Values at Work, Heidi Hartman and the Institute for Women's Policy Research, Moms Rising, and Zero to Three.

My allies in defense of the hungry included Reverend David Beckmann, Mark Bittman, Kelly Brownell, Mariana Chilton, Tom Colicchio, Dr. Debra Frank, Reverend Douglas Greenaway, Michael Jacobson, Lucy Nolan, Jim O'Hara, Marlene Schwartz, Billy Shore, Ellen Teller, Tianna Gaines-Turner, Ellen Vollinger, and Jim Weill. These are people who believe deeply that nutrition matters and hunger is unacceptable. At the U.S. Department of Agriculture, Kevin Concannon and Audrey Rowe were such champions, understanding the importance of food stamps and nutrition. And the coalition of organizations that joined to put pressure and raise cain included the Alliance to End Hunger, Bread for the World, Catholics in Alliance for the Common Good, Center for Science and the Public Interest, Children's Defense Fund, Coalition on Human Needs, End Hunger CT, Feeding America, Feed the Children, Food Policy Action, Food Research & Action Center, Meals on Wheels, National WIC Association, Pew Charitable Trusts, Rudd Center, Share Our Strength, Thousand Days, Witnesses for Hunger, and World Food Program USA.

Lilly Ledbetter was the remarkable person who exposed the unacceptable structure of discrimination against women at work, but she became my partner in the battle to pass Paycheck Fairness. I also want to thank Jody Calemine, Page Gardner, Norma Gattsek, Michele ("Mike") Leber, Rachel Lyons, Jocelyn Samuels, and Ellie Smeal. Deep in the fight were the American Civil Liberties Union, Business and Professional Women Foundation, Family Values at Work, Feminist Majority, Institute for Women's Policy Research, Leadership Conference on Civil Rights, Moms Rising, NARAL, National Committee on Pay Equity, and Women's Voices Women Vote.

The battle to defend our faith, particularly for the Catholic members, required a lot of counseling, soul searching, and collective action. In that I want to acknowledge the good work of Ambassador Elizabeth Bagley, Bob Bennett, Sister Joan Chittister, E.J. Dionne, Frances Kissling, Father John Langan, Cardinal Theodore McCarrick, Father Tom Reese, James Salt, Rabbi David Sapperstein, Doug Tanner, Jim Wallace, and Alan Wolfe. We also had a lot of help from Catholics in Alliance for the Common Good and Faith and Public Life, as well as from Pope Francis, while we're at it.

Defending people who get sick produced the fight and intense battle to deal with preventive health care, abortion, and women's health in the Affordable Care Act. The forces arrayed against us were daunting, and so that's why it is important here to thank

Donna Crane, Ruth Katz, Nancy Keenan, Rachel Laser, Terri McCullough, Amy Rosenbaum, Laurie Rubiner, Ron Pollock, Reva Price, Dana Singiser, Judy Stein, Dan Turton, and Tim Westmoreland.

In defense of children, Janice Mays played such a big part in the Ways and Means Committee. Outside, I need to acknowledge the Century Foundation, Center on Poverty and Social Policy at Columbia University School of Social Work, Citizens for Tax Justice, and Zero to Three.

In defense of the unemployed there are no greater champions than Connecticut's Joe Carbone of Workplace and Bill Villano of the Work Force Alliance. They keep you focused on what matters. If you are serious about work, then you have to be serious about infrastructure, and so many people helped elevate the role of an infrastructure bank, including Marcia Hale, Robert Reich, Governor Ed Rendell, Felix Rohatyn, and Bernard Schwartz, and, critically, the BlueGreen Alliance and the National Employment Law Project.

So, many people and organizations joined my efforts in defense of fair trade. This is personal to me, folks who mentored me on organizing, and some of whom I am honored to stand shoulder-to-shoulder with. This was a huge effort. I want to thank John Barto, Ben Beachy, Jared Bernstein, Michael Beune, Josh Bivens, Khristyn Brimmeier, Tom Buffenbarger, Peter Chandler, Larry Cohen, Barbara Coufal, Mia Dell, Celeste Drake, Tom Flynn, Kevin Gallagher, Tefere Gebre, Leo Gerard, Brett Gibson, Matthew Groch, Mary Kay Henry, James Hoffa, Roy Houseman, Karin Johannson, Lise Johnson, Roger Johnson, Simon Johnson, Sylvia Johnson, Shane Larson, Thea Lee, Andrew Linhardt, Bob Martinez, Dan Mauer, Josh Nassar, Bruce Olsen, Ben Palumbo, Jonathan Parker, Barbara Patterson, Laura Peralta, Jeffrey Sachs, Bill Samuel, Elizabeth Schuster, Robert Scott, Chris Shelton, Nicole Brenner Schmidt, Liz Shuler, Ilana Solomon, Arthur

Stamoulis, Joseph Stiglitz, Richard Trumka, Lori Wallach, John Walsh, Mike Wessel, John Wilhelm, and Patrick Woodall.

The defeat of TPP took an unprecedented coalition that I worked with until President Obama pulled back because we denied him the votes. I want to acknowledge the work of the AFL-CIO, AFSCME, AFT, Boilermakers, Carpenters, Catholics in Alliance for the Common Good, Coalition for Better Trade, CWA, Center for Economic and Policy Research, Center for Food Safety, Citizens Trade Campaign, Doctors Without Borders, Economic Policy Institute, Food and Water Watch, Global Development and Environment Institute of Tufts University, International Association of Machinists, International Brotherhood of Electrical Workers, National Farmers Union, National Nurses United, Network, Public Citizen—Global Trade Watch, Roosevelt Institute, SEIU, Sierra Club, Teamsters, United Auto Workers, United Food and Commercial Workers, International Union of Painters and Allied Trades, and United Steelworkers.

I want to thank the members of the Connecticut congressional delegation. We have one another's backs. This was true when I first served in 1991 and now when I am serving with Joe Courtney, Elizabeth Esty, Jim Himes, and John Larson in the House, and Richard Blumenthal and Chris Murphy in the Senate.

I also need to need to acknowledge plain luck or serendipity and how I ended up being able to make these fights for people. I worked with John Wilhelm in 1971 in union-leader Vinnie Sirabella's campaign for mayor of New Haven—a campaign where Bill Clinton had volunteered. John was one of the most innovative union organizers in the country, who organized the Yale employees and would eventually head the hotel and restaurant workers nationally. I had fallen out with Mayor Frank Logue, whom I had helped elect, and served as his chief of staff. While in the doghouse, I successfully organized a management union for city employees, and John offered me a job with his union. To push me out, the mayor proposed that I head the New Haven Coliseum Authority, which shocked those that controlled that male-dominated sports world. After the *New Haven Register* described me as "a helluva gal around the office," I got an education about women seeking to lead.

That is when Chris Dodd asked me to run his campaign for the U.S. Senate, and then to be his chief of staff in Washington, joining a handful of women in that role. I paused to fight ovarian cancer and my surgeon was Dr. Peter Schwartz, a world-renowned gynecological oncologist at Yale. He saved my life, and he walks on water. We are lifetime allies in the battle for women's health. And then, I decided I had to make an impact on my own.

I was aggressively recruited by Marge Tabankin, Bob Borosage, and Chuck Blitz to run Countdown '87, the national campaign to defeat Contra Aid. Chuck sent me chocolate chip cookies every day, and that's what did it. I learned something about the dedication and effectiveness of outside progressive organizations, particularly the faith groups, and members of Congress and their committed staff—Steve Champlin, Cathy Gille, Jerry Hartz, George Kundanis, and John Lawrence—working together to achieve change. That's when I got to know George Miller and David Bonior, who were liberal giants.

Then, Ellen Malcolm asked me to be the first executive director of Emily's List, and that is when I decided to run for Congress myself. Ellen is such a force and played a historic role in shifting the momentum for women leaders in America. She pushed me over the edge. Thank you.

I also want to thank Archbishop John Francis Whealon. He demanded that Lauralton Hall, my high school alma mater, remove me from their board of directors because of my views on abortion, or be decertified as a Catholic institution. I resigned and penned a detailed, unapologetic letter of resignation. It clarified my thinking about my Catholic faith and what the priorities of my church should be.

Before going to Washington, I had breakfast with Nick Aiello, head of the Amalgamated Clothing and Textile Workers Union in Connecticut. He had organized the women in the garment industry in New Haven, and he sent me off with this advice: "You'll be successful if you never forget the people."

I lost the election for Democratic Caucus chair by one vote, and, believe it or not, I say "thank you," every time I think about it. Caucus chair is a normal path to leadership in the House. Instead I pressed ahead to impact policy from the Appropriations subcommittees and created the public policy dinners at my house in Washington. I host about twenty-five to thirty members twice a month for off-the-record discussions with journalists, academics, bestselling authors, and policy experts.

And I want to thank President Obama for not selecting me as Secretary of Labor. I think it is pretty obvious now that I was not a great fit, and I could not have joined the battles described in this book.

Stan and I were blessed to develop a close group of friends in D.C. that grew closer as all of us worked in our ways to advance our values and put Democrats in a position to do the right thing in Congress and the White House. The "Wednesday night group" had dinner every Wednesday night, and it included at various times Rahm Emanuel and Amy Rule, Pat and Abby Griffin, Marcia Hale, Tom Nides, Doug Sosnik and Fabiana Jorge, Stan, and myself.

I also depend tremendously on my Connecticut friends—too numerous to list. I am home every weekend, and they are both my cheerleaders and my confidantes. Thank you, Barbara and Jimmy, Ellen and Bob, Ellen and Les, Emily and Steve, Fran and Jamie, Joyce, Kay and Gerry, Robert, Tina, and Gerald.

Stan and I have built deep bonds with friends abroad: Halton and Josephine Cheadle, Delicia Forbes, and Wilmot James in South Africa; Wendy Braverman and Phillip Kremen, Jane Cheadle, and Tessa Baird in London; and Isabella Zambon, Margharita Mascolo, and Monica Aonzo in Italy. They provide so much support and sometimes a place to write, too.

I hope after reading this book that readers will have a greater appreciation for the critical role of congressional staff in making progress. I was a staffer, so maybe I am more alert to them, but every policy breakthrough depends on them.

From my first election, my chiefs of staff, state directors, and legislative directors have been amazing and committed. I didn't pay a lot of attention to proper committee jurisdiction, so my staff in Washington supported me expertly on every crazy thing I took on. My staff in Connecticut were on top of the thousands of cases of real people looking for somebody who would listen. They kept me focused on how these issues would impact people in Connecticut. My staff came to live and breathe my parents' model of politics. I want to particularly thank Beverly Pheto and Eric Anthony in Washington, and Jennifer Lamb in New Haven.

I have to mention Ashley Turton. I first hired Ashley as my press secretary and she became my chief of staff. She was with me on the House floor during some of the biggest battles for the vulnerable. I wish she had stayed in the House of Representatives that she just loved, but she left Congress for her family and to work in the private sector. She died in a fiery car accident. She is always in my heart and my head.

Any royalties from this book will be contributed to two organizations that do special work in Connecticut. For one hundred years, the Clifford Beers Clinic has supported the mental health of children and families. And the Connecticut Food Bank is the biggest supplier of charitable food and works with hundreds of partners and programs to fight hunger.

My parents, Luisa and Ted, shaped me in every possible way. For better or worse, I owe them my personality, my values, and my model of politics. They had such big aspirations of their own, but their dreams were with me. I was the center of their universe and living up to their expectations was a challenge. I didn't want to disappoint.

Luisa and Ted were special because so much of what they did, they did together and shared, just as Stan and I get to share in each other's work today.

Our children, Anna, Kathryn, and Jonathan Greenberg, were on the stage with me on that freezing cold November day when I announced that I would run for the U.S. Congress. They were my stepchildren, and stepmothers don't fare well in fairy tales and real life, but we defied convention. They learned to eat anchovies and artichokes. We had so many travel adventures. And they were so excited about my being coliseum director so they could hang out with pop stars. They worked in my campaigns and cried when I lost my race for caucus chair because they knew I wanted it.

They were so involved and supportive with every up and down, but they were each doing amazing things in their own lives and creating their own families. Anna Greenberg became an accomplished pollster who has helped elect some of our country's most impressive Democratic leaders, and worked with the biggest labor unions and progressive groups to help them succeed. Anna is marrying Dana Milbank, accomplished writer for the *Washington Post*, and I welcome him into our family. Jonathan played at an early age on Stan's computers in the basement and was on a high-tech track when he decided to go to culinary school and open his brilliant restaurant in Brooklyn, Roscoe's. He uses Luisa's meatball recipe. And then he married Justine Gardner, a copy editor in her own right, and they are just great. Kathryn Greenberg's first real job after school was with a nonprofit, but job after job took her to city agencies helping the most vulnerable, and now she owns her own company helping major progressive nonprofits and institutes succeed. We are all blessed she married Ari Zentner, a financial and management consultant who is so attentive to the children and a brilliant traveling companion.

My grandchildren are precious to me, and they are the promise of the future, now more than ever: Rigby Maya Zentner, Sadie Liberty Delicath, Teo Isaac Zentner, and Jasper Samuel Delicath (and soon to be joined by Paola Catherine Milbank). They are young, of course, but they campaigned for me and met with voters, and they are damn sophisticated and engaged with what's going on. They've taken the oath of office with me on the floor of Congress every year it was possible and view that with responsibility. What a joy seeing them raise their hands and what joy seeing them point at the Capitol dome and say, "That's where Bubbie works." And they have brought their classes to the Capitol because they are conscious of law-making and the potential of the U.S. Congress in making a good society. I see them determined for America to do better on climate change, food, and the poor.

My journey with Stan began with coffee with milk and two sugars and a love of anchovy pizza that got us seated together in our first campaign. That journey of shared love and friendship continues. We are both sons and daughters in families that struggled to achieve and, like Ted and Luisa, we strive to achieve in our own worlds but benefit from what we share and do together. Sometimes we pinch ourselves on where our careers have taken us. Stanley is a brilliant academic and pollster and I am not. He has helped elect some of the world's greatest leaders, espousing "A better life for all." I was in South Africa when history was made and Nelson Mandela was elected president. It was thrilling and I felt such pride in Stan's work.

The greatest source of tension in our marriage was the NAFTA agreement. Stan was for; I was against. I was right. My clothes shopping can cause some angst.

Stan has been a rock from the first, encouraging me to take up new heights and opportunities. Go to work for Chris Dodd in D.C. Help me survive ovarian cancer. Run for Congress. Write a book.

The success of all of these efforts includes the two of us. There is no way to say thank you.

Rosa L. DeLauro
New Haven
February 18, 2017

Notes

Introduction: Our Safety Net

1. Larry DeWitt, "The Development of Social Security in America," *Social Security Bulletin* 70:3 (2010), www.ssa.gov/policy/docs/ssb/v70n3/v70n3p1.html.

2. Howard Markel, "69 Years Ago, a President Pitches His Idea for National Healthcare," *PBS NewsHour*, November 19, 2014.

3. Alfred M. Landon, "'I Will Not Promise the Moon': Alf Landon Opposes the Social Security Act, 1936," *History Matters*, accessed on October 18, 2016, historymatters.gmu.edu/d/8128.

4. Sahil Kapur, "Social Security And Medicare Would Destroy Freedom Too?," *Talking Points Memo*, April 4, 2014.

5. Kirsten Downey, "The Woman Behind the New Deal: The Life of Frances Perkins, FDR's Secretary of Labor and His Moral Conscience," *Democracy Now!*, March 31, 2009.

2. Breaking the Contract with America

1. *Personal Responsibility Act of 1995*, HR 1214, 104th Cong., www.congress.gov/bill/104th-congress/house-bill/1214.

2. Associated Press, "500 Protesting School Lunch Plans Block Gingrich's Speech," *LA Times*, March 7, 1995.

3. James Warren, "Ubiquitous Bonior Doggedly Campaigns Against Gingrich," *Chicago Tribune*, December 29, 1996.

4. Saul Friedman, "Gray Matters: Armey of One Marshals Forces Against Medicare," *Newsday*, October 30, 2009.

5. Michael Wines, "Gingrich Promises Big Medicare Cut With Little Pain," *New York Times*, May 8, 1995.

6. Alexander Nazaryan, "Newt Gingrich, Crybaby: The Famous Daily News Cover Explained," *New York Daily News*, January 6, 2012.

3. In Defense of Working Families

1. Irin Carmon, "Why Democrats' Doomed Family Leave Bill Matters," MSNBC, December 12, 2013.

2. Stephanie Armour, "Family Medical Leave Act at Center of Hot Debate," *USA Today*, May 27, 2005.

3. "Family Caregivers Need Paid Sick Days," National Partnership for Women & Families, February 2016, www.nationalpartnership.org/research-library/work-family/psd/family-caregivers-need-paid-sick-days.pdf.

4. "Healthy Families Act Introduced in Congress," National Partnership for Women & Families, April 27, 2005, www.nationalpartnership.org/news-room/press-releases/healthy-families-act-introduced.html.

5. "Americans' Views on Income Inequality and Workers' Rights," *New York Times*, June 3, 2015.

6. Jen Kuznicki, "The Problem with Rubio's Family Leave Policy," *Conservative Review*, October 9, 2015.

4. In Defense of the Hungry

1. "Recovery Act Third Quarterly Report—Tax Relief and Income Support Provisions," Council of Economic Advisers, accessed October 16, 2016, www.whitehouse.gov/administration/eop/cea/factsheets-reports/economic-impact-arra-3rd-quarterly-report/section-4.

2. *A Bill to Amend the Food and Nutrition Act of 2008; And for Other Purposes*, HR 3102, 113th Cong., 1st sess., *Congressional Record* 159, docs.house.gov/billsthisweek/20130916/BILLS-113hr3102ih.pdf.

3. Ron Nixon, "House Republicans Pass Deep Cuts in Food Stamps," *New York Times*, September 19, 2013.

4. "The Supplemental Nutrition Assistance Program," Congressional Budget Office, April 12, 2012, www.cbo.gov/publication/43173.

5. Dottie Rosenbaum, "SNAP Is Effective and Efficient," Center on Budget and Policy Priorities, March 11, 2013, www.cbpp.org/research/snap-is-effective-and-efficient.

6. Dottie Rosenbaum and Brynne Keith-Jennings, "SNAP Costs and Caseloads Declining," Center on Budget and Policy Priorities, March 8, 2016, www.cbpp.org/research/food-assistance/snap-costs-and-caseloads-declining; "SNAP/Food Stamp Participation Data," Food Research & Action Center, July 2016, frac.org/reports-and-resources/snapfood-stamp-monthly-participation-data.

7. Bryce Covert, "What 7 States Discovered After Spending More Than $1 Million Drug Testing Welfare Recipients," *ThinkProgress*, February 26, 2015.

8. Brittany Alana Davis, "Florida Didn't Save Money by Drug Testing Food Stamp Recipients, Data Shows," *Tampa Bay Times*, April 18, 2012.

9. Paul Waldman, "Scott Walker Wants to Drug Test Food Stamp Recipients. That Shows Why He'll Never Be President," *Washington Post*, July 16, 2015.

10. "8th District of Tennessee (Rep. Stephen LeeFincher)," Environmental Working Group, accessed October 18, 2016, farm.ewg.org/progdetail.php?fips =TN08&progcode=totalfarm&regionname=8thDistrictofTennessee(Rep .StephenLeeFincher).

5. In Defense of Women

1. *An Act to Amend the Fair Labor Standards Act of 1938 to Provide More Effective Remedies to Victims of Discrimination in the Payment of Wages on the Basis of Sex, and for Other Purposes*, HR 1338, 110th Cong., 2nd sess., *Congressional Record* 154, www.congress.gov/bill/110th-congress/house-bill /1338/cosponsors.

2. U.S. Congress, House, Subcommittee on Workforce Protections, *Paycheck Fairness Act: Hearing Before the Committee on Education and Labor*, 110th Cong., 1st sess., Congressional Record 153, www.gpo.gov/fdsys/pkg /CHRG-110hhrg36467/html/CHRG-110hhrg36467.htm.

3. Lilly Ledbetter, "Lilly Ledbetter Says the President Can Do More For Equal Pay: Sign an Executive Order," *Washington Post*, January 17, 2014.

4. "Remedies for Employment Discrimination," U.S. Equal Employment Opportunity Commission, accessed October 18, 2016, www.eeoc.gov/em ployees/remedies.cfm.

5. Kay Bailey Hutchison from Texas, Olympia Snowe of Maine, Susan Collins of Maine, and Lisa Murkowski of Alaska.

6. "Unmarried Women: A Demographic and Economic Profile," Women's Voices Women's Vote Action Fund, accessed October 18, 2016, www.wvwvaf.org /what-we-do/awareness/unmarried-women-demographic-economic-profile.

7. "#WomenSucceedBusTourWrappingUp, MakingHeadlines,"Democratic Congressional Campaign Committee, June 5, 2014, archive.dccc.org/news room/entry/womensucceed_bus_tour_wrapping_up_making_headlines.

8. When you factor in hours worked at home, working mothers rack up more total working hours than working fathers.

6. "Two Women on the Ticket": Notes on Ending Sexism

1. "Women in the United States House of Representatives," *Wikipedia*, en .wikipedia.org/wiki/Women_in_the_United_States_House_of_Representa tives.

7. Politics and Faith

1. Daniel Burke, "Helping Democrats Bridge the 'God Gap,'" *Washington Post*, October 21, 2006.

2. David R. Obey, "My Conscience, My Vote," *America Magazine*, August 16, 2004.

3. Sister Simone Campbell, "Obamacare Is No Threat to Religious Freedom," CNN, March 22, 2016.

8. In Defense of People Who Get Sick

1. *An Act to Amend the Public Health Service Act to Revise and Extend the Programs of the National Institutes of Health, and For Other Purposes*, Public Law 103-43, *U.S. Statutes at Large* 103 (1993).

2. Steven Waldman, "Breaking: The Common Ground Abortion Bill (Full Summary of New Ryan-DeLauro)," *BeliefNet*, accessed October 18, 2016, www.beliefnet.com/columnists/stevenwaldman/2009/07/breaking-the-com mon-ground-abo.html.

3. Bernie Becker, "House Democrats Seek Moderate Ground on Abortion," *New York Times*, July 23, 2009.

4. Ruth Marcus, "Let's End the Fear-Mongering Over Abortion," *Washington Post*, September 9, 2009.

5. David M. Herszenhorn and Jackie Calmes, "Abortion Was at Heart of Wrangling," *New York Times*, November 8, 2009.

9. In Defense of Children

1. Irwin Garfinkel et al., "Doing More for Our Children," The Century Foundation, March 16, 2016, tcf.org/content/report/doing-more-for-our -children.

2. "Mapping Family Change and Child Well-Being Outcomes," Social Trends Institute, 2015, www.childtrends.org/wp-content/uploads/2015/09 /2015-39WorldFamilyMap2015.pdf.

3. James Gerstenzhang, "Bush Unveils Tax-Credit Plan for Child Care," *LA Times*, March 16, 1989.

4. Steve Gardner, "Proposed Child Care Bill Is Better Than Bush's Plan, Dodd Says at Y," *Deseret News*, March 28, 1989.

5. Sheila B. Kamerman and Al Kahn, *Starting Right: How America Neglects Its Youngest Children and What We Can Do About It* (New York: Oxford University Press, 1995).

6. Greg J. Duncan and Katherine Magnuson, "The Long Reach of Early Childhood Poverty," *Pathways*, Winter 2011, inequality.stanford.edu/_media /pdf/pathways/winter_2011/PathwaysWinter11_Duncan.pdf

7. David B. Harris, "The Child Tax Credit: How the United States Underinvests in Its Youngest Children in Cash Assistance and How Changes to the Child Tax Credit Could Help," (PhD dissertation, Columbia University, 2012), academiccommons.columbia.edu/catalog/ac%3A175200.

8. They also fixed the combat pay provision for the refundable CTC. What was the problem there? Troops in a combat theater don't pay federal income tax. This is a good thing—except for families who got more back in taxes than they paid in, with a refundable CTC and EITC. For these families, the parent would ship off to Iraq or Afghanistan, and no longer be eligible for their CTC and EITC, potentially losing thousands in tax credits.

9. Internal Revenue Service, "Katrina Emergency Tax Relief Act of 2005," www.irs.gov/uac/katrina-emergency-tax-relief-act-of-2005.

10. Rosanne Altshuler et al., "Tax Stimulus Report Card: Conference Bill," Urban-Brookings Institution Tax Policy Center, February 13, 2009, www.tax policycenter.org/publications/tax-stimulus-report-card-conference-bill.

11. Irwin Garfinkel et al., "Doing More for Our Children," The Century Foundation, March 16, 2016, tcf.org/content/report/doing-more-for-our -children.

12. Harris, "The Child Tax Credit: How the United States Underinvests in Its Youngest Children in Cash Assistance and How Changes to the Child Tax Credit Could Help."

10. In Defense of the Unemployed

1. Motoko Rich, "Jobs Report Offers a Mixed Bag, but Little Comfort," New York Times, February 4, 2011; "The Trap," The Economist, January 16, 2010, 32.

2. Bill Marsh, "Jobless, Sleepless, Hopeless," New York Times, September 6, 2009; Michael Luo and Megan Thee-Brenan, "Poll Reveals Trauma of Joblessness in U.S.," New York Times, December 15, 2009.

3. Jack Karston and Darrell M. West, "How Robots, Artificial Intelligence, and Machine Learning Will Affect Employment and Public Policy," TechTank, October 26, 2015, www.brookings.edu/blogs/techtank/posts/2015 /10/26-emerging-tech-employment-public-policy-west.

4. "Hiring Discrimination Against the Unemployed," National Employment Law Project, July 12, 2011, www.nelp.org/content/uploads/2015/03/un employed.discrimination.7.12.2011.pdf.

5. Juliet Eilperin, "300 Communities Pledge to Help Unemployed," Washington Post, January 31, 2014.

6. Ammar Campa-Najjar, "Labor Department Reports Short-Time Compensation Saved 570K Jobs, Provided 22 States with $266M in Reimbursements

from 2012–2015," U.S. Department of Labor, April 6, 2016, www.dol.gov/newsroom/releases/eta/eta20160406.

7. "Bipartisan Budget Act of 2013," U.S. House of Representatives, December 10, 2013, budget.house.gov/the-bipartisan-budget-act-of-2013.

8. Ben Casselman, "Cutting Off Emergency Unemployment Benefits Hasn't Pushed People Back to Work," *FiveThirtyEight*, May 22, 2014, fivethirtyeight.com/features/cutting-off-emergency-unemployment-benefits-hasnt-pushed-people-back-to-work.

9. "The Economic Impact of the American Recovery and Reinvestment Act: Five Years Later," Council of Economic Advisers, February 2014, www.whitehouse.gov/sites/default/files/docs/cea_arra_report.pdf.

10. Michael Grunwald, "Paul Ryan and the Stimulus: A Match Designed to Make My Head Explode," *Time*, August 13, 2012.

11. Bob Herbert, "Our Crumbling Foundation," *New York Times*, May 25, 2009.

12. Harold Meyerson, "The Road to America's Economic Recovery Starts in L.A.," *Washington Post*, March 10, 2010.

13. "Infrastructure Highlighted During Opening Plenary of NGA Annual Meeting," National Governors Association, July 18, 2009, www.nga.org/cms/home/news-room/news-releases/page_2009/col2-content/main-content-list/infrastructure-highlighted-durin.html.

14. Sheryl Gay Stolberg and Mary Williams Walsh, "Obama Offers a Transit Plan to Create Jobs," *New York Times*, September 7, 2010.

15. Chuck Marr and Chye-Ching Huang, "Repatriation Tax Holiday Would Lose Revenue and Is a Proven Policy Failure," Center for Budget and Policy Priorities, June 20, 2014, www.cbpp.org/research/repatriation-tax-holiday-would-lose-revenue-and-is-a-proven-policy-failure.

11. In Defense of Fair Trade

1. Ana Radelat, "DeLauro Breaks with Obama, Big CT Firms on Pacific Trade Deal," *Connecticut Mirror*, January 12, 2015.

2. Christopher Ingraham, "Interactive: How Companies Wield Off-the-Record Influence on Obama's Trade Policy," *Washington Post*, February 28, 2014.

3. Radelat, "DeLauro Breaks with Obama, Big CT Firms on Pacific Trade Deal."

4. Ana Radelat, "DeLauro 'Guest' at State of the Union Turns Activist," *Connecticut Mirror*, January 21, 2015.

5. David Dayen, "Obama Is Selling the TPP Trade Deal Just Like Al Gore Sold NAFTA," *New Republic*, April 29, 2015.

6. Wenonah Hauter, "FSIS Catfish Inspection Program Stops Another Unsafe Shipment from Vietnam," Food and Water Watch, August 9, 2016.

7. "Bipartisan Group Presses for Consumer Protections in Trade Negotiations," Office of U.S. Representative Rosa DeLauro, November 29, 2012, delauro.house.gov/media-center/press-releases/bipartisan-group-presses-con sumer-protections-trade-negotiations.

8. "Food Safety and the Proposed Trans-Pacific Partnership," Southern Shrimp Alliance, March 8, 2012, www.shrimpalliance.com/food-safety-and -the-proposed-trans-pacific-partnership.

9. Lori Wallach, "NAFTA on Steroids," *The Nation*, June 27, 2012.

10. Robert E. Scott, "U.S.-Korea Trade Deal Resulted in Growing Trade Deficits and More Than 95,000 Lost U.S. Jobs," Economic Policy Institute, May 5, 2016, www.epi.org/blog/u-s-korea-trade-deal-resulted-in-growing -trade-deficits-and-more-than-95000-lost-u-s-jobs.

11. *An Act to Amend Section 241(i) of the Immigration and Nationality Act to Deny Assistance Under Such Section to a State or Political Subdivision of a State That Prohibits Its Officials from Taking Certain Actions with Respect to Immigration*, HR 3009, 114th Cong., 1st sess., *Congressional Record* 161, www.congress.gov/bill/114th-congress/house-bill/3009/text.

12. Jonathan Weisman, "House Rejects Trade Measure, Rebuffing Obama's Dramatic Appeal," *New York Times*, June 13, 2015.

13. Emma Dumain, "House Passes Trade Promotion Authority Bill," *Roll Call*, June 18, 2015, www.rollcall.com/news/home/house-vote-trade-promo tion-authority-bill-tpa-trade-deals.

14. Emma Dumain, "Obama Gets Trade Win: Democrats Give In on TAA," *Roll Call*, June 24, 2015, www.rollcall.com/218/obama-trade-win-democrats -give-in-taa/.

12. Paul Ryan's Assault on the Poor

1. Richard Kogan and Joel Friedman, "Ryan Plan Gets 69 Percent of Its Budget Cuts From Programs for People With Low or Moderate Incomes," Center for Budget and Policy Priorities, April 8, 2014, www.cbpp.org/re search/ryan-plan-gets-69-percent-of-its-budget-cuts-from-programs-for-peo ple-with-low-or-moderate.

2. Paul Ryan and Tim Scott, "A Republican Cure for Liberal Failures on Poverty," *Wall Street Journal*, January 7, 2016.

3. Vanessa Rancano, "In Defense of Food Stamps: Why the White House Sings SNAP's Praises," *NPR's The Salt*, January 29, 2015. Also per FRAC: 4.9 million people in 2012.

4. Rosenbaum and Keith-Jennings, "SNAP Costs and Caseloads Declining,"; "SNAP/Food Stamp Participation Data," Food Research and Action Center, July 2016, frac.org/reports-and-resources/snapfood-stamp-monthly -participation-data.

5. Edwin Park and Matt Broaddus, "Ryan Block Grant Proposal Would Cut Medicaid by More Than One-Quarter by 2024 and More After That," Center for Budget and Policy Priorities, April 4, 2014, www.cbpp.org/research /ryan-block-grant-proposal-would-cut-medicaid-by-more-than-one-quarter -by-2024-and-more.

6. Rosa DeLauro, "The Disastrous Ryan Budget: Labor, Health, and Education Programs," Office of U.S. Representative Rosa DeLauro, accessed October 18, 2016, delauro.house.gov/sites/delauro.house.gov/files/Ryan-Budget -Report.pdf.

7. Comparing 2016 totals to 2014 totals. These estimates assume that NIH spending as share of non-defense discretionary spending remains proportional to the 2014 level. Figures used in the calculations are adjusted for inflation and presented in 2014 dollars.

8. Chris Wallace, "David Plouffe Talks Energy, Elections; Rep. Paul Ryan Defends GOP Budget plan," Fox News, March 25, 2012.

9. "Paul Ryan: On the Choice Before Voters This Fall," MacIver Institute, August 2, 2012, www.maciverinstitute.com/videos/2012/08/PR2012-choice.

10. Danielle Kurtzleben, "What Is Paul Ryan's Opportunity Grant Proposal?," Vox, October 8, 2015.

Conclusion: Ten Policies for an American Twenty-First Century

1. Kali Holloway, "American Parents Are Miserable: Moms and Dads Alike Face a Massive 'Happiness Gap,'" Salon, June 23, 2016, www.salon .com/2016/06/23/american_parents_are_miserable_partner/.

2. Jared Bernstein and Lori Wallach, "The New Rules of the Road: A Progressive Approach to Globalization," The American Prospect, September 22, 2016.

Index

About the Author

Rosa L. DeLauro has served as congresswoman from Connecticut's Third District since 1991. She is a member of the House Democratic leadership and co-chair of the Steering and Policy Committee, the ranking member on the Labor, Health, Human Services, and Education Appropriations Subcommittee, and a member of the subcommittee responsible for the FDA and agriculture, where she oversees nutrition and drug and food safety. She lives in New Haven, Connecticut.

Celebrating 25 Years of
Independent Publishing